CALCIUM BENTONITE CLAY

Nature's Pathway to Healing
Balance, Detox, Stimulate, Alkalize

Perry A~

Revised Edition

ISBN: 978-1-951131-98-2

Revised Edition

Published by As You Wish Publishing
www.asyouwishpublishing.com
connect@asyouwishpublishing.com

DEDICATION

This book is dedicated to Ron Nielsen, a long-time friend who patiently guided me through the book publishing world for many years. He and his son David Nielsen made book publishing easy and advised me on all my books. To Jim Hoover of Austin who connected me with valuable resources I needed to establish a firm foundation in the business world when I didn't have a clue what I was doing. To Cheryl McCoy, my Webmaster, cover designer, friend and so much more who patiently edited my last-minute changes and gave me a presence on social media. To Kyle Johnson who began working for me out of college and stuck with me through hard times and eventually became my partner. To our fabulous staff who were dedicated to upholding standards for quality products and excellent customer service that made our company highly respected in the clay world. To Elizabeth Davis for her wise business council. To my Master Mind group, Mary Helen, Martha and Leslie, who supported my dreams and helped me believe all things are possible. To all the clay users and lifelong friends, I have made across the world who have shared their success stories and their creative ideas for mixing and using clay. To my daughters, Ashley and Allyson, who accepted my plan to step away from job security and follow my passion to become a successful entrepreneur. Finally, to my #1 sales person, my grandson Jack Shaver who tells friends and strangers, "Wow! You need to put some clay on that!" And always, my gratitude to God for this wonderful journey.

Contents

FOREWORD

Karen Atkins

In my 20 years as an educator and practitioner of holistic medicine, one of my all-time favorite cure-all healing tools is a Calcium Bentonite Clay. Older than traditional Chinese medicine, there is evidence of clay being used by kings and pharaohs in ancient Egypt. Clay has continued to be revered throughout the centuries for its ability to treat countless health concerns.

I started using a Calcium Bentonite Clay after the Fukushima nuclear power plant crisis in Japan to detox from radiation. Even if we have a pristine diet, we still have to manage the toxins in our environment. Acting like a magnet, clay draws toxins and pathogens to it, binds with them and pulls them out of the body. It is successful in clearing out chemicals, infections, viruses, molds, yeast and radiation. It also does remarkable work in restoring deficient organs. It is one of the safest, most inexpensive, powerful healing aids I know.

The original Living Clay: Nature's Own Miracle Cure has been an essential reference tool within my practice and personal health regime for years. In this new book, Calcium Bentonite Clay: Nature's Pathway to Healing Balance, Detox, Stimulate, Alkalize, Perry A~ shares more scientific research documentation, enlightening new information on the energy of clay, its applications, and the plethora of benefits it brings. In addition there are new testimonials, recipes and a chapter devoted to pets. In this new book, we are introduced to new techniques in administering the clay, as well as upgraded protocols.

For decades, Perry A~ has been a student of and advocate for the wonders of Calcium Bentonite Clay. Dedicated research and a multitude of anecdotal experience make her an invaluable resource in understanding this prized panacea. Calcium Bentonite Clay, Nature's Pathway to Healing, gives you the tools to care for your body naturally — with proven results. I invite you to turn the page and take the next step toward transforming your health.

Blessings to you on your journey!

Karen Atkins, Lifestyle and wellness educator, international lecturer, award-winning songwriter and troubadour.

About the Foreword Author

Karen Atkins specializes in helping people take better care of themselves and find their optimal state of being on all levels.

Through "Restore Your Soul" (www.restoremethod.com), an awareness based business, Karen supports lifestyle education and transformation through nourishment, Qi Gong, essential oils, BodyTalk, music, and other therapeutic methods.

She has recently been featured on Ted Talks and Good Morning America.

INTRODUCTION

I was a skeptic at first – "Eat dirt? You have got to be kidding!" That was my first response in 1994, many years ago, when a friend offered me my first drink of liquid clay. Today I eat, drink, bathe in, and apply topically, Living Clay. My experience has been the same as that of millions – to use it is to love it.

Welcome to the first revised printing of Calcium Bentonite Clay: Nature's Pathway to Healing Balance, Detox, Stimulate, Alkalize. This book contains changes, clarifications and much new information to the original version of Living Clay Nature's Own Miracle Cure, printed in 2006. It has been almost nine years since the first printing, and during that time my knowledge of Calcium Bentonite Clays, Living Clays from the Smectite family of clays has expanded. I have learned more effective ways of mixing, using and applying clays. Now it is time to share this new knowledge with you.

I am a layperson with no medical training. Although I do have a Bachelor of Science degree in Agriculture, with numerous classes in Chemistry, Biology, Bacteriology, Veterinary Science, Anatomy and Physiology that has helped me understand the complicated chemistry of clays. I feel blessed not to have been encumbered with a formal medical education. Had I been, I feel certain that somewhere along that trek some well-meaning, in-the-know soul would have instructed me that no good could come from eating clay. Fortunately for me, I've spent the past 20 years eating clay and learning the truth.

I feel a serendipitous connection with the clay. It's like the clay picked me to write about it and educate people to its healing benefits. It is so much more than 'dirt' and my life has been so enriched because of my connection to it.

Today I consider myself one of the leading advocates of this modern-day, yet age-old pathway to healing! Not just any clay, but more specifically a natural Calcium Bentonite Clay.

Since my introduction, awakening and conversion in 1994, I have been on a personal crusade to inform others of the inherent miracles and safety of this unique type of clay.

Throughout this book you will learn about the miracles for yourself. I will remind you from time to time that it is of utmost importance to use the clay yourself. I drink liquid clay daily. I apply hydrated clay to cuts, bruises, burns, bites, rashes and abrasions. I brush my teeth and pack my gums with clay. I use clay as a facial cleanser in the shower, even shampooing my hair with it. I give myself the luxury of detoxifying and refreshing clay baths. Needless to say, I believe in the benefits of cleansing my body inside and out with Calcium Bentonite Clay.

From this book you will learn the hard science behind Calcium Bentonite Clays as we know it and why it is effective for so many ailments. You will discover how clay is different from mainstream drugs. You will understand how it works to support the whole body. You will see where it gets its diversity of actions that work synergistically to bring amazing and fast results. You will be amazed at clay's simple function that keeps the body from building up a resistance to its benefits. You will learn that each clay deposit has different characteristics and strengths. You will learn what to look for when selecting a quality clay.

You will also hear from physicians, Medical Doctors, Doctors of Osteopathic Medicine, scientists, laypeople, academics, children and even animals – well, at least the animals' owners. There is no other substance on our planet that does what a Smectite Clay can do. You will learn about the 6,000 years of documented history of clay uses.

Use Smectite Clay and the quality of your life will improve, and that's the bottom line for all of this. I am referring to improved physical health, improved insight, improved mental acumen, and even a deeper sense of your own spiritual connection.

This information is not intended to be used as traditional medical reference work. If you are seeking medical advice – as defined by the U.S. Food and Drug Administration's criteria for "medical advice" – please consult a physician. This book is about an all-natural element that supports the body in healing itself – Calcium Bentonite Clay.

All referenced protocols are recommended by practitioners who have used calcium Bentonite Clays with successful results. I invite you to make your own decisions about using this remarkable clay.

The study of Smectite Clays is intriguing. Dive in and discover for yourself why Calcium Bentonite Clay has been providing a pathway to healing since time immortal.

Now, go drink some clay!

Chapter One

ABOUT CALCIUM BENTONITE CLAY

"From the good earth one regenerates one's health."

C. Louis Kervan, Biological Transmutations

WHAT IS CALCIUM BENTONITE CLAY?

I'll begin with the most basic fact of all – Bentonite clay is volcanic ash, the core of Mother Earth with all the impurities burned out from the tremendous heat of a volcanic eruption. The clay particle is made up of 60-80 trace minerals, fused together by heat and charged with a powerful electromagnetic energy and a strong negative ionic charge. When a volcano erupts and the lava flows down the side of the volcanic cone, the ash is blown high into the sky. Slowly it settles to the ground, sometimes nearby, sometimes hundreds of miles away, and in extreme cases it can encircle the globe. Volcanic ash landing in inland lakes and seas evolves over millions of years into various stages of Bentonite clay maturity and types.

Bentonite and Montmorillonite clays are trade names from the Smectite family of clays, which are known for their remarkable ability to change. The book Earth Cures makes several references to clays being alive or a living earth. Louis Kervran's book Biological Transmutations determined that clays contain beneficial living microorganisms and with the help of enzymes, clays can make chemical interconversions that sustain life. Smectite clays are 2:1 layer clays that expand and have the largest surface area and the highest Cation Exchange Capacity, I refer to them as "Living Clays" because of their ability to make changes. A Living Clay is one capable of change through balancing, transforming, stimulating and the interactive exchanging of elements and energy. A rock, on the other hand, is incapable of transforming itself from within. It can only change from outside influences including weathering by heat, wind and water. The short version is that Calcium Bentonite Clay is like the garbage truck picking up the trash (body toxins) and taking them to the trash dump. It has an electromagnetic force to take it where it needs to go, allowing the body to maintain balance and equilibrium to stay afloat. Used topically, it stimulates by drawing blood flow and oxygen to the skin surface to promote healing and by its powerful ability to remove toxins from the body.

My intent is to reduce some relatively complicated scientific explanations into everyday language using analogies that we all can understand. However, the fact is because of clay's multifaceted nature, understanding the mechanics of clay is still a mystery to most researchers, biologists, chemists, physicists and healers.

BENTONITE CLAY AS A CATALYST

Clay acts as a catalyst and assists the body in returning to and maintaining a state of balance and well-being through amazing processes that are not fully understood. As a catalyst, it provides activation energy to the body. A catalyst is an agent that provokes or speeds significant change or action. Without the help of a catalyst, the amount of energy needed to spark a particular reaction is high. When the catalyst is present, the activation energy is lowered, making the reaction happen more efficiently. Unlike other reagents, substances that produce a chemical reaction, a catalyst is not consumed by the reaction itself. It generally works by either changing the structure of a molecule or by bonding to reactant molecules, causing them to combine, react and release a product or energy.

Enzymes are biological catalysts or assistants. They consist of various types of proteins that work to drive the chemical reaction required for a specific action or nutrient. Enzymes might be the factors that give clay its amazing and unexplained abilities. "Enzymes are large biological molecules responsible for the thousands of chemical interconversions that sustain life. They are highly selective catalysts, greatly accelerating both the rate and specificity of metabolic reactions, from the digestion of food to the synthesis of DNA. Enzymes catalyze the forward and backward reactions equally. They do not alter the equilibrium itself, but only the speed at which it is reached." [59]

HOW CALCIUM BENTONITE CLAYS WORK

Calcium Bentonite Clays work in a multitude of interactive ways. Professor C. Louis Kervran formulated the biological transmutation hypothesis as the change of one chemical element into another, a nuclear transmutation occurring in a living organism.

His theory is explained in this story from his book about the Niphargus shrimp, giving credence to the deficiency theory:

"It has been known a long time that living organisms inhabit clay while having no organic supply from the outside. This fact has intrigued research workers, and an important study was made in a laboratory installed in the cave of Moulis, France. Let us note the case of the Niphargus shrimp, a small shrimp half an inch in length that lives in the clay caves. If a shrimp is given organic matter (meat, etc.), it vegetates and dies. It also dies if it is not kept in humid clay. Experiments have shown that it grows normally in pure clay to which nothing has been added. Research workers therefore thought the shrimp lived on clay and nothing but clay, an impossibility according to the laws of biochemistry. It cannot live thus in clay alone, but this clay contains microorganisms which work for the shrimp, making vitamins and various mineral products, nitrogen, phosphorus, and calcium, etc." [30]

In addition, "Research has shown that several organic substances formed by a combination of two or more molecules can be bonded to the surface of clay minerals. Several investigators think the adsorptive properties of certain clays may have played a crucial role in the origin of life. The hypothesis arises as a result of the effort to simulate the conditions under which amino acids may form proteins within the human body. Experiments showed simple amino acids formed into the longer chains called peptides on the surface of clay particles. It is thought that clay acts as a catalyst for the formation of long peptide chains, or proteins. (Georges Millot, "Clay," Scientific American, April 1979)

This is further validated by a recent Cornell University study:

"We propose that in early geological history, clay hydrogel provided a confinement function for biomolecules and biochemical reactions," said Dan Luo, a professor at Cornell University.

The statement from Cornell further suggests that, "over billions of years," clay could have "confined and protected" certain chemical processes, much like cell membranes do today. Then, the protected chemicals "could have carried out the complex reactions that formed proteins, DNA and eventually all the machinery that makes a living cell work."

"To further test the idea, the Luo group has demonstrated protein synthesis in a clay hydrogel." Thus Bentonite Clays are able to combine with enzymes to create amino acids and produce proteins and other elements the body is deficient in that do not exist in the clay itself. [35]

FOUR PRIMARY ATTRIBUTES OF CLAY

There are four primary attributes of clay. It balances, detoxes, stimulates and alkalizes. Although there are other factors that contribute to clay assisting the body in returning to a state of wellness, these primary attributes of clay work independently and yet synergistically.

Clay in a nutshell:

Balances — It is homeostatic and strives to return the body to a state of wellness. A balanced body is designed to heal itself. This state of homeostasis is how clays balance pH levels rather than over alkalizing.

Detoxifies — Its strong negatively charged ions (anions) pull, hold and capture positively charged ions (cations), which are found in toxins, viruses, mold, yeast, heavy metals and radiation. This is made possible by its tremendous absorption ability.

Stimulates — It draws blood flow and oxygen, stimulating circulation and the flow of energy necessary for cellular revitalization and repair. It awakens latent cell energy.

Alkalizes — Clay has a high alkaline pH in the 8.5 to 10 point range.

Internally, Calcium Bentonite Clay works from the mouth-south through the alimentary canal, providing a very effective cleansing and detoxing capability even though it is not absorbed through the colon wall into the blood stream. It can, however, capture freshly ingested toxins before they are absorbed into the body. This is the ultimate prevention. More importantly, most of these clays have a high alkaline pH and act to bring balance and equilibrium so the body can return to its natural state of well-being.

Externally, clay baths are the safest, most effective detox protocol for removing heavy metals, toxic chemicals and radiation stored in the body. Miriam Jang, M.D. [8]

"I have put a huge number of patients on these clay baths and the levels of heavy metals - mercury, lead, arsenic, aluminum, and cadmium - have come down dramatically ... I have been monitoring the levels of metals using all three methods TD DMPS (transdermal dimercapto-propane sulphonate), Oral DMSA (dimercapto-propane sulphonate) and clay baths, and the clay baths are way faster in the removal of metals ... One particular patient had very high levels of mercury and levels of lead that were off the charts. In 3 months of twice weekly clay baths, the lead came down dramatically and the mercury disappeared. The muscle weakness associated with high lead levels improved dramatically. Interestingly enough, another 5 months of these clay baths showed even lower levels of lead, but the mercury reappeared. This supports the theory that mercury is sequestered in different areas of our body, and it takes time to get it all out." (Dr. Miriam Jang, "Breakthroughs in the Evaluation and Treatment of Autism," 2009)

Clay works on the whole body when taken internally as the energy in clay stimulates latent cell energy.

Clay's ability to alkalize helps the body to stabilize and balance itself. A balanced body can heal itself. When it is out of balance, there is a loss of energy. This loss of equilibrium contributes to a weakness and vulnerability to illnesses arising from mental stress as well as physical abuse, poor eating habits and poor life style choices.

This quality of homeostasis is explained as the ability of a system or living organism to adjust its internal environment by several complex biological mechanisms that operate via the autonomic nervous system to maintain a stable equilibrium.

How is this possible? Well, clay is a nanocrystal. Crystals are capable of memory, reorganization and holding energy. These Smectite Clays communicate with the body and act as needed. In other words, they assist the body in regaining equilibrium, and thus the normal flow of energy returns.

MYSTERIES OF BENTONITE CLAYS

In Earth Cures, French naturopath Raymond Dextreit says it this way: "Clay acts on all organs of the body — on the whole organism. Everything unhealthy and emitting positive cations are irresistibly attracted to clay and become subject to immediate elimination. Wherever there is a deficiency, clay seems to supply the needed substance regardless of whether or not the clay itself is rich in that substance"

Both U.S. Government Bureau of Mines Booklet #609, and an edition of the Dispensatory of The United States of America, an official compendium, give Bentonite high praise. We quote from an addition of the U.S. Dispensatory: "In aqueous suspension, the individual particles of Bentonite are negatively charged, this resulting in a strong attraction for positively charged particles and being responsible for the ability in Bentonite to clarify such liquid as contains positively charged particles of suspended matter. In addition to the growing number of external uses for Bentonite, it has been reported to be of value as an intestinal evacuant when used in the form of a liquid."

Modern science confirms that minerals derived directly from the earth can be more effective than supplements synthesized by man. In the 1960s, when NASA was preparing to conquer space, experiments showed that weightlessness induced very rapid bone depletion. They funded a range of pharmaceutical companies to develop calcium supplements. But Benjamin Ershoff of the California Polytechnic Institute found that the most efficacious treatment was the tried-and-true eating of clay. He reported that "the calcium in clay ...is absorbed more efficiently and that it contains some factor or factors other than calcium which promotes improved calcium utilization and/or bone formation." He added, "Little or no benefit was noted when calcium alone was added to the diet." http://researcharchive.calacademy.org/calwild/2005winter/stories/mud.html

Mud, Mud, Glorious Mud by Suzanne Ubick. Another miracle of Calcium Bentonite Clay is that it acts so gently and subtly that you are not aware of the healing actions until you see or feel the positive results. For many, the fact that it works and that no one has ever died from taking clay is enough.

"Clay is effective through a dynamic presence far more significant than a mere consideration of the substances it contains. It is a catalyst rather than an agent in itself. This is possible because clay is alive — 'living earth.' We cannot always penetrate Nature's secrets, we must merely acknowledge and use them," Dextreit said in Earth Cures.

Calcium Bentonite Clay therapy is the ideal detoxification method because it is both safe and effective. Take control of your body by safely detoxing to help regain and achieve your pinnacle of health! Are you beginning to have a new respect for this simple clump of earth? Scientists have long given up trying to replicate clay given its composition of minerals and ionic charges. Clay is a product of Mother Nature, God's Pharmacy.

Never underestimate what Calcium Bentonite Clay can do in supporting well-being. The simple version is that clay knows where to go and what to do to improve the well-being of the body. Trust the clay.

Chapter Two

THE SCIENCE OF CLAY

Remember when you were young and you played with horseshoe magnets. When you placed like poles together – negative-to-negative and positive-to-positive – the two magnets repelled. When you placed opposite poles together – negative to positive – they pulled toward each other and stuck together.

The process by which substances are absorbed or adsorbed is through their ionic charge. The ionic charge of pure, natural Calcium Bentonite Clay is highly negative. This unique clay adsorbs and absorbs positively charged ions (cations). Almost everything that attacks our bodies – bacteria, viruses, fungi, diseases, toxic chemicals, insect venoms, radiation, etc. is of a positive ionic charge. The beauty of a Living Clay or Calcium Bentonite Clay is that it is blind. It doesn't know an eczema molecule from a staph bacteria molecule or a viral molecule. What it does know is a positive charge. As we apply hydrated Calcium Bentonite Clay topically to our bodies or drink liquid Calcium Bentonite Clay, one of its primary functions is to draw to itself positively charged cations, which it holds like a magnet, both internally and externally. Calcium Bentonite Clay literally removes the positively charged molecules that attack our bodies.

One thing to keep in mind is that the amount of minerals exchanged in the Cation Exchange Capacity, or CEC, are in small amounts and not sufficient to supply daily minimum supplement requirements. Therefore, Living Clays are not an adequate source of mineral supplements.

ADSORPTION VS. ABSORPTION

The two words look alike but their difference is critical in understanding the functions of clay minerals. Adsorption is the process by which substances stick to the outside surface of a clay molecule, similar to the way a strip of Velcro works. This is also where cation exchange takes place. Absorption is the process by which the positive ionic particles are drawn into the structural body of the clay molecule, much like a sponge soaks up liquid. Smectites are known as expanding clays.

The net charge of the clay particle is negative, and this must be balanced exactly by adsorbed cations, adsorbed because they are not internal to the particle but at its surface. They are also referred to as exchangeable cations because when the free water flowing around the particle contains a different type of cation, it may be exchanged with those adsorbed on the clay particle. The extent of isomorphous substitution varies in different clay minerals, giving them varying cation exchange capacities.

CATION EXCHANGE CAPACITY

An important piece to understand about clays is CEC, Cation Exchange Capacity. CEC is the amount of negatively charged ions (anions) in clay that are available to bind positively charged ions (cations). Bentonite Clay particles contain two sources of negative charge, permanent and variable. Permanent or fixed charge is located within the structure of the clay particles - absorption. Variable charge is located on the outer edges of clay particles - adsorption. The basic cation minerals in Calcium Bentonite Clay - calcium, potassium, magnesium and sodium - are bound on the edges of the adsorption layer to the negative surface charges of clay particles. These minerals can then be exchanged to take on the positive cations, the toxins, i.e. cation exchange. Smectite Clays have the highest CEC of the healing clays.

THE SEVEN FAMILIES OF CLAYS

Clays fall into seven separate and distinct family groups. Within these seven families are thousands of different types of mineral compositions, each unique and serving vastly different purposes in our world. This book is primarily about the Smectite family of clays.

Kaolin, a non-expanding clay also known as "China Clay," is a white to pink, soft, plastic clay mainly composed of fine-grained plate-like particles. It is chemically inert, nonabrasive and has low heat and electricity conductivity. Kaolin clays are 1:1 structured clays, with one tetrahedral layer and one octahedral layer. They are best known for their uses in anti-diarrheal products such as Kaopectate. Although it absorbs toxins and bacteria to a limited extent, as do most clays, Kaolin clay acts primarily as a bulking agent. It has the lowest Cation Exchange Capacity of 3-15 meq 100 g-1. Their specific surface area is 5-20 m2/g.

Illite is a non-expanding clay. It is a phyllosilicate or layered alumino-silicate. It has a 2:1 structure that is constituted by the repetition of tetrahedron-octahedron-tetrahedron layers. The interlayer space is mainly occupied by poorly hydrated potassium cations responsible for the absence of swelling. It is sometimes a dark green mineral clay found in marine settings. Some cosmeceutical companies use this clay in their "mud" formulations because of its high content of long dormant microbials and other sea life residue. Pure finds of Illite are rare. They have no expanding lattice characteristics and thus are low in water absorbency. Illites have a low Cation Exchange Capacity of 10-40 meq 100 g-1. Their specific surface area is 80-100 m2/g. (Earnest CN. 1991)

Chlorite Clays also are 2:1 structure clays and are non-expanding. They are known for their abrasive and cleansing properties. Cleaning and scrubbing powders are typical products made from this clay. Never use this caustic, abrasive clay on your body. They have a Cation Exchange Capacity of 20-30 meq 100 g-1. Their specific surface area is 80 m2/g.

Vermiculites are expanding clays and have a 2:1 structure of primary mica minerals. Vermiculites contain either Al^{3+} or Mg^{2+} and Fe^{2+} as normal octahedral ions, and tetrahedral sheets in which Al^{3+} occurs as a substituted ion in place of some of the Si^{4+}. Vermiculite differs from the micas in that it contains hydrated cations rather than un-hydrated K^+ in the interlayer space. The weak bonding afforded by these ions allows vermiculite to expand on wetting. Expansion, however, is less than in Smectite clays. Vermiculite is widely used in the construction and automotive industries, for horticultural applications, and for high-temperature and industrial insulation uses. They are also used for making china, pottery and similar applications such as porcelain finishes on metals. Vermiculites are not recommended for use on the body. They have a Cation Exchange Capacity of 100-150 meq 100 g-1. Their specific surface area is 500-700 m2/g.

Mixed group clays occur when a volcano spews ash from several different internal plate formations. It is not uncommon to find mixed group clay formation at many mines and quarries.

Lath-formed clays are yet another mixed form and are typically used to fire bricks for construction. It is not suitable for use on the body.

Smectites: Smectites are characterized by their expandable properties and a Cation Exchange Capacity of 80-100 meq 100 g-1, meaning they absorb and adsorb. They also have the largest specific surface area of 700-800 m2/g. Smectites are known as dioctahedral 2:1 structured clay; it has two tetrahedral sheets, with the unshared vertexes of each sheet pointing toward each other and forming each side of the octahedral sheet in between them. When the clay is hydrated with water, the space between these layers expands allowing the toxins to flow through and be captured.

"The Cation Exchange Capacity CEC and the Specific Surface area of Smectites are considerably larger than other families of clays being as they are predominately 2:1 clays." Its absorption capacity is as much as eight times as great as other clays. [31]

According to Robert T. Martin, Ph.D., "Clay's particles being shaped like a 'calling card' with the wide surfaces negative and the edges of the card positive and have many times more negative than positive pulling power. The very minuteness of the particles of Bentonite gives a large surface area in proportion to the volume used, thus enabling it to pick up many times its weight in positively charged particles. One gram of Bentonite has a surface area of 80 square meters." [38]

For a visual, one gram of Bentonite is 1/4th of a teaspoon and its surface area of 800 square meters is 1/5th of a football field or to the 20-yard line. Therefore, one teaspoon would have the surface area of 3,200 square meters reaching the 80 yard line of a football field.

Smectites are a family of nonmetallic clays primarily composed of hydrated calcium sodium aluminum silicate. Alumino silicates are crystalline compounds made up of silicon, aluminum and oxygen-aluminum oxide. As long as the aluminum is bound in this form, it poses no health risk.

Smectite clays include Calcium Bentonite, Sodium Bentonite, Wyoming Bentonite, Montmorillonite, Calcium Montmorillonite, Sodium Montmorillonite, or Fuller's Earth and even Magnesium or Potassium Bentonites and are often referred to as living clays. In addition, they go by a multitude of brand names. Make sure the label distinguishes if it is a calcium or a sodium.

Smectites comprise 99% of all clays used for health purposes today. It is the favored clay for health and dietary use as well as for many industrial applications. This is because Smectites are more complicated clays, having a higher Cation Exchange Capacity (CEC), a larger surface area and are considered expanding clays. The sheet of atoms in Smectites are much thinner and more easily separable in water. "That is why they occupy more surface area than other clays. This property is known as dispersibility, which is unique to swelling type of Smectites." http://www.mineralco.net/index/product/productdetail. [9]

Bentonite, Montmorillonite and Fuller's Earth are used synonymously as names for clays in the Smectite family. Bentonite is a clay generated from the alteration of volcanic ash, consisting predominantly of Smectite minerals. Other Smectite group minerals include hectorite, saponite, beidellite and nontronite. Calcium Bentonite is a useful adsorbent of ions in solutions, as well as fats and oils.

As mentioned earlier, the most common subfamilies are Bentonites and Montmorillonites. It's from the Smectite family tree that we find the broadest spectrum healing modality on our planet.

Montmorillonite Clay was named after the town of Montmorillon in France where it was first identified. Its common name is French Green, and you will see it packaged under several different brands today and available in many health food stores. Green swelling clays are known for their remarkable healing properties. Not to say that non-swelling clays are not good also, but due to the molecular makeup the swelling clays have a greater drawing or detoxing potential.

Bentonite Clay was named after the town of Fort Benton, Wyoming, where this clay was first identified by a local miner. The name Bentonite began to stick for other deposits of Smectite Clays in the area. Today, most Smectite Clays are referred to as Bentonite or Montmorillonite regardless of the location of the deposits.

There are few 100% Montmorillonite deposits to be found

today, and the original mine in Montmorillon, France, is no longer in operation. Almost all clays have some properties of Montmorillonite and Bentonites in them. However, most are in very small amounts. Montmorillonite and Bentonite have now become buzz words for people marketing their clays. Remember, each clay deposit has a different mineral composition and therefore has different strengths and weaknesses.

Over the years the names Montmorillonite, Bentonite and Fuller's Earth have been used synonymously and interchangeably much like all facial tissues are commonly referred to as Kleenex because that was the first widely known brand name.

Calcium Bentonite Clay is the rarest form of clay in the Smectite family. Sodium Bentonites are the most prevalent deposits. Even though Sodium Bentonite and Calcium Bentonite Clay are cousins from the same family genesis, they are as different as night and day in efficacy and intended uses. Sodium Bentonites primarily throw off sodium from the cation exchange layer, while Calcium Bentonite will exchange the dominant minerals, calcium and magnesium. High sodium tends to have a thick, gooey, plastic-like consistency. Taken internally, some high sodium clays may cause nausea and diarrhea. If you want to take a sodium look for a lower sodium content clay.

The only important difference between Sodium and Calcium Bentonites is the relative proportions of the two cations in the inter-laminar region. In Calcium Bentonite, the divalent calcium ion predominates. "The ionic radius of Ca2+ is 99 pm, which is almost identical to that of Na+. Although the ions occupy the same volume in space, the charge density of the Ca2+ ion is twice that of the Na+ ion. [5]

In physical terms this impacts greatly on physiochemical characteristics of the two minerals, since the negatively charged lattice sheets are more tightly held together by the calcium ions. Most Sodium Bentonites come from industrial producers. Their processing often introduces problems. Their operations are geared for commercial, not natural or health, products and contamination is a possibility. Calcium Bentonite Clay's swelling activities can be damaged by the addition of salt or certain impurities in the clay. Introduction of impurities tends to displace sodium ions and to lower the electrical imbalance in the flakes. It is important to identify purity of clays for wellness purposes.

Chapter Three

SELECTING A HEALING CLAY

ALL CLAYS ARE NOT CREATED EQUAL

It is important to know that all clay deposits differ in mineral content and therefore produce different results. Within each clay family there are thousands of types of clays, each consisting of 60 to 90 minerals in different amounts. Most clays are used for industrial purposes, but some are good for pottery making, agriculture, cosmetics and healing. Clays will vary in their areas of strength, even regarding one specific use. In the alternative health field some are for topical uses only, and some are better for internal use. Then there are those few high-quality clays that are excellent for both uses. It is important to know your clay.

IMPORTANT QUALITY FACTORS WHEN CHOOSING YOUR CLAY

It is very important that the clay be pure, clean and natural, and direct from the source mine — preferably a subsurface mine that has been protected from the natural elements. Some companies are so far removed from the original clay source that they have little knowledge about what they are promoting and how it works. Avoid Bentonite/Montmorillonite clays that do not specify whether they are a Calcium or a Sodium.

Many clays that claim to be 100% pure have been cleaned, using either a heat process or a hydration process to "wash" out impurities. Both processes can reduce the effectiveness and strength of the clay. In their attempt to make a purity claim, some companies are actually destroying the natural healing properties. Read labels carefully for any notation of the clay having been cleaned, processed, filtered, recharged or tampered with in any fashion other than milling.

Calcium-based clays are the most popular healing clays for internal and external use. Most Sodium Bentonites are suitable for commercial and industrial use, such as sealing farm ponds, sealing asphalt and in oil rig mud pits. The high sodium clays tend to be a plastic-like, gooey, thick clay. A few Sodium Bentonites with lower levels of sodium are used for internal consumption. If taking Sodium Bentonite internally, be alert to feelings of nausea and constipation. Some Sodium Bentonites contain 18% sodium!

Clays are all milled to various degree of "fineness." This fineness number typically runs from 50 to 400 screen mesh. A 50-screen mesh feels like fine-grain sand, while a 400 mesh is almost as fine as talcum powder. These finer milled clays are smoother and more easily hydrated when water is added.

The pH of your Calcium Bentonite Clay is crucial. One of the clay's greatest blessings to your health is its ability to increase your pH from acid to alkaline. Although almost all clays are alkaline, some are acidic. I recommend you select Calcium Bentonite Clay within the higher range between 8.5 and 10.0

pH. Naturally, you want a tasteless, odorless clay that is creamy smooth when hydrated. Unprotected clays tend to pick up odors. Be wary of clays with strong odors.

Remember, the purpose of clay when used on a daily basis is to continually remove positively charged ions – the things that attack our bodies. The very best clay to accomplish this goal is a pure, natural clay with a large surface area and a high Cation Exchange Capacity.

I've looked at two clays and swore by looking at them that they were the same. And yet, the swelling properties were quite different, as were the tastes and textures. This can make a monumental difference in the clay's efficiency. Below are a few tests you can perform at home to determine the differences between clays efficiency levels or whether you have purchased a quality effective clay.

Compare the clays, side by side, by mixing each clay as a hydrated mask or mud paste using the products' directions. Remember to shake well; do not stir when mixing clay. Compare them. You want a smooth texture expanding clay that absorbs water to make a creamy paste.

Hold each jar of clay mask one at a time on the flattened palm of your hand. Tap the side of the jar. Notice whether you feel a vibration. The vibration shows its absorption/swelling and I like to believe it shows energy in the clay.

Compare the texture. Which one is gritty, and which one is smooth and creamy? Apply them covering half your face with one clay and half with the other. When the clays dry, does one side feel tighter than the other? Does the clay stay on the face, or does it turn powdery and brush off easily? Which maintains the strongest pull? The stronger and tighter the hold, the stronger the pull and detox potential.

Next, compare in liquid form, again by using the products' directions. Mix clay and water in a glass or food-grade plastic bottle with a plastic lid. BLEND or SHAKE WELL. Let stand for 30 minutes. Once fully mixed, does the clay water stay emulsified or does it separate? All clays will have some heavier particles that settle to the bottom. You want a clay that stays evenly emulsified. The clay and water should have about the consistency of chocolate milk. It should be tasteless. When holding it in your mouth you will only feel cool, not sweet, salty, bitter or sour. After swallowing, you may notice a slight chalkiness that will wash away with a sip of water. If you pour the liquid mixture in a glass and swirl it around, it should leave a thin, slick coating on the glass.

As you can see, knowing what clay to use becomes the paramount question. Kinesiology (muscle testing) is an inexpensive, widely accepted practice, and there are many alternative health practitioners who can test your body's response to several different brands of clay to help you find the best clay for you.

To determine levels of heavy metal contamination in the body, I recommend a hair analysis or a blood test for metal sensitivity. The Melisa Test is one that measures your immune system's (lymphocyte) activation when exposed to specific heavy metals. Now go find your clay and get started supporting your immune system the natural way.

QUESTIONS TO ASK WHEN SELECTING A QUALITY HEALING CLAY

Now that you know how important it is to select a quality clay, below are a few questions to ask when selecting a clay for topical or internal use for health purposes.

Is it from the Smectite family of clays?

Is it a calcium-based Bentonite/Montmorillonite Clay?

Is it an all-natural clean clay that came directly from the source mine and has not been processed or purified in any fashion?

Is it a clay from a mine protected from the elements?

Are the products in professional packaging with instructions and a list of ingredients?

Does the company provide a phone number and website for easy contact?

Is the company a reputable and helpful source that provides Mineral Analysis documentation along with Quality Control Reports to ensure the purity of the product?

Is it a naturally non-gritty clay milled to at least a 325-400 screen mesh?

Is the pH at least 8.5 or above?

Is it a clay capable of adsorbing and absorbing?

Is it considered a green swelling clay?

Is it tasteless and odorless and non-staining clay?

As with anything, there are exceptions to the rules. There are some low sodium Bentonite Clays that are acceptable for internal use. Though green clays have long been known for their healing properties, there are some other colored clays that have healing properties as well.

Chapter Four

CLAY FACTS AND FREQUENTLY ASKED QUESTIONS

Some things bear repeating. Though these statements are found throughout the book, I felt it necessary to group them to have a reference point for these important facts and protocols. I do like keeping things simple.

Things You Should Know

Take prescription medications away from the internal clay. Ask your pharmacist how long it takes your medicines to be absorbed.

The protocol for each person may be different depending on the degree of dis-ease and individual sensitivity.

When mixing with water, NEVER STIR clay. ALWAYS BLEND OR SHAKE THOROUGHLY.

Follow the manufacturer's directions for your specific brand of clay.

Do not leave clay in prolong contact with metal.

The thicker the clay poultice, the stronger the detoxing and healing process.

When speaking of taking the clay internally or drinking the clay, I am referring to the amount of pre mixed liquid clay in ounces that you drink.

Drinking LOTS water during the day is important to flush the body of eleased toxins. Wait 30 minutes after taking the liquid clay to start your water regime.

Constipation: Most people have three regular bowel movements a day when taking the liquid clay. Some people may experience constipation from the clay pulling out old putrefied fecal matter out. In this case take whatever you need to keep your system running smoothly or another alternative is to take over the counter Magnesium Oxide tablets 250 mg. from the grocery store.

The purpose of the hot bath is to open the pours of the skin for more effective detoxing. With a hot bath only stay in 15-20 minutes and drink water or an electrolyte drink so as not to become dehydrated.

Not all protocols call for a hot bath.

Clay is not a drug.

Clay is a catalyst.

All clay deposits are different. Know your clays.

Clay works in a multitude of ways.

A HEALING CRISIS may be experience as the body adjusts to the rate of detoxification. See Chapter 7 for information on a

Healing Crisis.

Clay captures and removes rather than kills.

Clean Calcium Bentonite clay will not destroy or damage body organs.

The clay particle size of 2 μm is too large to be absorbed through the colon wall. Therefore, it does not go into the blood stream.

It would be very difficult to overdose on a quality internal use clay, and no one has ever died from taking clay.

It is important to mix correctly and follow instructions.

Disclaimer: This educational information is meant to supplement and not be a substitute for professional medical care or treatment. This information has not been evaluated by the FDA.

The facts and protocols listed in this book are only recommendations. Feel free to use clay in any fashion that best suits your own personal needs or preferences. It is recommended to use it as a stand-alone product. Some people want to mix it with oils. Oils are designed to soak into the skin; clay pulls things out. Now you have two products at odds with each other in their primary functions. It's a push me, pull you effect, if you will. Salts added to clay cause the clay to lose its ability to expand and stay emulsified. It will cause separation from the water. Lemon juice or vinegar added to clay will cause a bubbly gas reaction. They are an acid and clay is alkaline so they fight each other.

Frequently Asked Questions About Calcium Bentonite Clay

The information in this piece is meant to supplement and not to be a substitute for professional medical care or treatment. This information should not be used to treat a serious ailment without prior consultation with a qualified health-care professional.

1. Question:

What is a living clay?

Answer:

A living clay is one capable of change through bio-transmutation, transformation and interactive exchange of elements and energy. A rock on the other hand is incapable of transforming itself from within. It can only change from outside influences of weathering by heat, wind, and water.

Clay is a catalyst* that assists the body in returning to and maintaining a state of well being. Clay helps to balance the body with its alkaline pH and its electromagnetic charge that stimulates and revitalizes latent cell energy

2. Quesiton:

What is a Catalyst?

Its high negative ionic charge gives living clay a strong drawing, pulling, absorbing, and capturing ability, a substance that enables a chemical reaction to proceed at a usually faster rate or under different conditions as at a lower temperature) than otherwise possible. An agent that provokes or speeds significant change or action.

3. Question:

In a nutshell what does clay do?

Answer:

Detoxifies –Both internally and externally. Its strong negatively charged ions pull, holds, and captures positively charged ions, which are toxins, viruses, mold, yeast, heavy metals, and radiation made possible by its ability to adsorb and absorb.

1. Cleanses – Internally it pulls old build ups of mucoid plaque and putrefied fecal matter and parasites that are lodged in the crevasses of the colon out with the feces making better absorption of supplements and nutrients. Externally it draws out impurities and infections through the pores of the skin.

2. Balances - Clay is homeostatic. It brings the body into balance. A body in equilibrium can heal itself.

3. Alkalizes – It has a high alkaline pH in the 8.5-to-10-point range. Reduces over acidity in the body.

4. Stimulates - It draws blood flow and oxygen stimulating circulation that is needed for cellular revitalization and repair.

5. Energizes - It has an electromagnetic energy that resonates with the life force energy of the body to propels it to a higher state of wellbeing.

Never underestimate what clay can do in supporting wellbeing.

4. Question:

How does a Living Clay remove toxins from the body?

Answer:

Clay detoxes the whole body from different applications; internal, external
(topical applications) and clay baths. All three work together in unison. Taking the clay internally acts to absorb any fresh toxins ingested before they are passed into the blood and body. This lightens the workload of the body's filtering systems (the lymphatic system, liver and kidneys). Applying the clay externally to the skin acts to stimulate latent cell activity and revitalize the cells which will help the cells release the toxins. Next, the clay baths pull the stirred-up toxins from the body through the pores of the skin. A 'living clay' with a strong electromagnetic power pulls it from the soft tissue deposits and its **large absorption capacity** holds the toxins captive and eliminates them from the body. Imagine the toxins sucked up into a vacuum cleaner and trapped in the bag. This is just the short, condensed answer. It does so much more to benefit the body's return to wellness.

5. Question:

Is Calcium Bentonite Clay safe for internal use?

Answer:

It depends on the clay. Some clays are acidic, and some have been contaminated from environmental sources. Some have been subjected to chemical treatments or extreme heat processes to clean the clay, taking away the natural clay's strength and effectiveness.

In his book, *Earth Cures*, Raymond Dextreit explains it this way. "It is not possible to foresee exactly what will happen with clay applications especially at first, (it reacts different to each individual's body chemistry and needs) but in every case, there is a remarkable improvement, if not a complete healing. As there are no dangers to fear, there is no reason to oppose giving it a try, even for an extended period of time."

All clays are different and not all clays pass a purity test. It is important to know your clay and to request a Laboratory Quality Control Report on the clay in question. Unfortunately, an all natural clay is not currently recognized by the FDA as an internal dietary supplement. To read the article," Criteria for Selecting a Quality Healing Clay," go to page 102.

6. Question:

Are metal minerals in clay dangerous?

Answer:

No, the trace minerals in clay are bound tightly together and make up the whole of the clay molecule. The clay particle size is too large to pass through the colon wall into the blood stream. Two limited studies have addressed the leaching and bioavailability of metals from clays [34] No significant differences were observed in the contents of aluminum, antimony, barium, bromine, caesium, calcium, cerium, chromium, cobalt, copper, dysprosium, europium, hafnium, iron, lanthanum, lutetium, magnesium, manganese, neodymium, nickel, samarium, scandium, selenium, sodium, strontium, sulfur, tantalum, tellurium, terbium, thorium, titanium, uranium, vanadium, ytterbium, zinc, or zirconium in the brain, kidney, liver, or tibia from pregnant SD rats dosed with 2% sodium montmorillonite or calcium montmorillonite clay compared with animals fed the basal diet. The main element components of the clays were aluminum (10%), iron (3%), and magnesium (0.5%) (as well as sodium in the sodium montmorillonite, 1%), with small amounts (usually less than 0.1%) of barium, caesium, manganese, strontium, zinc, and zirconium. The authors concluded that at this dietary level, the clays did not liberate significant amounts of trace elements

7. Question:

Is Aluminum in Clay Dangerous?

Answer:

No. Myths about clay and the elements that make up a clay molecule are rampant. One deals with aluminum. Clay is a **super stable compound. All of the elements that make up clay are bound together and act as a whole.** Aluminum silicate is a crystal compound and cannot be utilized by the body. Aluminum in clay is an oxide form that makes it safe. As long as the aluminum is bound in this form, it poses no health risk. The aluminum in clay is never in an isolated form and is not absorbed into the body. Processed aluminums or free aluminum are positively charged toxins and are the ones absorbed into the body that cause harm.

8. Question:

Is it true clay responds differently to different people?

Answer:

Yes. Clay is an adaptogen. Different people will have different health problems and different responses to the clay. For some they notice more regular bowel movements and others may not have this success. Some get instant results and others may take several weeks to see progress. It will depend on your condition and degree of toxicity.

9. Question:

How much clay do I need for a detox bath?

Answer:

It depends on the clay. Some cheaper clays have impurities, in other words they are not as pure in clay content. This reduces their expansion properties; thus they draw and hold smaller amounts of impurities and toxins. Since all clays are different and vary in their abilities to draw and hold, it is difficult to precisely say an amount that will apply to all clays. One autism treatment center recommends 2 baths per week for 10 weeks using 2 cups of a Living Clay for metal toxicity. For maintenance and muscle relaxation baths, 1 cup is usually sufficient. When it comes to cost, remember you are talking about ridding your body of serious harmful toxic elements. The price of a pound of quality clay is much cheaper than bottles of side-effect riddled prescription medications or of invasive chelation processes. Clay is a natural chelator. It is recommended that you get a blood or hair analysis test before you start so you can monitor your progress.

10. Question:

I was told by the place where I had my amalgam fillings removed that you cannot detox mercury by just internal use of clay, that you must do baths as well. Is that true?

Answer:

Yes. If your amalgams have been leaking over time and the kidney and liver are in overload from processing out the baddies in your system, the toxins become stored in the soft tissues and joints of the body. As the toxins build up, they can cause a variety of health problems. Clay baths will open the pores of the skin and draw out the toxins. Full body wraps with clay and infrared sauna clay sessions are also recommended. Internal use of clay will only bind and remove any mercury from the amalgam removal process that might be taken into the digestive track before it is absorbed into the body, as well as toxins we ingest on a daily basis.

11. Question:

Will Bentonite clays leach nutrients and vitamins from the body?

Answer:

No. Weston Price, D.D.S. and author of *Nutrition and Physical Degeneration*, drew the conclusion that clay increases the body's ability to absorb nutrients. He drew this conclusion from studying cultures that used clay as a daily part of their diet. Whether in fact this is due to the cleansing and purifying effect of clays, or a whole combination of related actions in the body, is unknown.

What is certain is that clay does not leech valuable vitamins and minerals from the body. Of further note, Raymond Dextreit, after 50 years of clinical research in natural medicine, has found no indication that clay negatively affects the nutritional system, although it CAN interfere with drugs being taken internally. Independent experiments designed to find out how much such adsorption might adversely affect the growth and health of experimental animals indicated no ill effects when the intake of Bentonite was 25% of the total diet. [4]

Since liquid clay is mostly water with only a proportion of Bentonite, to reach this state of toxicity it would mean projecting the results of this experiment to where the person would have to consume each day a supply designed for 1032 days. In other words, mathematically for the Bentonite to reach the toxic level of 50% of the diet it would be necessary to consume a three year supply each day over an extended period.

12. Question:

Why does it not interfere with the absorption of minerals in your food? Why only "bad" minerals, i.e. mercury-lead-etc.?

Answer:

Clay is selective. It has a strong negative charge and seeks the positive charged baddies. It is drawing the minerals that are of a toxic nature that have the positive ion. These heavy metal minerals in man processed form are broken down from their natural state. It seems that clay has, among other properties, the ability to either stimulate a deficiency or absorb an excess. It is a catalyst more than an agent. As a catalyst, clay favors the transformations and operations of synthesis, thus allowing better use of the absorbed elements like vitamins and minerals we take or get from the food we eat.

The Indians said it this way, 'Clay has a wisdom of its own and it knows where to go and what to get.' Clay seems to have a universal intelligence, or you can call it chemistry.

13. Question:

Does clay disrupt your natural flora?

Answer:

No. Aside from its absorbent and revitalizing properties, clay is also a catalyst when taken orally, for it favors the transformation of foods into nutritive elements.

In his book, *Earth Cures*, Raymond Dextreit wrote, "Clay is incomparable for maintaining or re-establishing a good normal flora, for it favors the development of useful ferments, while opposing the growth of pathogenic bacilli"

Bentonite clay also promotes good digestion even though it forces the waste out. This is because Bentonite clay has microorganisms and certain enzymes that help the digestive system regain its natural flora. Remember that the digestive system has its own set of good bacteria that helps maintain the natural flow in the body. With the use of colon cleanse products, there is a chance that this flow may be interrupted. But Bentonite clay prevents this from happening, making the process of colon cleansing effective as well as safe.

If you have a concern, feel free to take probiotics and enzymes.

14. Question:

Should clays be taken as dietary supplements?

Answer:

No. Although very small amounts of the dominant minerals (i.

e., calcium, magnesium, sodium and potassium) in clays might be exchanged in the adsorption layer, it is not enough to meet daily requirements.

15. Question:

Is it safe to brush my teeth with clay each day and pack my gums weekly if I have mercury fillings, bridges with titanium, and gold crowns?

Answer:

Yes. Clay is safe for dental hygiene uses and will not affect the dental restorative materials. Because of the diversity of chemicals and chemical components going through our oral cavities, not to mention widely fluctuating pH readings, the dental materials are developed not to break down or dissolve when exposed to different substances. Be sure to use a finely milled, non-gritty clay.

16. Question:

Is Montmorillonite clay the same as calcium Bentonite?

Answer:

There are very few true 100% Montmorillonite clays. Montmorillonite is a name given to a certain clay originally found in Montmorillon, France. Some Montmorillonite properties (mineral compositions) are found in different percentages in most all clays. It has become a buzz word by association. It is often found in your Bentonites but also in Illite, Kaolin's and Chlorites as well, all to different degrees.

Montmorillonite clays and Bentonite clays have been used

interchangeably over the years.

Today people are throwing the word around loosely. There is a good article in Criteria for Selecting A Quality Clay on page 102 that is very educational in understanding clay differences.

17. Question:

Will clay draw moisture from the body and cause constipation?

Answer:

No. When clay is fully hydrated it will not turn into little clay bricks in the intestines. Clay in and of itself does not cause constipation. Hydrated clay is extremely slick. There are many reports that clay has helped stop constipation and an equal number of reports that it stops diarrhea. This is because clay reacts differently in different body systems and in response to different health problems. Clay is all about homeostasis. Homeostasis is the ability of a system or living organism to adjust its internal environment to maintain a stable equilibrium; such as the ability of warm-blooded animals to maintain a constant temperature. It is a dynamic equilibrium or balance. A balanced system is essential for maintaining good health.

If you experience constipation when taking clay, it is because the clay is pulling the old mucoid, putrefied plaque that is lodged in the lower colon. As it cleanses the colon of this build up, it is thrown into the colon canal to be discharged from the body. Another cause is too much white bread and pasta that cover the vilia in the small intestine where absorption takes place. It is a gooey build up combined with heavy meats not properly chewed and digested that are the major culprits.

If you experience constipation take whatever you need to keep your Janitorial Services working. A safe solution is Magnesium Oxide tablets 250 mg. The tablets can be cut with scissors to get the amount that works for you. At the same time, it is important to drink lots of water daily when taking clay to help flush out the toxins and soften the old fecal matter.

18. Question:

Should I worry about draining bath clay into my septic system?

Answer:

No. Not if you add the clay in a liquid form and make sure there are no lumps. We asked an expert who was a former designer of residences. He is a licensed builder and has constructed many residences on septic systems. He stated that if your septic was designed adequately and is working properly, the heavier clay particles will never get to the leach field. They'll settle by their own weight to the bottom of the septic tank compartments.

If you do the math related to tank volume and frequency of your baths and amounts of clay used, it would take years of clay baths before significant build up would dictate tank pumping. Since a cubic foot of clay would occupy only 1,728 square inches (at a one-inch thickness) and there are approximately 7,200 square inches of tank space on a flat bottomed concrete tank, it would take 4.16 years, to accumulate a mere inch of deposit, not in my opinion an amount that would be deleterious to the tank's function. (Information provided by Lawrence (Luke) Luecking, a career builder and construction consultant.)

Below is a testimony from one person's experience with clay and a 50-year-old septic tank:

I've been giving my daughter, who is recovering from Asperger's, SID and Pandas, an average of 3 baths a week for the last year, with 3-4 cups of clay in each one. I don't use a strainer; I wash every bit of it down the drain and I haven't had the first bit of trouble. In fact, it seems like all my drains work better now than they did before clay. I used to get the drains unplugged a couple times a year for other reasons but haven't had a problem since I started using clay. I'm on a septic system that is 50 years old, and I've used several different kinds of clays. Darla S.

19. Question:

What causes the lingering effects of clay? Clay continues to work for days after washing it off or after stopping taking it internally. How does it do this?

Answer:

It is one of the many mysteries of clay. It likely has to do with several factors.

1. Balancing the system and pH. An alkaline pH will not simply revert to acidic overnight.

2. The re-entry of toxins entering the body through the intestines might take several days to overload the liver and kidneys.

3. The vibrational resonance of the electromagnetic energy of clay in stimulating blood flow and circulation has a lingering

essence.

It's somewhat like forgetting to plug your cell phone into a charger. It may take a few days to completely lose the charge. Clay is like a charger that keeps the body balanced and in equilibrium and thus energized. It is best to take clay on a daily basis and keep a steady balance in your body.

20. Question:

Is it good to add magnesium oil to a clay bath?

Answer:

No. Clay draws out, magnesium oil soaks in. It's best to use them separately as their primary functions are different. For the same reason, it's not recommended to use clay in conjunction with DMSO.

21. Question:

What is the best way to prepare the liquid clay?

Answer:

For a single serving, mix a rounded teaspoon of clay powder in 2 ounces of water and shake well. This 2 oz. amount is a single serving.

For larger batches, place 4 cups of water in a blender and add 1/2 cup of the clay powder and blend on high until thoroughly mixed. Pour it into a glass or food grade plastic bottle with plastic lid. Wash the blender immediately, taking care to clean the blades.

For a smaller amount, add ¼th a cup of clay powder to 16

ounces of water and shake until all lumps are gone. When you get to the residue in the bottom add more water, shake well and water your plants. They love clay too.

***Always shake but not stir clay when mixing.**

22. Question:

Can I use distilled water with clay?

Answer:

You can but it is not the best choice. Distilled water may be acidic and is stripped of minerals. It tends to dry the skin when mixed with clay for topical use. Try a purified, filtered water.

According to the Environmental Protection Agency (EPA), distilled water has a pH of between 5.6 and 7, because distilled water reacts with carbon dioxide in the air and forms carbonic acid. This weak acid, as it is called, actually lowers the pH levels.

23. Question:

Once mixed, how much liquid clay is considered to be one serving?

Answer:

For a single serving is 2 ounces of the liquid clay. However, some people need more.

For 4 cups of water add ½ cup of dry powder clay In a blender for 30 seconds, or follow manufacturer's directions for your specific clay.

For general detox: Drink 2 oz. of the premixed liquid clay

morning and night for 14 days.

For heavy metal detox: Drink 2 oz. of the premixed liquid clay 3 times a day for 14 days.

For maintenance regime: 2 oz. of the premixed liquid clay daily.

More may be taken if desired, for more severe problems.

If taking prescription medications, check with your pharmacist and tell him you are wanting to take a 8.5-10 pH Calcium Bentonite Clay. Also ask how long it takes to absorb your medicines and take the clay after absorption has taken place.

24. Question:

Should clay be taken on an empty stomach or with food?

Answer:

It may be taken at any time. It varies with your needs. If you are eating rich, high fat foods or may have food allergies, it is recommended to take some before and after eating. Taking it on an empty stomach for a first time clay cleanse is better without interference from food. Clay is drawn to where it is most needed.

"Clay does act with wisdom—it goes to the unhealthy spot. Used internally, whether absorbed orally, anally or vaginally, clay goes to the place where harm is; there it lodges, perhaps for several days, until finally it draws out the pus, black blood, infection etc. with its evacuation." The Healing Clay, Michel Abehsera,

Just get some in you or on you and it works 95% of the time. It is difficult to overdose on clay. It is much like Vitamin C.

25. Question:

Can I take clay if I am taking prescription medication? Does anyone specifically know what the problem is?
Answer:

It is mostly precaution because there might be a conflict with the medicine and the clay. If you are taking medicines, ask your pharmacist if taking a Calcium Bentonite Clay with a 8.5-10 pH will interfere with the medicine. Secondly, ask how long it takes to absorb your medicines and take the clay after absorption has taken place. The clay particle is too large to pass through the colon wall into the blood stream.

26. Question:

Is it better to take clay in a liquid or gel state than a tablet or capsule?

Answer:

To obtain maximum effectiveness in the human body, the clay should be in a liquid or colloidal-gel state. In this activated state, the body responds immediately, as soon as the clay enters the mouth. Therefore, it is not recommended to take clay in capsules or in a tablet form. Doing so slows the activation of the clay and the mouth and esophagus miss the direct effects of the clay. It will require time for the stomach acid to dissolve the capsule coating and then require water to fully hydrate the clay to an active state. The water you took with the capsule has long passed through the stomach. Now you have a lump of clay in the stomach, and it is not as effective at coating the stomach and intestinal track. You can always mix the liquid clay with juice or in a smoothie.

27. Question:

What is the easiest way to prepare dry clay for a clay bath?

Answer:

Sprinkling clay over the bath water can be dusty and leave lumps that may stop up the plumbing. There is a quick and easy way to mix the clay and eliminate this problem. The only equipment you need is a blender.

For a two-cup clay bath, mix in the blender:

4 cups of water
1-2 cups of clay powder and top off with water leaving an inch of space at the top.

Hit the start button and blend until smooth and all lumps are gone.

Add the liquefied clay mix to the hot bath water and rinse the blender under the tap, getting all the clay out. It is important not to leave any clay in the blender on the metal blades. Wash it thoroughly and then go jump in the tub for a 15–30-minute soak. You will be glad you did.

28. Question:

Why do they say not to store or leave metal in clays?

Answer:

Clay is known to draw toxic metals (metals that deteriorate). A cheap kitchen spoon left in clay overnight was found to have rust on the edges the next day. Titanium (as is used in internal staples), gold and other such metals don't seem to pose a problem. Metals such as canning jar lids and coffee cans will deteriorate rapidly when in placed in contact with clay. It's fine to use a blender with metal blades or a wire whisk to mix clay. Just make sure to wash them immediately after use.

29. Question:

In general, is more clay concentration better? For example, when taking a bath – does it pull more toxins out of your body if you use 10 cups of clay vs. only 2 cups?

Answer:

On a wound, thicker applications are better. For baths, it depends on the type of clay. The purer the clay the stronger it is. Smectites can adsorb as well as absorb. All families of clays do not have the high cation exchange capacity of Smectites. If you know you are dealing with some serious heavy metals and toxicities it is better to be more aggressive.

On the other hand, if you ever have an opportunity to take a full body clay mud bath, do it! Native Americans used to bury themselves in hot sand or clay muds for healing. Get a Kiddie pool and make a thick mud bath. Submerge yourself for an hour. Cover with a tarp and reuse several times. You might experience a healing crisis form purging toxins rapidly. Results may be faster, however. 10 cups or 4 pounds of clay in a bathtub is unnecessary when using 2-3 cups of a premium clay and that much mud will likely clog the pipes. Again, this depends on the type and purity of the clay you are using. The general rule of thumb is: if you are not getting the results, you want to use more clay.

30. Question:

What is the best way to warm clay?

Answer:

For small amount, holding it in your warm hands for a short while will work. Or put it in a plastic storage bag and warm it in a bowl of hot water. Then, snip one corner and squeeze it out.

31. Question:

Do Living Clays have calories?

Answer:

No. Clay has a zero glycemic index and is not a digestible food substance so it would have no calories.

The glycemic index (GI) is a ranking of carbohydrates on a scale from 0 to 100 according to the extent to which they raise blood sugar levels after eating.

32. Question:

Will a living clay help allergies?

Answer:

Clay will help if the allergies are due to clogged detoxification channels (liver, kidney, lung, large intestine).

If they are due to histamine reactions, if won't help. However, it could tone the reaction down if your allergies are part true histamine response, part clogged detox channels. Clay does not stop a histamine reaction. This occurs in the blood.

Clay attracts toxins from the small and large intestine and pulls them out of the body, speeding up the natural elimination process that may be suffering from some blockages. Because your toxic load is reduced, you will feel a lessened symptomatic expression of the reaction.
So. the answer is yes and no.

33. Question:

Is clay safe for elderly and pregnant women?

Answer:

Yes. Elderly people have accumulated more toxins over the years and as they get older, they get out of balance and usually more acidic. Clay will support them in returning to a state of equilibrium.

In many aboriginal tribes, the pregnant women craved eating clay. They did not eat balanced meals and take pregnancy vitamins, so they were drawn instinctively to eating clay to meet their needs. They believed it would help them get pregnant (cycling in) and thought it would help support a strong healthy fetus. They also used it topically to turn an out of position baby and to rub on their breasts to bring down their milk.

It is always important however to have a pure clean clay for internal use. As always consult with your pharmacist if you are taking medications.

34. Question:

What is the difference between Sodium and Calcium Bentonites?

Answer:

Two types of Bentonites are generally identified. One is called the swelling type or Sodium Bentonite, which has single water layer particles containing Na+ as the exchangeable ion. The other has double water layer particles with Ca++ as the exchangeable ion. It is called Calcium Bentonite or non-swelling type.

The only important difference between Sodium and Calcium Bentonites is the relative proportions of the two cations in the inter-laminar region. In Calcium Bentonite, the divalent calcium ion predominates. The ionic radius of Ca2+ is 99 pm [5] which is almost identical to that of Na+. Although the ions occupy the same volume in space the charge density of the Ca2+ ion is twice that of the Na+ ion. In physical terms this impacts greatly on physiochemical characteristics of the two minerals, since the negatively charged montmorillonite lattice sheets are more tightly held together by the calcium ions.

Calcium Bentonite, having a better "glue" in between the lattice sheets in the form of calcium ions, does not disperse in water as readily as sodium bentonite, meaning that hydration (swelling) does not occur to the same extent. Flocculation and settling for Calcium Bentonite are much more rapid than for Sodium Bentonite, since the calcium ions cause faster re-association of the lattice sheets. Both have their special uses. High Sodium content is definitely for industrial uses.

35. Question:

What is the Difference between Zeolite and Clay?

Answer:

There is quite a bit of difference between zeolite and clay. Zeolite is a crystal and acts as a filter. Clay both absorbs and adsorbs and has a higher cation exchange rate. Some zeolites might have a little clay in them. Bentonite clays are far superior as a digestive aid and as a healing stimulant as well as a detoxifier of heavy metals. Both zeolite and clay are used to detoxify heavy metals though clay does so much more.

Zeolites are classified as tectosilicates consisting of interlocking tetrahedrons. The zeolite structure provides vacant spaces that form channels of various sizes allowing movement of molecules into and out of the structure. KEYWORDS - INTO AND OUT OF.

There are no references to using zeolite for facials, drawing out infections from wounds, for acne, rashes and skin diseases, for healing burns, stopping toothaches, as a digestive aid, and in reducing swelling, inflammation and pain of arthritis.

www.zeolite.com/lvsp.phpfor information on Liquid Zeolite

If you choose to use zeolite get the micronized zeolite as traditional milling destroys their crystalline cage structure.

36. Question:

I've heard that clay can be taken with meals, but since it's so alkaline & your stomach needs an acid environment for digestion isn't that a contradiction.

Answer:

Given clay's goal is to clean house and restore balance most of what it does is the result of that ability. Which is the answer to the acidity and digestion question. Clay has a wisdom we cannot understand or process without a pH in chemistry. Our normal pH should be in the 7.0 – 7.4 range. With all the clay I have taken, my pH stays at the 7.0 level. Balance being the key word. How it does it, we many never fully understand. Here is my best attempt. Clay is considered homeostatic.

Homeostasis is a term that is used to both describe the survival of organisms in an ecosystem and to describe the successful survival of cells inside of an organism. Organisms and populations can maintain **homeostasis** in an environment when they have a steady level of births and deaths.

Homeostasis:

The tendency of an organism or cell to regulate its internal conditions, such as the chemical composition of its body fluids, so as to maintain health and functioning, regardless of outside conditions. The organism or cell maintains homeostasis by monitoring its internal conditions and responding appropriately when these conditions deviate from their optimal state. The maintenance of a steady body temperature in warm-blooded animals is an example of homeostasis. In human beings, the homeostatic regulation of body temperature involves such mechanisms as sweating when the internal temperature becomes excessive and shivering to produce heat, as well as the generation of heat through metabolic processes when the internal temperature falls too low.

37. Question: "Do you have any concerns about petro leaching when packaging your clay in plastic containers?

Why not glass?"

Answer:

Anytime you package a food or supplement in plastic, leaching is always a concern. This is especially concerning when it comes to Bentonite, it being a highly absorptive substance. The trick is in knowing what types of plastic are safe. We have found that as long as the clay is stored in food grade plastics of the highest quality, engineered against leaching of petro chemicals, that plastic can be a safe and desirable material for clay storage. We will only use PETE and food grade HDPE (as some HDPE is not food grade) plastics for both our packaging in our production equipment. These types are designated by the numbers 1 & 2 on the bottom of our containers. Attached is a very helpful document about the types of plastics. A more valid concern is the storage of Bentonite in contact with metal as it can diminish the ionic charge of the clay, therefore, plastics are a must in the handling and production of Bentonite products (so even if you find a clay packaged in glass I promise you it wasn't mined, milled, mixed, etc. with glass utensils, more likely it was metal or plastic). Non- food storage grade plastics should never be used with Bentonite, we often warn customers against picking up clays at farmer's markets that may be packaged in Ziplock bags.

We would agree that glass would be an elegant and superior presentation of our products, but it is also very impractical. Glass is heavy and fragile, increasing shipping cost and damage in transit. We distribute our clay products all over the world and all glass packaging just wouldn't be practical choice for our packaging needs

These questions were compiled by Perry A~, author of Calcium Bentonite Clay, Nature's Pathway to Healing, In *answer to questions most often directed to her. She is a frequent contributor to Natural News and other health publications. She has been an ongoing student in the study and research of Bentonite Clays since the early 1990s. She is available for radio interviews, talks and for questions about clay. She can be reached at 1-512-773-0335 or perrya@perrya.com*

Chapter Five

CLAY ARTICLES

The information in these articles is meant to supplement and not to be a substitute for professional medical care or treatment. This information should not be used to treat a serious ailment without prior consultation with a qualified health-care professional.

Perry A~ Arledge is the author of numerous articles and books on Calcium Bentonite Clays, her most recent *is Calcium Bentonite Clay Nature's Pathway to Healing Revised*. She is a frequent guest on health talk radio shows. She is dedicated to spreading the word about clay's healing potential and putting attention on safe healing with Bentonite Clay. She is available for lectures, workshops, interviews, and answering questions on clay therapy. For more clay information go to www.BentoniteClay Info.com Perry A~ can be reached at perrya@perrya.com.com, 1-512-773-0335.

A SOLUTION FOR PRESSURE AND DIABETIC ULCERS

Pressure Ulcers and Diabetic Ulcers are a serious problem for our elderly bedridden population. Weak and immobile pressure points develop in areas that support most of the body's weight and the constant pressure cuts off the flow of oxygen rich blood to the area necessary for healthy skin and tissues repair.

The information below is from http://www.skinsight.com/adult/pressureUlcerDecubitusUlcer.htm

Bedsores (pressure ulcers), also known as pressure sores or decubitus ulcers, result from prolonged pressure that cuts off the blood supply to the skin, causing the skin and other tissue to die. The damage may occur in as little time as 12 hours of pressure, but it might not be noticed until days later when the skin begins to break down. The skin is especially likely to develop pressure sores if it is exposed to rubbing (friction) and moving the skin in one direction and the body in another (shear), as in sliding down when the bed head is raised. Dampness (such as from perspiration or incontinence) makes the skin even more liable to developing pressure sores.

The solution is Calcium Bentonite Clay straight from Mother Earth's Pharmacy. So, what is this clay and how can it help? Living Clay is an all-natural and very pure Calcium Bentonite Clay. It evolved from volcanic ash. In other words, it is the core of Mother Earth with all the impurities burnt out. Nothing is left but tightly bound trace minerals with a strong electromagnetic charge that resonates to stimulate circulation, blood flow and oxygen to rebuild damaged tissues and cellular repair. Clays have a strong negative ionic charge and are considered a very powerful drawing agent. It is a catalyst that works with the body. In addition, Living Clay has a 9.7 pH and is homeostasis. It works with the body to bring about balance and equilibrium.

Clay is a natural detoxing and cleansing agent. It draws toxins, viruses, molds, fungus, chemicals, heavy metals and even pesticides and poisons from the body through internal and external means. The beauty of clay is that it holds and binds what it draws and carries out of the body. It is the Pac Man gobbling up the baddies. The cleansing effect is very gentle, yet it can pull out old dried fecal matter that has lodged in the colon that hinders the absorption of nutrients, vitamins and even medications. In addition, it will draw out many parasites and carry them out of the body.

Topically clay's drawing power pulls blood flow, circulation and oxygen necessary to heal ulcer wounds. Clay can and has stopped many needless amputations from diabetic ulcers. Most women have had a clay facial and experienced the firming and tightening as the clay dries and pulls out impurities and removes the dead skin cells by exfoliation revealing a soft and glowing skin.

Pressure ulcers can be treated in two ways. As a poultice or just apply the dry powder clay direct on the wound several times a day. When applying the clay paste, cover the area thickly and cover with Saran Wrap of a piece of Glad wrap to hold the moisture in. Change the application 2-3 times a day. Results will be noticed with in 3-4 days showing signs of improvement.

An important fact to know about clay is that all clays are different in their mineral composition and what they will accomplish. Since most clays have been used for commercial purposes, they may not be a pure clean grade. For information on selecting a clay go to www.BentoniteClayInfo.com for the article Criteria for Selecting a Quality Healing Clay by Perry A~

ACNE'S WORST NIGHTMARE - BENTONITE CLAY!

Bentonite Clays are the one natural remedy that is acne's worst nightmare. The fine particles of clay carry a strong negative charge that attracts toxins and flushes them out of our system.

It is imperative that acne sufferers understand that:

The skin is the largest organ of our body and it's the outward reflection of what's happening inside. On the outside of your body, you have orifices that can permit the entry of dangerous toxins, bacteria, viruses, and various other poisonous substances. And such toxins come from your food, cigarette smoke, vehicular traffic, smog, drugs, alcohol, air pollution, and generally any form of pollution itself.

1. Bentonite Clays cleanse the system internally and the skin shows it.

2. Bentonite Clay promotes balance and well-being without dangerous side effects.

3. The human body gets rid of toxins through various chan-

nels of elimination. [33]

A. The internal channels of elimination for toxic substances are the anus and urethra. Most of the unwanted waste is passed out in your urine or fecal matter. This is where the problem for acne patients begins right in the small and large colon. The problem arises when the small and the large colon become congested. When the walls of your intestines are impacted with mucoidal waste, the absorption of nutrition from your food and supplements and the expulsion of by-products into the intestinal tract are both seriously reduced. This is exactly why acne patients feel "sluggish", and experience lethargy, headaches, lack of energy. Taking Calcium Bentonite Clay internally is a natural gentle colon cleanse resulting in better nutritional absorption and more energy.

B. The other channel of elimination is externally though the skin. Used topically and in clay baths the skin releases toxins as the clay draws impurities, excess sebum and even heavy metals lodged in the pores and soft tissues and joints of the body.

Say goodbye to acne, heavy metal problems and more with a living Bentonite clay. It is the Toxic Garbage Disposal your body needs!

All that being said all Bentonite clays are not alike. Bentonites belong to the Smectite family of clays which have a higher Cation Exchange Capacity for attracting more toxins. They are also considered 'living clays' which means they are capable of chemical changes making them a catalyst that works with the body. For more information, read "Criteria for Selecting a Quality Healing Clay".

BENEFITS OF CALCIUM BENTONITE CLAY FOR PREGNANCY

A pilgrim from El Salvador and her grown-up daughter browsing among the market stalls around the basilica enthusiastically claimed that they ate the holy tables (clay), and when asked, "Do they do you any good?" the woman's sparkling eyes and instant response was: "Of course they do: I have eight children!" [26]

A mother-to-be sometimes has strange cravings. For no apparent reason, her body suddenly feels starved for certain inedible substances such as charcoal, chalk or plain dirt. She will go out of her way to eat them, sneaking into the backyard to scoop up a tiny bit of mud in her hand to suck on, or running into the front yard to peel park off a tree and chew it as if it were a piece of gum. If you ask her why she does this, she may shrug or say, "I don't know, no special reason," or she might say, "I just like it."

Even though these pregnant earth-eaters may not be able to explain their reasons, I believe their actions hold a purpose. Intuitively, the body makes its needs known through physical cravings. When they are responded to, our bodies are "fulfilled" and we are compensated with health. In this case, the mother and her newborn are rewarded.

Well, here's good news for those mothers who run to the backyard to grab a handful of dirt but don't know why: There is a type of dirt they can safely eat – clay. Calcium Bentonite Clay eating is most common during pregnancy, and it is said to be the most favorable practice a mother can undertake for herself and her unborn child.

The following reports explain the many uses of clay by pregnant women everywhere.

Before Pregnancy

Eaten by women who want to bear children. The clay is supposed to have an effect during normal menstruation, before conception has occurred. It is taken as a means of encouraging future pregnancy.

- Recommended for women who are sterile.
- Good for cleaning the body, creating a better environment to house an infant.

During Pregnancy

- It is believed that the unborn infant benefits from it.
- Promotes healthy digestion.
- Prevents and/or counteracts morning sickness.
- Among the women in one culture, it is thought the fetus will be bigger if the mother eats clay.

· Helps with minor discomforts.

· Has mineral rich nutrient contents.

· Gives the fetus "good bones and teeth."

· Protects against any unfortunate mishap during pregnancy.

· Calcium Bentonite Clay will calm stomach acidity.

· Calcium Bentonite Clay adsorbs metabolic toxins such as steroidal metabolites associated with pregnancy.

Delivery

· The clay is placed on the tongue of a woman in the belief it facilitates delivery and expulsion of the afterbirth.

· The fetus rises in the womb, making delivery easier.

· Calcium Bentonite Clay eases labor pains, accelerates the delivery, and strengthens the expectant mother.

Breastfeeding

· Women rub their breasts with a paste made from clay to stimulate the secretion of milk.

· Taken internally, it is considered good for lactation.

Before I go any further, you may already be wondering, "That's fine that so many women take clay. But how do I know it is really safe for me and my child?"

Yes, eating is a safe and suitable practice that can be maintained during pregnancy. But, as I have emphasized throughout the book, it is important to find the *right* clay. Not all clays are good for eating. You want a clean, natural, Calcium Bentonite Clay. Throughout pregnancy, drink 1 ounce liquid Calcium Bentonite Clay daily and take a weekly clay bath.

PREMENSTRUAL SYNDROME – PMS

Eating clay is therapeutic in cases of menstrual cramps. By drawing the metabolic waste products and improving intestinal health, clay helps prevent cramps and lessen the related symptoms (headaches, bloating, irritability). Many naturopaths agree that menstrual crams are not only a hormonal matter but are partly due to constipation. One ounce of liquid Calcium Bentonite Clay taken twice per day will be helpful.

If major troubles occur – if the menstruation is very abundant, insufficient, too painful or accompanied by several clots, or mucosities, apply a clay poultice on the lower abdomen every night before going to bed, which should be kept on overnight unless it causes discomfort. For minor troubles it is sometimes sufficient to apply these poultices for 10 days preceding menstruation. Interrupt the application during the menstrual period, after that, resume applying them.

The applications can be continued even if the menstruation takes the form of hemorrhage; be sure to slightly warm up the poultices in order not to create a congestive state.

For long-term sufferers of the emotional roller coaster, which oftentimes precedes a menstrual cycle, we recommend drinking liquid Calcium Bentonite Clay as a daily lifestyle practice.

When tackling the symptoms of PMS, for the first 7 days, drink 2 ounces liquid Calcium Bentonite Clay twice daily. Following that, drink 1 ounce liquid Calcium Bentonite Clay as a lifetime practice.

PREGNANCY FROM THE HEALING CLAY

Clay, in combination with a natural diet, is highly beneficial for the formation of the fetus and in the preparation for childbirth.

If the child is badly situated, do not hesitate to apply clay poultices on the belly. For the sake of prudence, it is preferable to apply it symmetrically during the last month of pregnancy. Also place tepid clay poultices on the lumbar region if pain appears.

Cold poultices applied on the stomach just after the childbirth will prevent all subsequent troubles (principally, the risk of infection) and is the best remedy for the imperfect elimination of the afterbirth.

Clay drinking favors nursing.

BENTONITE CLAY TO THE RESCUE!

I went to a young friend's wedding as an honorary adopted grandmother and before the night was over, I was dancing with all the kids. When you are 70 years young, they all seem like kids, but the ages ranged from 6 yrs to well I just told you... It was at the Wildflower Center in Austin. A really nice place for a small family wedding. Any who the music was great and the body seemed willing. Not as much motion as in my younger years but I found the beat and move it I did. It was after being still in the car with the AC full blast on the way home that the body started letting me know it was feeling abused. I had an early morning flight the next day to go visit my daughter Allyson in Dallas for the weekend. I knew I needed a clay bath if I was going to make it through the weekend.

I drew a hot bath, mixed my clay water in a blender (the fast method) as it was already past my bedtime. As I eased my body into the tub, I let out a sigh of relief. Nothing feels better to a physically abused body than a clay bath. I had a bottle of cold water and made a pillow for my neck with a towel and settled in. I felt my body let go and relax. I was purring in contentment. I dozed off a time or too and lost track of time. It didn't matter. I was in heaven. I didn't want to get out and leave my sanctum, but the water was getting cold and my fingers were thoroughly pruned.

By now I did not know I had a body. All aches and screaming muscles were at peace and I set the alarm and slipped between the cool sheets. My head hit the pillow, and I fell into a deep sleep. I am happy to say my newly revitalized body was up for a weekend of fun with my daughter. Clay to the rescue one more time.

BIO-TRANSMUTATION AND LIVING CLAY

The Smectite family of clays are called 'Living Clays' because of their ability to make chemical changes. Internally, Calcium Bentonite clay, Living Clay, provides an awesome cleansing and detoxing capability. It can get freshly ingested toxins out before they get in the body. More importantly most these clays have a high alkaline pH and act to bring balance to the body so it can heal itself.

Louis Kervran formulated the biological transmutation hypothesis. A biological transmutation is defined as a nuclear transmutation occurring in a living organism. Such transmutations are strongly believed not to occur according to mainstream physics, chemistry and biology; however, proponents of the hypothesis claim to have empirical evidence that they do. [1] In addition these clays are capable of bio-transmutation.

Every piece of clay retains a considerable amount of energy from the large and powerful magnetic entity of the Earth. It seems that clay has, among other properties, the ability to either stimulate a deficiency or absorb an excess in the radioactivity of the body on which it is applied. On an organism, which has suffered and still retains the radiation of radium or any other intensive radioactive source, the radioactivity is first enhanced and then absorbed. Clay could, in this way, ensure the protection of an organism overexposed to atomic radiation. [13]

Clay is simply a catalyst that supports the body through amazing processes understood fully by no one on earth yet. A catalyst is any substance that works to accelerate a chemical reaction. For any process to occur, energy, known as activation energy, is required. Without the help of a catalyst the amount of energy needed to spark a particular reaction is high. When the catalyst is present the activation energy is lowered, making the reaction happen more efficiently. The catalyst generally works by either changing the structure of a molecule or by bonding to reactant molecules causing them to combine, react and release a product or energy.

The tremendous amount of energy in clays is from the electromagnetic actions and intense thermodynamic heat of the volcanic eruption. You might say it is super charged.

This was shown by a chemist in France who attached a patch wired to a machine to read electromagnetic response to the bottom of a man's foot. The minute the liquid clay entered his mouth is showed a responsive reading on the machine. Thus, an example of how clay resonates and revitalizes cells of the body. This stimulating action pulls blood flow and oxygen needed for cellular repair.

The miracle of Calcium Bentonite Clay is it acts so gently and subtly you are not aware of the healing actions until you see or feel the positive results. For many, the fact that it works and that no one has ever died from taking clay is enough.

All clays are different, and it is important to know your clays. For more information read Criteria for Selecting A Quality Clay on page 102.

CALCIUM BENTONITE CLAY – THE NATURAL BODY pH BALANCER

PH is the new buzz word these days regarding health as we have begun to discover the pitfalls and dangers when our bodies are over acidified from many sources. The result is diseases begin to manifest as we feed acid loving pathogens and enhance their proliferation by providing the perfect acid and oxygen-free medium they need to multiply. A balanced body will heal itself. When balance goes acidic the body is too stressed and overburdened to return to a state of balance without outside help.

Nancy Appleton, Ph. D, a nutritional consultant, stated in an article, "The state of balance (homeostasis) is the key to health. If your body is in homeostasis, it is healing. When it is out of homeostasis, it is on the degenerative disease process, in a recent article by Ethan Huff he said, "Maintaining pH balance in the body has become an important subject of modern health research as it is being concluded that general wellness is predicated upon it." Have you ever made Amish Friendship bread with a yeast starter that is fed with 1 cup of flour, 1 cup of sugar and 1 cup of milk, mixed well and left on the kitchen cabinet to ferment for 5 days? In the process of fermentation oxygen is released as bubbles, the bag expands, and you have to crack the bag and release the gaseous mixture. So, the oxygen is burned off, so to speak, leaving an acidic, anaerobic environment which is ideal for the rapid growth of yeast to take place.

[51] "Fermentations in food processing typically refers to the conversion of sugar to alcohol using yeast, or a combination thereof, under anaerobic conditions."3 A more general definition of fermentation is the chemical conversion of carbohydrates into alcohols or acids. It also states that ethanol fermentation is a form of anaerobic respiration used primarily by yeasts when oxygen is not present in sufficient quantity for normal cellular respiration.

So, when we eat excessive amounts of sugar, yeast breads and carbohydrates, acid sodas and acid producing foods we are in effect weakening the body's natural defenses to heal itself.

Robert O. Young tells us in *The pH Miracle*, that just about all health problems stem from being acidic. This is because parasites, bad bacteria, viruses, and Candida overgrowth - all of which are the root causes of what we give thousands of disease names - thrive in acidic environments. But those problems don't do well in an alkaline environment.

Kim Evans is a natural health writer and author of *Cleaning Up!* In her article*, Acid or Alkaline: Why Your Health Depends on It,* that appeared in the Natural News on September 4, 2009, reported that: "It's been found that cancer doesn't do well in an alkaline environment, and is most often found in bodies with a pH around 4 or 5, which is highly acidic. The fact that forty percent of the population is expected to have a problem with cancer is very telling about the acidic nature of people these days, and the problems with our standard diets."

pH is essentially a measure of oxygen to hydrogen, therefore, substances in the body with more oxygen than hydrogen will be on the alkaline side. On the pH scale 7 is neutral, and anything above 7 is alkaline; anything below 7 is acidic.

There are lists all over the internet, and books as well, that tell you how to eat for an alkaline pH. What most people want to know is how to eat right when they're on the go. Let's face it most menus support high carbs and greasy meats, so what can you do?

The answer is really very simple. Just eat or drink high alkaline hydrated or liquid Calcium Bentonite Clay daily and before you eat or drink something acidic. Look for clay in the 8.5 or higher pH range.

Why clay, you ask? Clays, for the most part, have a naturally high alkaline pH. Clay is homeostatic. One of its major functions is to act as a catalyst to assist the body in returning to a balanced state. It accomplishes this in a variety of beneficial ways. Of course, clay's alkaline pH factor is the primary one.

Calcium Bentonite Clay, birthed from volcanic ash, has an extremely high negative ionic charge due to the thermodynamic heat from the volcano. In essence this clay is tightly bound together trace minerals. Clays hold their integrity meaning the mineral components of clay stay bound together to make the clay molecule and they act as a whole clay unit. This high negative ionic charge makes clay a force to be reckoned with in drawing and capturing toxins and pathogens. Because of the high negative charge, some clays can adsorb and absorb toxins pulling them into the interior layers of the clay and holding them captive, then carrying the toxins out of the body through the feces.

Clay has the power to attract and either absorb or stimulate the evacuation of toxic and non-useful elements. Clay considerably reduces the toxicity of harmful substances.

The knowledge of these properties would be insufficient to explain clay's active power if we did not understand that clay is a powerful agent of stimulation, transformation and transmission of energy. We have extraordinary energy resources which normally remain dormant. Clay awakens them. When life force energy flows the body will balance itself. When the flow stops necrosis kicks in and a burden is placed on the body as the cells cannot get nourishment.

The molecular structure of the clay molecule is too large for the particle to pass through the colon wall and be absorbed into the blood stream. So, once they capture the toxins they are eliminated as they cannot be absorbed into the body to do harm.

In addition. Calcium Bentonite Clays are from the Smectite family of clays. Smectite is characterized by its expandable properties. Unlike the other clays, only Smectite can absorb as well as adsorb toxins. This qualifies its structural uniqueness and sets it apart from all other clays.

[13] Every cell in our body excretes waste material that becomes toxic and poisonous to our bodies if it is allowed it to build up faster than it can be eliminated by the body. Clay's

pH and electromagnetic charge allow it to adapt to its host's dominant needs.

Now that you know what clay is and some of what it does, next comes what you can do to keep your pH in the normal or slightly alkaline range. Knowing sodas are between 2.4 and 4.0 acidity, drink 1 ounces of pre-mix liquid clay or eat a ½ teaspoon of hydrated clay before you indulge. This goes for alcoholic beverages also. Be safe and take just a little more afterwards. If you find yourself eating greasy, fried foods, repeat the clay dosage. Not only will you balance your pH but you will keep the body from absorbing cholesterol and excess grease and fats. This will cleanse the internal track of newly ingested toxins and help rid parasites in the colon as well. To bring yourself into a pH balanced state, start with 2 ounces of pre-mix liquid clay 3 times a day and 2 clay baths a week. For maintenance, 1 ounce 2 times a day plus 1 ounce before or after indulging in acidic eating, and one clay bath a week is sufficient.

Taking clay baths is another popular method of safe detoxing of heavy metals and chemical toxins that influence our body balance. The clay's strong drawing power will pull toxins lodged in the soft tissues of the body that the kidneys and liver could not filter out, through the pores of the skin.

To monitor your progress, get some saliva or urine pH strips. You can do a Google search for them online or check with your pharmacy. They are inexpensive and help you regulate your progress.

Clay is God made and all natural. There are 7 families of clay, and all clays are different in color, texture, mineral content, energy and absorption. There are specific things to look for in securing safe clay. Look for a reputable company with easy access to phone numbers and contact information. Ask for specific information as to the pH of the clay and the type and family of clay. Some clay can be acidic so be sure to ask. Ask for proof of purity of the clay (certified lab test results of microbial, yeast and mold tests). Look for a non-gritty, fine milled 325-400 screen mesh. You want virtually tasteless, odorless clay. A slightly swelling Calcium Bentonite Clay is best, preferably a virgin natural clay that hasn't undergone any treatment (not processed, washed, heated or gamma rayed). Look for professional packaging, avoid Ziploc bags and ask for clay mineral analysis sheet.

In conclusion, give clay a try at lowering and maintaining a lower pH. Raymond Dextreit in his book, *Earth Cures,* explains it this way. "It is not possible to foresee exactly what will happen with clay applications especially at first, It reacts different to everyone's body chemistry and needs, but in every case, there is a remarkable improvement, if not a complete healing. As there are no dangers to fear, there is no reason to oppose giving it a try, even for an extended period."

Our Earth is the source of infinite means for restoring and maintaining good health. The study of nature is fascinating and rewarding. We have so much readily available at our fingertips. Increasingly we are awakening to the value and safety of these natural resources. Enjoy your journey to healthy living.

CALCIUM BENTONITE CLAY A CATALYST FOR ENRICHING BLOOD

Many experiments have confirmed the useful role of clay in the reconstitution of blood. Spectacular improvements in the composition of blood have been observed following a protocol of clay and improved diet.

As the old adage goes," You are what you eat." Most of our physical ailments are the result of our life style of poor eating habits and lack of exercise. Most of what we put in and on our bodies contributes to a buildup of acidity, clogged arteries, high blood pressure and imbalance in pH Levels and numerous diseases.

One theory for the origins of life proposes that clay particles acted as a catalyst, converting simple organic molecules into more complex structures. [1] This is important to note because revisions in diet alone is not enough by itself to solve the problems associated with poor nutrition. The body needs a catalyst to aid in transforming the nutritive elements, contributing to their assimilation, fixation and storage in the body. Calcium Bentonite Clay is that important catalyst.

With good nutrition and help from a quality, Calcium Bentonite Clay, you will be amazed at how quickly you can begin to rectify the ills we have inflicted on our bodies. The green healing clays from the Smectite family of clays known as Living Clays have long been respected for healing properties. Some of these clays draw as much as 33 times their molecular weight.

Living clay works with the body to reduce acidity by balancing the pH level, cleansing the colon, ridding parasites from the colon, detoxing environmental contaminants and enriching the blood. Applied topically, clay stimulates the flow of blood containing oxygen needed for cellular repair and thus speeds the healing process. Additionally, the powerful drawing power of clay's negative ionic charge, some as much as 33 times it molecular weight, makes clay baths both popular and highly effective in removing toxins

Recent studies of blood samples under high powered microscopes show what acidity can do to our blood. Blood cells tend to cluster and clump together and often the background is filled with parasites and nano crystal build-up. After six weeks of good nutrition and taking the clay internally the blood samples instead show a clear background and individual round cells surrounded by a glow, evidence that an alkaline pH has been restored.

Slide 1, below are some blood samples that illustrate this progression: These are beginning slides of acidic blood samples showing the clustering of the blood cells. Acidity causes the cells to stick together and impedes the delivery of oxygen to the cells. The debris and lines in the background denotes the presence of parasites and nano acid crystal lines and particles that can contribute to kidney and gall stones.

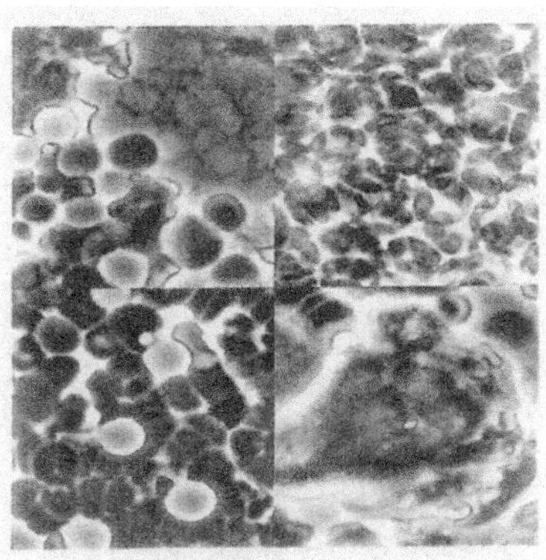

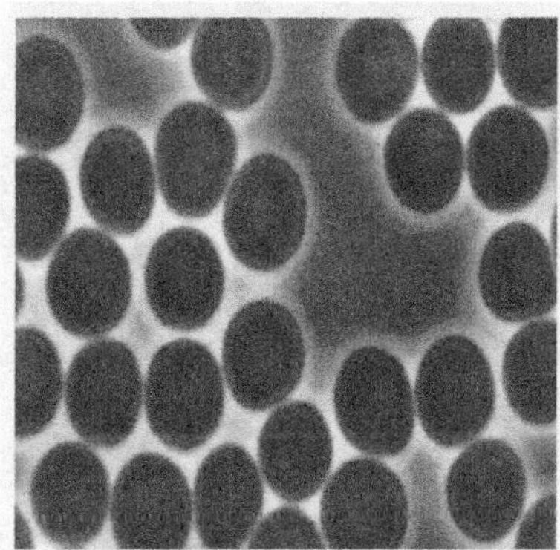

See slide 2 showing the progress of the blood cells six weeks later when cells are becoming better defined and healthier.

The renowned French natural healer Raymond Dextreit he states, "Clay is particularly rich in certain diastases and enzymes. Some of these diastases, the oxidases, have the power of fixing free oxygen, which explains the purifying and enriching action of clay in the blood."

All this being said not all clays are alike or suitable for healing purposes. For more information about the Criteria for Selecting A Quality Clay go to page 102. Only nature can make clay.

It cannot be replicated in laboratories or by pharmaceutical companies.

CHEMOTHERAPY DETOXIFICATION PRE AND POST CARE AND DETOX

Clay therapy, both internal and external, during the crucial rest time between chemotherapy treatments is important. This detox strategy will assist the patient to and stabilize in time for the next treatment.
After the chemotherapy treatments are finished, the critical convalescing period begins.

Check with your physician as to when the radiation and Chemo have completed their work.

It should be noted that Calcium Bentonite Clay might allow some patients to complete the series of chemotherapy treatment that they would otherwise withdraw before completion. This is where Calcium Bentonite Clay goes head-on against the dangerous accumulation of toxic waste and all the debilitating side effects.

Examples of this detox/healing process will start with topical oral hygiene: gums, mouth sores, tongue, lips, and throat. External will be the obvious skin problems: infection, fungus, and yeast infections.

1) Clay for Mouth Sores – Clay is excellent for healing mouth sores. Swish with liquid clay 2-3 a day. Brush your teeth a little hydrated clay on top of a little toothpaste. For bleeding gums and mouth ulcers put the dry powder clay between the cheek and gums. Saliva will cause it to adhere to the area. Sleep with it in the mouth as needed.

2) Full Body Wraps – Use daily with slightly warmed clay. Put some hydrated clay in a zip lock bag and put the bag in a sink of warm water for a few minutes. Apply head to toe and allow it to dry in a warm room. Even a partial treatment, such as face or neck, an upper or lower body, or only legs and feet, would be of value to the stressed patient. However, a full-body treatment is an exceptional and favoured tactic to dramatically reduce the flood of toxic poisoning that is overwhelming and literally choking the patient's system. Wrap in a warm sheet if necessary while drying.

3) Detox Clay Bath – Use twice a week or as needed. Mix the dry powder clay according to directions. Pour the liquid mixture and swish around as the bath water is filling. Soak for no more than 30 minutes. You may use this method as a stand alone or use after a full body wrap. The hot water will open the pores, and the clay will draw out the toxins.

4) Clay Drink – Drink Liquid Clay, 3 ounces, three times a day. To prepare the liquid clay in a blender, add 4 cups of water to ½ cup of powder Clay and mix well. Pour into a glass or food grade plastic Quart bottle with a non-metal lid. From this premixed liquid, the recommended ounces can be added to juice or a smoothie. Make sure to drink plenty of water during the day as well. Drinking Calcium Bentonite Clay is great for settling and balancing a nauseous stomach, acid reflux, stopping diarrhea and balancing the pH.

5) Calcium Bentonite Clay Suppositories – Use as needed. Clay suppositories aid in hemorrhoid, vaginal and anal fistula treatments, along with feminine hygiene needs. Take some hydrated clay and mix a little clay powder in it for a workable and firm consistency. Form into bullet-shaped suppositories and allow them to dry slightly until firm enough to insert as a suppository. Re-wetting lubricates for easier insertion.

The cancer chemotherapy patient is in dire need of detoxification and wound healing – which are provided by the soothing properties of Calcium Bentonite Clay. A patient's whole system has been in a physical, emotional, and chemical wreck; the patient is totally exhausted and full of poison.

Antibiotics are of little value. The patient's immune system is desperately depressed and in overload. It just can't deal with the bacterial and toxic assaults.

The body needs help to absorb and adsorb the mass of toxins and poisonous waste that any person's system isn't designed to handle. The ailing body needs assistance in searching out, capturing, and removing the destructive bacteria, which are growing by about one billion every hour.

It seems that clay has, among other properties, that of either to stimulating a deficiency or absorbing an excess in the radioactivity of the body on which it is applied. On an organism that has suffered and still retains the radiations of radium or any other intensive radioactive source, the radioactivity is first enhanced and then absorbed. Clay could, in this way, ensure the protection of organisms over-exposed to atomic radiations. This radioactive effect has been researched: today when everyone is forcibly submitted to many artificially provoked radioactive aggressions, such as dust in the atmosphere from bomb testing, everything increasing this danger should be avoided. Experiments made with the Geiger counter have demonstrated that dry clay absorbs a very important part of this surrounding radioactivity. [1]

Clay can absorb/adsorb infection in tissue and acts as nature's referee so your body can heal itself. Remember, Calcium Bentonite Clay can't be used incorrectly. Drink it, put it on your body, and bathe in it.

If taking life-sustaining medicines, check with your pharmacist to see if there is a conflict of medications. Allow 4-6 hours after taking medicine to take clay internally to make sure you have absorbed your medicine and that clay will not interfere with it.

CLAY A LIVING CATALYST SUPPORTING THE BODY

French Naturopath Raymond Dextreit is the most famous and most experienced clay therapist known in the history of the world. The following is from his book, *Earth Cures*. [13]

"One of clay's peculiarities is based on its physical-chemical domination. From a thermo-dynamic point of view, we must admit that clay cannot be the sole source of energy of the phenomena it produces. Clay is effective through a dynamic presence far more significant than a mere consideration of the substances it contains. It is a catalyst rather than an agent in itself. This is possible because clay is alive – 'living earth'." [1]

Howard Hughes Medical Institute (HHMI) researchers have discovered that clays may have been the catalysts that spurred the spontaneous assembly of fatty acids into the small sacs that ultimately evolved into the first living cells.

One theory for the origins of life proposes that clay particles acted as a catalyst, converting simple organic molecules into more complex structures. [2]

As a catalyst clay, through biological transmutation, can and does redesign itself through chemical changes that make elements in the clay's composition synchronize with the body and its needs to improve bodily function. Though clay is inert it is still capable of chemical and physical changes that break down the clay minerals to provide necessary enzymes, amino acids and even peptide chains that make available protein absorption. In this way clay is a 'Living' matter.

Clay is particularly rich in certain diastases and enzymes. Some of these diastases, the oxidases, have the power of fixing free oxygen, which explains the purifying and enriching action of clay in the blood. [13]

Many experiences have confirmed the useful role of clay in the reconstitution of the blood. Lab analysis of blood samples has given visual proof to the speculation of the role clay plays in cleansing and rebuilding the blood through its adaptability to the body's needs.

CLAY BATHS – THE SAFE METHOD FOR DETOXING YOUR SYSTEM

by Cheryl McCoy

"Detoxing" – the myriad and sundry ways of removing metals, toxins, and other nasties from the body - is becoming increasingly popular in alternative and natural medicine and appears to be inching its way into the more traditional medical arenas as well. The beneficial health results produced by these procedures cannot be ignored. As a result, it seems that everywhere you turn, there are companies claiming to have the best product for detoxing your system. "Clay and water...those two lifelines are all you will often need to return your body to a state of optimal health," states Perry A~

According to clay expert Jason Eaton:

"There are many methods available in both alternative and natural medicine that are designed to 'detoxify the body.' However, nearly all of them do exactly the opposite: They stimulate the body to release toxic byproducts stored in fat, organs, and other tissues. The result is that these substances are dumped back into active metabolism. The body, then, is placed under a great deal of toxic stress, even to the point of toxic shock. This poses quite a problem, for the body has stored these substances for a very specific reason: It has been incapable of eliminating the substances without causing significant damage. Therefore, the short cut "quick fix" methods to detoxify the body can be quite dangerous, and the natural and comprehensive methods can require a lot of attention, hard work, and anywhere from six months to three years to accomplish and are often accompanied by uncomfortable symptoms as the body cleans itself." What is lacking is an avenue to get the released toxins out of the body.

So, what's a person to do? Many experts recommend clay baths for detoxing used especially in treating lead or mercury poisoning).

Clay baths have been safely used for centuries. These days, clay baths are used to treat everything from tired, achy muscles to heavy metal poisoning, radiation and chemical/pesticide exposure. Very recently, some surprising and encouraging results have been reported when using clay baths to treat Autism.

Certain clays have the ability to remove toxins through the pores of the skin. Discussing clay baths in his book, *The Clay Cure*, Ran Knishinsky states, "It is a fairly simple procedure, and it can do a lot of good in a relatively short time. Because of clay's excellent drawing effect, the clay has the power to literally pull toxicities through the pores of the skin in the bath." In addition, Wendell Hoffman, author of *Using Energy to Heal*, found that bentonite clay baths draw out toxic chemicals through the pores of the skin.

Taking a therapeutic clay bath, lasting anywhere from 15 minutes to two hours, is one of the most effective methods in existence to help assist the body in the elimination of toxic substances which have accumulated in the body. Clay baths stimulate the lymphatic system and deeply cleanse the body's largest breathing organ (the skin). Acting both directly on the body and acting as a systematic catalyst, clay used in this manner interacts directly with the body's immune system and helps to remove the toxic burden placed on the major organs of the body.

Dr. Miriam Jang, M.D., author of "Breakthroughs in Autism," a synopsis of the DAN protocol, says:

"I have put a huge number of patients on these clay baths and the levels of heavy metals – mercury, lead, arsenic, aluminum, and cadmium have come down dramatically... I have been monitoring the levels of metals using all three methods (TD DMPS, oral DMSA and clay baths) and the clay baths are way faster in the removal of metals...One particular patient had very high levels of mercury and levels of lead that were off the charts. In 3 months of twice weekly clay baths, the lead came down dramatically, and the mercury disappeared. The muscle weakness associated with high lead levels improved dramatically. Another 5 months of these clay baths showed even lower levels of lead, but the mercury reappeared. This supports the theory that mercury is sequestered in different areas of our body, and it takes time to get it all out." [27]

Clay baths may be used for heavy metal toxicity, general chemical toxicity, radiation and chemotherapy recovery, general systemic support by stimulating the lymphatic system, comprehensive cleansing protocols, as well as simply for relaxation and enjoyment. They are wonderful for relieving stress and helping to relax, especially in the evening before bed.

Choosing the Right Clay:

It's important to choose carefully when selecting clay for your clay baths. While certain clays are ideal, and others are acceptable though not as good, still others should be avoided all together. For clay baths, the experts agree that clean, raw, natural Smectite clays, which adsorb and absorb, such as Calcium Bentonites, often referred to as Living Clays, are the best. It's vital to avoid any contaminated clays, as well as any clays with additives. Clay should be stored in containers that are completely sealed and kept away from petroleum chemicals. Clay should not come into prolonged contact with metals.

Preparing a Clay Bath:

The preferred method is to add 1 cup of water to a 6-7 cup blender, then add 1-2 cups of clay powder, (2 cups for heavy metal removal and 1 cup for general maintenance), next top off with water to within 1 inch of the top and blend until smooth. Pour the liquid clay into the bath and rinse the container. Be sure to wash the blender blades immediately to prevent rusting. A clay bath should last ideally between 15-20 minutes in hot water (longer in a less hot bath). Submerge as much of your body as possible during the bath. For hot baths drink water or a Gatorade type drink to replenish the electrolytes. The more clay that is used in the therapy, the more powerful the response.

In some rare, severely toxic cases, the clay may turn dark and gooey. If so scoop the gooey part out and dispose of it. If the water has not turned dark, scoop some of the clay water out after your bath to water your plants. Rinse the tub thoroughly. A quality clay will clean the pipes and is safe for septic systems.

It is recommended nothing be added to the clay bath – no herbs, oils, fragrances, etc. Herbal treatments or other skin treatments can be done after the clay bath if desired.

Cheryl McCoy designed the website www.BentoniteClayInfo.com an informational and educational resource for the various uses of healing clay. She discovered the amazing benefits of this clay and has been an ardent advocate for this clay ever since with clay baths being one of her favorites. She is now retired and has moved to Oregon.

CLAY, A HORSE OF A DIFFERENT COLOR

Clay is a horse of a different color. It is not a drug. Its actions are varied and being a catalyst adds to the mystery of how it can do all it does. It is synergistic and its multiple actions work together with the body to co-create amazing healing results.

The Smectite family of clays is called "Living Clay" because of their ability to make changes. A Living Clay is one capable of change through balancing, transforming, stimulating, and the interactive exchange of elements and energy. On the other hand, a rock is incapable of transforming itself from within. It can only change from outside influences including weathering by heat, wind and water.

Living Clays act as a catalyst and assist the body in returning to and maintaining a state of balance and well-being, through amazing processes not fully understood by anyone as of yet. A catalyst is an agent that provokes or speeds significant change or action. For any process to occur, energy known as *activation energy* is required. Without the help of a catalyst the amount of energy needed to spark a particular reaction is high. When the catalyst is present the activation energy is lowered, making the reaction happen more efficiently. Unlike other reagents, substances that produce a chemical reaction, a catalyst is not consumed by the reaction itself. It generally works by either changing the structure of a molecule or by bonding to reactant molecules causing them to combine, react, and release a product or energy.

Enzymes are biological *catalysts* or assistants. They consist of various types of proteins that work to drive the chemical reaction required for a specific action or nutrient. Enzymes might be the factors that give Living Clays its amazing and infinitely unexplained abilities. "Enzymes are large biological molecules responsible for the thousands of chemical interconversions that sustain life. They are highly selective catalysts, greatly accelerating both the rate and specificity of metabolic reactions, from the digestion of food to the synthesis of DNA. Enzymes catalyze the forward and backward reactions equally. They do not alter the equilibrium itself, but only the speed at which it is reached." [54]

Clays do not fit the healing modalities of standard drugs. Until the research scientist quit looking at it as a drug in an in vitro study, they will never understand the miraculous healing potential Living Clays offer.

In vitro, studies require sterilization and this messes with the natural microorganisms in the clay reducing its effectiveness. The "killing power" of Living Clays are limited, it seems, to gram negative organisms. And yet, while clay is a very, very effective treatment for conditions such as food poisoning (E Coli for example), clay doesn't kill this organism. There are many other avenues, or 'modes of action" that living clays use as co-healers with the body to cure conditions, and very little of clay's amazing power is in its ability to kill things.

The microbiologists at BYU noted that clay didn't kill the pathogenic bacteria they were studying but continued to study until they found the mechanism of action: In their study the clay adsorbed all of the endotoxin produced by the bacteria, which is what caused the bacteria to be pathogenic. Using clay prevented dehydration, and because the bacteria wasn't poisoning the body, the body's own immune system was quickly able to reduce population counts. Likely, but not demonstrated in the study, the clay absorbed much of the bacteria as well, eliminating it from the body without actually killing the organisms. [56]

With Living Clays, the proof is in the pudding, the results speak for themselves.

CLAY'S INFLUENCE ON CELL DEVELOPMENT

There is much known about the environment and composition of the early earth. However, there is even more which is uncertain and not known. Because of this, scientists are studying and searching for the conditions which they believe were present when life began. If we know these conditions, then perhaps we can discover the building blocks from which life came. [35]

Clays May Have Aided Formation of Primordial Cells

Howard Hughes Medical Institute (HHMI) researchers have discovered that clays may have been the catalysts that spurred the spontaneous assembly of fatty acids into the small sacs that ultimately evolved into the first living cells.

HHMI investigator Jack W. Szostak and his colleagues were prompted to perform their experiments by the earlier work of other researchers who had found that clays could catalyze the chemical reactions needed to construct RNA from building blocks called nucleotides. They reasoned that if clays could foster the formation of vesicles, it would not be inconceivable that clay particles that had RNA on their surface could end up inside such vesicles. If that were true, the result would offer conditions amenable to the eventual evolution of living cells that could self-reproduce.

"To what extent might clay minerals have been suitable as biomaterials, to make such things as the genes, the catalysts, and the membranes of the very first organisms?"

The proposal was that primitive forms of life appeared as the products of a prolonged series of chemical processes taking place under the conditions of the probiotic Earth. [53]

"Given the recognition that all extant organisms are themselves the products of a long process of evolution, the question arose also as to which of these common properties were more fundamental than others with respect to the early history of life on Earth."

Clay made animal life possible on Earth, a UC Riverside-led study finds. A sudden increase in oxygen in the Earth's recent geological history, widely considered necessary for the expansion of animal life, occurred just as the rate of clay formation on the Earth's surface also increased, the researchers report.

"Our study shows for the first time that the initial soils covering the terrestrial surface of Earth increased the production of clay minerals and provided the critical geochemical processes necessary to oxygenate the atmosphere and support multicellular animal life," said Martin Kennedy, an associate professor of sedimentary geology and geochemistry at UCR, who led the study. "Clays not only have the ability to grow and adsorb other molecules, but they can then incorporate the information from those molecules and use it to alter and change themselves. [53]

[27] Louis Kervran, the French scientist, world-famous for his provocative work on Biological Transmutations, writes about a shrimp that lives in clay: "It has been known for a long time that living organisms inhabit clay without any organic supply of food from the outside. The Niphargus shrimp lives in the clay of caves. Experiments have shown that it grows normally in pure clay to which nothing has been added. Research workers therefore thought that the shrimp lived on clay and nothing but clay, an impossibility according to the laws of biochemistry. It cannot live thus in clay alone, but this clay contains microorganisms which work for the shrimp, making vitamins, various mineral products, nitrogen, phosphorous, and calcium, etc." Therefore, clay is a live medium which helps generate and maintain life.

CRITERIA FOR SELECTING A QUALITY CLAY

In 1998, when I first Googled Bentonite Clays, I got 5,000 results. Today, in 2023, I get approximately 14,000,000 results. That's quite a significant increase.

To what can we attribute this increase? With the growing realization of the dangers of traditional medicines, the search for a natural and safe alternative has brought man back to this healing element that has been used for thousands of years by indigenous people around the globe.

With this rising popularity and recognition of clays being safe, natural and inexpensive, clay companies are popping up overnight. This alternative to prescription, side-effect-riddled medicine has everyone wanting to get in on this opportunity to make money - and some actually care about sharing this remarkable healing agent.

As with anything that grows too fast, the lack of education and knowledge about clays can pose a danger to society. Kitchens and garages become launch pads for home grown businesses, and new domain names flood the Internet with eager entrepreneurs in search of financial freedom. Common sense and safety in handling are ignored in eagerness to capture a corner of the market.

With these concerns in mind, it is extremely important to know your clays, what the law requires, and what the clay companies should provide in the way of service and information.

First, all clays are different, making it complicated to understand the many differences in clay families. For this article, let's focus on the Smectite Family of Clays known commonly as Bentonites. A unique trait of the Smectite Family of clays is their greater adsorption capacity over other clay families. Within the Smectite Family of clays, there exist predominately Sodium and Calcium Bentonites.

Sodium Bentonites are naturally high in salt – as high as 14%. They are the swelling or expanding clays, taking on more water when hydrated. These have been used primarily for industrial purposes (e.g., liner materials for landfills, binders for iron ore processing, suspension agents in oil well drilling, and water-proofing products for building materials).

In addition, all Calcium Bentonite Clays are not the same! They differ in composition of minerals, colors, textures, swelling capacity, taste, odor, grittiness and purity. The major differences lie in proportion of the trace minerals that make up clays. All clays contain from 60 – 70 trace minerals, and most in parts per million (ppm) and in insignificant amounts. The primary minerals determine the common names of many clays, as does the location of their source.

Calcium Bentonites are more widely known as healing clays

for detoxing, cleansing, drawing our impurities and are used in many products such as toothpaste, antacids, and cosmetics.

Today, clays are carving a significant niche in the natural health world. One of the major problems is that industrial clays are not mined with attention to purity and cleanliness. For industrial purposes, it is NOT important for the clay to be clean and pure. For these purposes, clays are dirt cheap (excuse the pun), as they are only scooped up, bagged, and sold (and usually only sold by the tonnage or truck load).

[60] The FDA has given all Bentonite clays a certification as GRAS: Generally Regarded as Safe. This refers to the exposure to clays during the milling process and for external uses. This does not mean, by any stretch of the imagination, that you can make health claims about clays LEGALLY. A clay company selling clay cannot legally say it will stop the pain of an insect bite, a Jellyfish sting, a tooth ache, clear up Acne, accelerate wound healing, stop Acid Reflux, diarrhea, or detox heavy metals until it has undergone one of the million-dollar tests performed to FDA specifications and gets the FDA's approval. Since Clays have been known to help with 50 -100 ailments, you would need a test for each ailment, and I think you can do the math on that one. Basically, clay has positive effects on so many ailments that it would take billions of dollars to get it approved for each and every health claim.

Clay companies making healing claims are riding on the edge of serious trouble as clays become more and more popular. It is only a matter of time before the FDA rears its head and starts investigating the healing claims and shuts them down and/or issues serious fines. Today, the FDA has other fish to fry, so they have not messed with these up-and-coming clay companies.

There are companies that sell clay for internal use legally, but some have had to have their clay processed to meet stringent requirements. When clays are processed, whether by heat, sterilization or irradiation, the efficacy (strength) of the clay has been greatly reduced.

So if you can't make healing claims, what can a company legally say about the clay they sell? They can legally say clay relieves, detoxes (can't say what), soothes, draws impurities (it is a known fact that clay is used by the wine and beer industry for drawing out impurities), stimulates, and a few other very safe generic terms with no definitive meaning.

Anytime a good thing comes along, there are those who recognize it as an opportunity to make money and will jump in and take advantage by pushing the rules. The misuse of the internet is a good example. More clays are pushing the edge of truth. Some are copying information verbatim from other sites and claiming it as their own.

One man claimed to be selling Dead Sea mud that was Illinois dirt laced with cornstarch. This is another interesting statement: *"Vegetables are not attacked by pests when grown with Brand X clay in the soil."* I would say to them, "Show me some proof." If you have a concern with a statement made by a clay company, question it and ask for an explanation.

My greatest concern with the influx of new clays is the lack of clay knowledge and the harm it will bring to the good reputation of quality clays.

There are many confusing and misleading statements to lure

you to a particular clay. KNOW YOUR CLAY. Do your due diligence by asking the company questions and for a lab test as to the purity, cleanliness and analysis of the primary minerals.

Criteria for selecting a quality clay and a reliable clay source:

1. A natural calcium Bentonite clay, pure and free of contaminants.

2. A pH of 8.5 or above.

3. A mineral analysis sheet.

4. A Quality Control Lab report showing the clay falls within the safety guidelines.

5. A living clay, Montmorillonite/Calcium Bentonite, from the Smectite family of clays.

6. A green swelling clay that Absorbs and Adsorbs.

7. A pure clay that is odorless and tasteless.

8. An all-natural vs. processed clay.

9. Professional packaging (no Ziploc bags or hand-written labels) with labels showing directions and ingredients.

10. A non-gritty clay milled to a 325-400 screen mesh.

11. A clay that expands to a 2 1/2 to 1 ratio in volume (2 1/2 parts water to 1 part dry clay).

12. A company that gives you direct contact information (a phone number, physical address and an e-mail address).

13. A company available to answer questions about their clay.

14. A reliable company that has been in business for several years.

15. A clay that does not stain material.

16. A clay from a subsurface type mine protected from the elements.

17. A clay direct from a source provider.

Continue to ask for proof and do your due diligence. Educate yourself and use common sense. If you cannot speak to a person from that company, consider it a red flag.

Now go find your perfect clay!

ERRONEOUS BELIEFS ABOUT CALCIUM BENTONITE CLAY

Before healing clays became so popular, there was very little information on the internet regarding these all natural, drug free, alternative healing modalities. Since the popularity of Calcium Bentonite Clays have increased, misconceptions about how they work have become rampant resulting in many erroneous beliefs. It is time to correct some of these common misconceptions.

1. MYTH: Taking clay internally will absorb nutrients, vitamins and minerals from daily supplements and foods you eat.

FALSE. Quite the contrary. Calcium Bentonite Clay molecules hold a strong negative ionic charge and are only attracted to substances that hold a positive charge like toxins and contaminants. The Clay cleanses the colon pulling out old putrefied fecal matter and mucoid plaque buildup that is blocking the absorption of vitamins, minerals, supplements, and nutrition from the foods we eat. Energy levels are known to increase in 1-3 days depending on the condition of the individual.

2. MYTH: Calcium Bentonite Clay will absorb all the good flora

bacteria in the digestive tract.

FALSE. No. Aside from its absorbent and revitalizing properties, clay is also a catalyst when taken orally, for it favors the transformation of foods into nutritive elements.

[27] "Clay is incomparable for maintaining or reestablishing a good normal flora, for it favors the development of useful ferments, while opposing the growth of pathogenic bacill."

3. MYTH: Aluminum in Clay is dangerous.

FALSE. Aluminum is part of the structural make up of all clays. The aluminum in clay is in a safe oxide form, not the dangerous man-made processed aluminum. The many trace minerals in Calcium Bentonite Clay are fused together into a super compound structure known as a clay particle which cannot break down and cannot be absorbed by your body.

4. MYTH: Clays are dietary supplements, like vitamins.

FALSE. Though very small amounts of the dominant minerals (i.e. calcium, magnesium, sodium and potassium) in clays might be exchanged in the adsorption ionic exchange layer, they are not sufficient as daily supplement requirements.

A little bit of incorrect knowledge can be very harmful. Help set the record straight on this multi-beneficial gift from Mother Earth. Now, go spread some good information.

EXCERPTS FROM CALCIUM BENTONITE CLAY, NATURE'S PATHWAY TO HEALING

1. Raymond Dextreit, French naturopath and fore runner in herbal healing states, [13] "Clay is effective through a dynamic presence far more significant than a mere consideration of the substances it contains. It is a catalyst rather than an agent in itself. This is possible because clay is alive, a living earth'. We cannot always penetrate Nature's secrets; we must merely acknowledge and use them."

2. Clay is a catalyst that assists the body in returning to and maintaining a state of balance and wellbeing. A catalyst is an agent that provokes or speeds significant change or action. Unlike other reagents that participate in the chemical reaction, a catalyst is not consumed by the reaction itself. It generally works by either changing the structure of a molecule or by bonding to reactant molecules causing them to combine, react and release a product or energy.

3. A catalyst is any substance that works to accelerate a chemical reaction. For any process to occur, energy, known as ac-

tivation energy, is required. Without the help of a catalyst the amount of energy needed to spark a particular reaction is high. When the catalyst is present the activation energy is lowered, making the reaction happen more efficiently. The catalyst generally works by either changing the structure of a molecule or by bonding to reactant molecules causing them to combine, react and release a product or energy.

4. Internally, Calcium Bentonite clay provides a very effective cleansing and detoxing capability even though it is not absorbed through the colon wall into the blood stream. It can, however, capture freshly ingested toxins before they are absorbed into the body. This is ultimate prevention.

5. Simply put, where there is a deficiency, clay seems to supply the needed substance regardless of whether the clay itself is rich in that substance. Clay does not merely remedy a deficiency. It goes further and stimulates the deficient organ and helps the restoration of the failing function. This is possible because clay is alive – " a living earth."

6. Smectite clays are capable of bio-transmutation. How else can you explain the fact that clay enriches and cleanses the blood, increases bone density, reduces inflammation, swelling and pain in joints, when taken internally, knowing that the clay particles do not pass through the colon wall into the bloodstream?

7. In *Earth Cures*, Raymond Dextreit says it this way, "Clay acts on all organs of the body – on the whole organism. Everything unhealthy and emitting positive cations are irresistibly attracted to clay and become subject to immediately elimination. Wherever there is a deficiency, clay seems to supply the

needed substance regardless of whether the clay itself is rich in that substance. [13]

8. The tremendous amount of energy in clays is from the electromagnetic actions and intense thermodynamic heat of the volcanic eruption. You might say it is super charged.

9. The miracle of Calcium Bentonite Clay is it acts so gently and subtly you are not aware of the healing actions until you see or feel the positive results. For many, the fact that it works and that no one has ever died from taking clay is enough.

10. The energy of clays and clay's ability to release energy are two critical points in how clays work. "If we go back to our base physical components, we can safely say that we are built from multitudes of particles held together by electrical bonds. Electrical forces are what hold atoms and molecules together. Chemical bonds and reactions depend on these electrical forces. Therefore, all chemical reactions are, in essence, reorganizations of electrical forces, which continue to be vital at body levels, i.e., tissues and organs. When this is all considered, a living organism is shown to be an extremely delicate and intricate electrical system." [16]

11. During illness, the vital force is weak and incapable of supporting the body and its functions. In health, however, the opposite occurs: the force is strong and is able to counteract sickness and decay. What keeps the immune system running is the energy that feeds it, the substance of life. The body will not run well or will at least run with all sorts of mechanical problems, when there is no energy to support it. When a Living Clay is consumed, its natural electro-magnetic energy is released into the body and mingles with the energy of the

body, creating a stronger, more powerful boost of energy in the body.

12. In order to create health, the body must be stimulated and re-stimulated by another working energy like clay. When the immune system does not function at its best, the clay stimulates the body's inner resources to awaken the stagnant energy. It supplies the body with the available magnetism to run well.

13. "The best-known characteristic of clay is that it "acts as needed." Living clay is said to propel the immune system to find a new healthy balance. Reactions are not forced, but rather triggered into effect, as they are needed. To put it in other words, clay strengthens the body to a point of higher resistance. In this way, the body's natural immune system has an improved chance of restoring and maintaining health." [13]

14. Due to its huge surface area and negative charge, clay maintains its molecular whole and does not break down or assimilate with the body.

15. We must accept the facts even if we do not understand their origin. And clay does act with wisdom – it goes to the unhealthy spot. Used internally, whether absorbed orally, anally or vaginally, clay goes to the place where harm is, there it lodges, perhaps for several days, until finally it draws out the toxins, disease, etc., with its evacuation.

16. From helping to prevent the proliferation of pathogenic germs and parasites to aiding with rebuilding of healthy tissues and cells, clay is a 'living' cure.

17. Bentonites are from the Smectite family of clays. Smectite

clays refer to a family of non-metallic clays primarily composed of hydrated calcium sodium aluminum silicate. Alumino silicates are crystalline compounds, made up of silicon, aluminum and oxygen-aluminum oxide. As long as the aluminum is bound in this form, it poses no health risk.

18. Smectites are characterized by their expandable properties and a Cation Exchange Capacity of 80-100 millequivalents 100 g-1. They also have the largest specific surface area of 700-800 m2/g.

19. Even though Sodium Bentonite, and Calcium Bentonite Clay are cousins from the same family genesis, they are as different as night and day in efficacy and intended uses. Sodium Bentonites primarily throw off sodium from the Cation Exchange layer while Calcium Bentonite will exchange the dominate minerals calcium and magnesium. High Sodiums tend to have a thick gooey plastic like consistency.

20. All clays are not created equal. Within the Smectite family there are thousands of different types of clays, each consisting of between 60 and 90 minerals in different amounts. Some clays are good for topical only and some better for internal use. Then there are those high-quality clays that are excellent for both uses. It is important to know your clays.

21. It is very important that the clay be pure, clean and natural direct from the source mine—preferably a subsurface mine that has been protected from the natural elements. Some companies are so far removed from the original clay source they have little knowledge about what they are promoting and how it works.

22. Long before recorded history, humans have used healing clays both internally and externally to cure illness, sustain life and promote general health. Ancient tribes of the high Andes, central Africa and the Aborigines of Australia used clay as a curative for healing purposes.

23. Another early clay user was the Greek lad who became the famous Dioscorides and was considered the engineer of medicine for the Roman Empire. He attributed a "God-Like-Intelligence" to the properties of healing clays.

24. In Malaysia, women who want to bear children eat clay to help secure pregnancy. In New Guinea, pregnant women eat clay because they believe it is good for fetal development. In Russia, pregnant women place clay on their tongue to expedite birth and to facilitate easier expulsion of the afterbirth. It is also used to combat morning sickness. Aborigine women were some of the first clay eaters. The pregnant women craved it and believed it helped develop the fetus.

25. As late as 1919, clay provided an invaluable medicine in the cholera epidemic that swept through China.

26. During WWI, German physicians offered clay therapy as a solution to food poisoning, dysentery, diarrhea, and battle wound infection that was rampant among troops on both sides, greatly reducing mortality rates.

27. Russian scientists used clay to protect their bodies from radiation when working with nuclear material. Because it absorbs radiation so well, Bentonite Clay was chosen to dump into the Chernobyl reactors after the meltdown there

28. In Switzerland and Germany, doctors made use of clay for

healing purposes. In Davos, an important center for treatment of tuberculosis, patients were usually treated with clay; the whole thorax was daubed with a paste of very hot clay and this pack was kept on overnight. This treatment was credited with miraculous healings.

29. One of living clay's healing properties is that of homeostasis, the ability to return to balance. Homeostasis is explained as the ability of a system or living organism to adjust its internal environment by several complex biological mechanisms that operate via the autonomic nervous system to maintain a stable equilibrium.

30. Unfortunately, with clay one size does not fit all. What gets amazing results for one person may get minimal results for another. Our systems are at different stages and the clay is an adoptogen and meets your body where it is. Therefore, it may be necessary to play around with applications and protocols and find your own unique 'Clay Happy Place.'

31. It is important to take it in a liquid form vs. a tablet or capsule. Clay begins working in the mouth and the life force energy of the clay will resonate with all the cells of the body immediately. Taking it in a capsule or pill form you miss the benefits to the mouth, gums, esophagus and it will take fluids from the body to fully hydrate. In a liquid or fully hydrated form it is activated ready to work immediately.

32. Precaution if taking medications, check with your pharmacist to determine if clay will interfere with any medications. Ask how long it takes for the body to absorb the medication, allow that time to pass between taking your medication and the clay.

33. The skin is the largest organ of our body and can be considered the outward reflection of what's happening inside. Used topically, Calcium Bentonite Clay pulls out excess oils and impurities, stimulates circulation and cellular revitalization and detoxifies. Whichever method you select, your skin will thank you for it!

34. Clay baths - Because the body detoxifies through the skin, clay baths are becoming more and more popular for drawing out toxins and cleansing the skin. Clay baths are beneficial in removing toxic build-up of heavy metals stored in the body. They also relieve sore muscles, body aches, stimulate lymphatic action and circulation, are very relaxing, and can promote a good night's sleep. Children with Autism are reported to be calmer, to maintain longer eye contact, and exhibit improved communication skills after a single clay bath.

35. When clay baths are not possible prepare a foot soak. Mix the clay at a ratio of 1 part clay powder to 6 parts of warm water (when possible) and mix in a blender until it is lump free. Pour the mixture into a plastic shoe box and soak feet for 30 minute intervals. The mix maybe used several times. Cover with an airtight lid between uses.

36. The dry powder Calcium Bentonite Clay application is the most basic. Simply apply dry powder by hand in the amount indicated by the treatment modality. Dry Powder Clay is excellent for open, bleeding wounds and oozing rashes. Packing the wound with the dry powder will stop the bleeding and keep infection out and keep people from bleeding out until they can get adequate medical help.

37. Most clays work best when taken over a long period of

time. Clay does not offer instant cures for all ailments, but history shows it can encourage the body to put up a better fight when taken over a long period of time. When clay is taken for indefinite periods of time, it has no addictive qualities. One can quit taking clay at any time. There are no withdrawal symptoms, and you will never need to enter a withdrawal program.

38. Healing clays are like a Swiss Army Knife. It is a combination of multiple tools in one product that function independently for greater effectiveness.

39. Clay is not a drug. It does not kill; it merely captures and disposes of toxins and infections that are detrimental to the body. So simple.

40. The important difference between sodium and calcium Bentonites is the relative proportions of the two cations in the inter-laminar region. In calcium bentonite, the divalent calcium ion predominates. The ionic radius of Ca2+ is 99 pm [5] which is almost identical to that of Na+. Although the ions occupy the same volume in space the charge density of the Ca2+ ion is twice that of the Na+ ion. In physical terms this impacts greatly on physiochemical characteristics of the two minerals, since the negatively charged Bentonite lattice sheets are more tightly held together by the calcium ions.

41. Bentonites belong to the Smectite Family of clays. Smectites are characterized by their expandable properties and a Cation Exchange Capacity of 80-100 meq 100 g-1, meaning they absorb and adsorb. They also have the largest specific surface area of 700-800 m2/g.

42. Bentonite Clay particles contain two sources of negative

charge, permanent and variable. Permanent charge is located within the structure of the clay particles- absorption. Variable charge is located on the edges of clay particles - adsorption.

43. Smectites (Bentonites) comprise 99% of all clays used for health purposes today. It is the favored clay for health and dietary use as well as for many industrial applications. This is because Smectites are more complicated clays having a higher Cation Exchange Capacity (CEC), a larger surface area and are considered expanding clays.

44. The sheet of atoms in Bentonite are much thinner and more easily separable in water. That is why Bentonite occupies more surface area than other clays. This property is known as dispersibility, which is unique to swelling types of Bentonites. [39]

45. Bentonite, Montmorillonite and Fuller's earth are used synonymously as names for clays in the Smectite family.

46. It is very important that the clay be pure, clean and natural direct from the source mine—preferably a subsurface mine that has been protected from the natural elements. Some companies are so far removed from the original clay source they have little knowledge about what they are promoting and how it works.

47. Many clays that claim to be 100% pure have been cleaned using either a heat process or a hydration process to "wash" out impurities. Both processes can reduce the effectiveness and strength of the clay. In their attempt to make a purity claim they are actually destroying the natural healing properties. Read labels carefully for any notation of the clay having been

cleaned, processed, filtered, recharged, or tampered with in any fashion other than milling.

48. Some research has shown that clays may have played an essential role in the formation of life. This hypothesis comes from experiments performed with clay to recreate the conditions under which amino acids may form proteins. The clay is thought to act as a catalyst for the formation of long peptide chains, or proteins.

49. Science has shown that the effects of detoxification on our body's cells are nothing short of miraculous. Time alone is not a disease or poison; it is the toxins that accumulate with time that the body cannot withstand and in turn causes deterioration.

50. Clay is a God given pharmacy. Pharmaceutical companies can't replicate it. It must go through an earth birthing of a volcano to make clay.

51. Most clays are alkaline. It is best to ask the pH levels of a clay. Many are acidic due to environmental exposure. Seek a pH between 8 and 10.

52. Never underestimate the power of clay. It is inexpensive and safe to boot. If clay is working for you, you will know it within a week. Be aware of improvements and additional benefits other than the reason you are taking it.

53. Can't get in and out of a bathtub easily to detox. Do a foot detox with the clay mask/mud. Coat the feet thickly and cover with Saran Wrap or Glad Press n' Seal then slip a sock on and sleep with them on at night. You might notice your corns and calluses pealing off too. Do this at least 3 times a week until

feeling better or retested for heavy metals and toxins.

54. A pure, clean natural Calcium Bentonite Clay can be used head to toe inside and out to support the body's immune system in multiple ways.

55. The feet have 500,000 sweat glands and can produce more than a pint of sweat a day. We naturally detox when sweating. Now add clay to those sweat glands covering the feet in a thick clay mask, prop your feet up and really detox.

56. Been on your feet all day? Rub a layer of Bentonite clay on your feet and ankles and prop them up for 15 minutes. You will feel like going dancing afterwards.

57. A number of investigators think the adsorptive properties of certain clays may have played a crucial role in the origin of life. The hypothesis arises as a result of the effort to simulate the conditions under which amino acids may form proteins within the human body. Experiments showed simple amino acids formed into the longer chains called peptides on the surface of clay particles. It is thought that clay acts as a catalyst for the formation of long peptide chains, or proteins

58. One of the most overlooked elements in clay is Silica; an element that is essential to the existence of life. [8] Prof. Adolf Butenandt, proved that life cannot exist without Silica.

59. The Silica in clay is what gives clays properties of nanocrystals. Crystals are dramatic examples of the capacity of matter to self-organize. They can also acquire and retain information.

60. The tremendous amount of energy in clay is from the electromagnetic actions and intense thermodynamic heat of the

volcanic eruption. The energy of clay and its ability to release energy are two critical points in how clays work.

61. When a living clay is consumed, its natural electro-magnetic energy is released into the body, creating a stronger, more vibrant boost of energy.

62. Clay particles are catalysts for stimulation and transformation capable of withholding and releasing energy on impulse. This magnetic action is the booster needed to help to rebuild vitality through the liberation of latent energy.

63. When the immune system is under attack and not functioning at its best, Calcium Bentonite Clay stimulates the body's inner resources to awaken the stagnant energy. It supplies the body with the necessary negative ionic charge to run well.

64. The Cation Exchange Capacity CEC and the Specific Surface area of Smectites are considerable larger than other families of clays being as they are predominately 2:1 clays. There absorption capacity is as much as 8 times greater than other clays. [28]

65. Clays fall into seven separate and distinct family groups; Kaolin, Illite, Chlorite, Vermiculites, Mixed Group Clays, Lath Formed Clays, and Smectite Clays. Within these seven families there are thousands of different types of mineral compositions, each unique and serving vastly different purposes in our world.

66. Clay-swelling activities can be damaged by the addition of salt or certain impurities in the water. Introduction of impurities tends to displace sodium ions and to lower the electrical imbalance in the flakes.

67. It is important to note that the clay particle maintains its molecular integrity. It does not break down and assimilate into the body as the individual mineral components.

68. Do not be alarmed by the presence of heavy metals in clays.

[52] Graham Cairns-Smith of Scotland's University of Glasgow suggests that clays are "proto-organisms" that could have served as the pattern for living systems. He notes that metals in clay lattices n form complexes with the precursors of proteins and DNA. These lattices provide the molecular structure that is necessary to store the energy needed to catalyze chemical reactions.

69. According to the FDA, natural products must comply or be subject to fines or company closure. Before healing claims can be made by a company, the product must have million-dollar scientific studies acceptable to the FDA. Bentonite Clays are however a horse of a different color. They are not a drug, and they are not a food. They really don't fit the scope of the FDA guidelines. "FDA Approved" means it has been tested and proven to make a specific claim as long as the public is informed of possible lethal and destructive side-effects. Personally, I think I'll go drink some clay. [52]

Fibrous Tumors in the Uterus-Painful Menstruation and Lymphatitis

[1] From The Healing Clay by Michel Abehsera. He quotes [58] Our Earth Our Cure: A Handbook of NaturalMedicine for Today by Raymond Dextreit too.

If major troubles occur—if the menstruation is very abundant, insufficient, too painful or accompanied by several clots, mucositis or skin, apply clay poultice on the lower abdomen every night before going to bed, which should be should be kept on overnight unless it causes discomfort. For minor troubles it is sometimes sufficient to apply these poultices only for 10 days preceding menstruation, Interrupt the application during the menstrual period, after that, resume applying them.

The applications can be continued even if the menstruation takes the form of hemorrhage; be sure to slightly warm up the poultices in order not to create a congestive state. According to Dextreit one of the best treatments for hemorrhage consists of applying fresh climbing ivy leaves on the top of the poultice, the stems against the clay. Renew the poultices every 2-3 hours during the day and every time the clay becomes warm during the night.

Of course, a good diet must absolutely be eaten. Also take plants such as marigold and nasturtium, which are rich in female hormones. Make infusions and drink 2-3 times a day. Sage is one of the best for this purpose.

Lymphatitis

This inflammation of the lymphatic vessels is treated as for abscess and carbuncles, as far as the general treatment of the organism is concerned. Treat the inflamed area with repeated applications of clay poultices, left on for 2-4 hours.

Fibrous Tumors in the Uterus

As for almost every disease, this one cannot be taken care of with only symptomatic treatment. No toxic foods of any sort should be provided. A good healthy diet should be eaten. Lemon is good for accelerating the elimination of substances in excess and for contributing to the fixation of useful elements. Take 2-6 lemons a day, depending on tolerance. Clay is an amazing remedy for fibrous tumors. It should be taken orally for the same reasons as the lemon. Take ½ glass of liquid clay once a day on an empty stomach.

Used externally, clay accomplishes wonders when accompanied by natural medicine and food. Dextreit tells of a woman with fibrous tumor in her uterus which caused

serious hemorrhages during menstruation which were treated with clay. She drank it and applied poultices on her lower abdomen. After 3 months of treatment, an examination in a hospital produced this conclusion: "uterus is in the condition of a person of twenty." The patient was 50 years old.

In another case of an ovarian cyst, even specialists feared the operation which seemed unavoidable. However, four months of clay applications resulted in a significant reduction of cyst (at first to the size of an ostrich egg—it had been much larger), making it possible to avoid the operation.

Applications of poultices continued until the total disappearance of the cyst.

Spectacular results were often registered after a few weeks of treatment; However, it should be made clear that usually it takes months and sometimes even years, (in the case of fibrous tumors that do not bleed) to get rid of it completely.

For the first two months apply a poultice a day on the lower abdomen, interrupting it only at the period of menstruation. The poultices must remain in place at least 2 hours. It can remain overnight if applied just before going to bed, unless it is too bothersome. The poultice must be approximately 10-12 inches large and 1 inch thick. The clay must be well against the skin (put a cheese cloth on hairy areas only). Begin first with cold clay; only if it is not tolerated should it be warmed up slightly.

In cases of heavy losses of blood prepare a decoction of oak bark. Use 4 oz. per quart. Boil 10-15 minutes and use as a very slow douche.

FIBROUS TUMORS IN THE UTERUS-PAINFUL MENSTRUATION AND LYMPHATITIS

From The Healing Clay by Michel Abehsera [1]. He quotes [58] Our Earth Our Cure: A Handbook of NaturalMedicine for Today by Raymond Dextreit too.

If major troubles occur—if the menstruation is very abundant, insufficient, too painful or accompanied by several clots, mucositis or skin, apply clay poultice on the lower abdomen every night before going to bed, which should be should be kept on overnight unless it causes discomfort. For minor troubles it is sometimes sufficient to apply these poultices only for 10 days preceding menstruation, Interrupt the application during the menstrual period, after that, resume applying them.

The applications can be continued even if the menstruation takes the form of hemorrhage; be sure to slightly warm up the poultices in order not to create a congestive state. According to Dextreit one of the best treatments for hemorrhage consists of applying fresh climbing ivy leaves on the top of the poultice, the stems against the clay. Renew the poultices every 2-3 hours during the day and every time the clay becomes warm during the night.

Of course, a good diet must absolutely be eaten. Also take plants such as marigold and nasturtium, which are rich in female hormones. Make infusions and drink 2-3 times a day. Sage is one of the best for this purpose.

Lymphatitis

This inflammation of the lymphatic vessels is treated as for abscess and carbuncles, as far as the general treatment of the organism is concerned. Treat the inflamed area with repeated applications of clay poultices, left on for 2-4 hours.

Fibrous Tumors in the Uterus

As for almost every disease, this one cannot be taken care of with only symptomatic treatment. No toxic foods of any sort should be provided. A good healthy diet should be eaten. Lemon is good for accelerating the elimination of substances in excess and for contributing to the fixation of useful elements. Take 2-6 lemons a day, depending on tolerance. Clay is an amazing remedy for fibrous tumors. It should be taken orally for the same reasons as the lemon. Take ½ glass of liquid clay once a day on an empty stomach.

Used externally, clay accomplishes wonders when accompanied by natural medicine and food. Dextreit tells of a woman with fibrous tumor in her uterus which caused

serious hemorrhages during menstruation which were treated with clay. She drank it and applied poultices on her lower abdomen. After 3 months of treatment, an examination in a hospital produced this conclusion: "uterus is in the condition of a person of twenty." The patient was 50 years old.

In another case of an ovarian cyst, even specialists feared the operation which seemed unavoidable. However, four months of clay applications resulted in a significant reduction of cyst (at first to the size of an ostrich egg—it had been much larger), making it possible to avoid the operation.

Applications of poultices continued until the total disappearance of the cyst.

Spectacular results were often registered after a few weeks of treatment; However, it should be made clear that usually it takes months and sometimes even years, (in the case of fibrous tumors that do not bleed) to get rid of it completely.

For the first two months apply a poultice a day on the lower abdomen, interrupting it only at the period of menstruation. The poultices must remain in place at least 2 hours. It can remain overnight if applied just before going to bed, unless it is too bothersome. The poultice must be approximately 10-12 inches large and 1 inch thick. The clay must be well against the skin (put a cheese cloth on hairy areas only). Begin first with cold clay; only if it is not tolerated should it be warmed up slightly.

In cases of heavy losses of blood prepare a decoction of oak bark. Use 4 oz. per quart. Boil 10-15 minutes and use as a very slow douche.

FIVE REASONS TO INTEGRATE CALCIUM BENTONITE CLAY INTO YOUR DAILY DIET

Bentonite Clay is Mother Nature's Pharmacy. Bentonite Clay is volcanic ash with all the impurities burnt out leaving tightly bound pure trace minerals. Clay is a nano crystal with a strong negative ionic charged surface area and electromagnetic energy from the thermodynamic heat of a volcano. It is highly regarded as a strong detoxifier.

All dis-ease begins in the digestive system. When the gut becomes out of balance the body's support system malfunctions and gradually the immune system becomes compromised and the body crashes in many ways. The weakened immune system becomes susceptible to all sorts of infections and attacks that the body can no longer defend itself against. Consider Calcium Bentonite Clay as your natural pathway to regaining stability and well-being.

Five Reasons to Integrate Calcium Bentonite Clay into your Daily Diet:

1. Clay is homeostatic.

As such it adapts where needed to bring balance and equilibrium to the body. A balanced body can heal itself. That is what the body is designed to do when it isn't overloaded.

2. Clay detoxifies through adsorption and absorption.

As a strong yet gentle detoxifier it begins by cleaning the body of infections, viruses, chemicals, toxins, parasites, poisons and even excess radiation. It simply cleans house by removing the 'baddies' that play havoc with our bodies.

3. Clay stimulates. The electromagnetic energy of the clay stimulates circulation, bringing blood flow and oxygen to revitalize cellular repair and awaken latent cell energy.

4. Clay Alkalizes.

Clay has a high alkaline pH in the 8.5-to-10-point range. Clay's ability to alkalize helps the body to stabilize and balance itself.

5. Clay is a Catalyst.

As a catalyst, it provides activation energy to the body. When the immune system is compromised clay supplies the body with the available magnetism to run well.

Since clay is not absorbed into the blood stream, total detoxification is by three methods:

1. Internally from drinking the liquid clay that works from the mouth south to clean, replenish digestive flora, and balance the alimentary canal from beginning to end. By cleaning house we are talking about removing harmful bacteria, viruses, molds, yeast, heavy metals and parasites.

2. Externally with clay baths that draw toxins, chemicals, heavy

metals lodged in the soft tissues and joints of the body, out through the pores of our skin.

3. Externally with thick clay poultices over targeted areas like the liver, kidneys, lower bowls, the throat and chest and topically on skin irritations, wounds, burns and infections.

Calcium Bentonite Clay therapy is the ideal detoxification method because it is safe, effective and inexpensive. Take control of your body by safely detoxing to help regain and achieve your pinnacle of health! Are you beginning to have a new respect for this simple clump of *earth*? Clay is a product of Mother Nature, God's Pharmacy.

Never underestimate what Calcium Bentonite Clay can do in supporting wellness. The simple version is that clay knows where to go and what to do to improve the well-being of the body.

Have you had your clay today?

GROUNDING WITH CLAY

Clinton Ober's new book, *Earthing*, is making a big hit in the alternative health common sense world. Here is a brief description of the principles of *Earthing* and grounding with the earth:

"The solution for chronic inflammation, regarded as the cause of most common modern diseases, has been identified! And it is not blueberries. It is something right beneath our feet-the Earth itself!"

Throughout most of evolution humans walked barefoot and slept on the ground, largely obliviously that the surface of the Earth contains limitless healing energy. Science has discovered this energy as free-flowing electrons constantly replenished by solar radiation and lightning. Few people know it, but the ground provides a subtle electric signal that maintains health and governs the intricate mechanisms that make our bodies work-just like plugging a lamp into a power socket makes it light up. Modern lifestyle, including the widespread use of insulated rubber or plastic-soled shoes, has disconnected us from this energy and, of course, we no longer sleep on the ground as we did in times past.

Earthing introduces the planet's powerful, amazing, and overlooked natural healing energy and how people can readily connect to it. This eye-opening book describes how the physical disconnect with the Earth creates abnormal physiology and contributes to inflammation, pain, fatigue, stress, and poor sleep. By reconnecting to the Earth, symptoms are rapidly relieved and even eliminated and recovery from surgery, injury, and athletic overexertion is accelerated."

He just described the actions of clay and its electro-magnetic energy. Why wouldn't clay work to restore energy flow to the body? After all it is what we are made from. No wonder clay baths work so well to calm autistic children and help them make eye contact and improve their verbal skills. The natural flow of energy has been restored.

Want to experience earthing with clay? I for one have grass on my yard and can't get down to the earth (dirt) beneath and who knows what fertilizers and herbicides might be in the dirt. So, get a plastic dish pan big enough for your feet and add two cups of dry power calcium Bentonite clay. Now sit with your feet in the dry clay for 30 minutes to an hour.

Store your dry clay between uses by covering the pan with a lid to prevent contamination.

HEALING IS A SPIRITUAL JOURNEY – CLAY IS A SPIRITUAL HEALING ELEMENT

Clay is a fine-grained mineral material of the earth. It is an important part of soil fertility that all plant and (ultimately) *all life depends upon*, and has been used since ancient times...

The two main uses of clay, *life from the soil*, and vessels, have a direct and profound significance to humanity.

The original Hebrew word that is translated as the "dust" that Adam was created from means clay, making God the first "potter," as was well known by the ancients. "Yet, O Lord, Thou art our Father; we are the clay, and Thou art our potter; we are all the work of Thy hand" Isaiah 64:8 RSV and "The Spirit of God has made me, and the breath of the Almighty gives me life... I too was formed from a piece of clay." Job 33:4,6 RSV

So, it is the loss of balance in the energy that makes up our bodies which results in illness. From this, it follows that to restore lost health, or to maintain the good health we may currently be having, we need to ensure a good balance of energy in our bodies. It is here that the silica crystal becomes useful, for it has been known to maintain such a perfect balance of energy in the body; thanks to some properties it has.

The Spirit of God has made me, and the breath of the Almighty gives me life... I too was formed from a piece of clay." Job 33:4,6 RSV

The Random House College Dictionary describes Bentonite rock as "a clay formed by the decomposition of volcanic ash." It describes clay as "consisting essentially of hydrated silicates of aluminum, regarded as the material from which the human body was formed."

The body is designed to heal itself. When it is out of balance, there is a loss of energy which results in illness. **This loss of equilibrium contributes to a weakness and vulnerability** to illnesses arising from mental stress as well as physical abuse, poor eating habits and poor lifestyle choices. One of Living Clays spiritual healing properties is that of homeostasis, the ability to return to balance. Homeostasis is defined as the ability of a system or living organism to adjust its internal environment by several complex biological mechanisms that operate via the autonomic nervous system to maintain a stable equilibrium. The Native American Indians simplified it by saying, "Clay has wisdom of its own. It knows where to go and what to do."

How is this possible you ask? Well, clay is a nano crystal. Crystals are capable of memory and holding energy. Living Clays communicate with the body and act as a catalyst that supports the body in healing itself by cleansing, detoxing, stimulating circulation and balancing body pH. In other worlds it assists the body in regaining equilibrium and thus the normal flow of energy.

Clay is volcanic ash – the burnt-out core of Mother Earth. Clay is a **super stable compound. All the elements that make up clay**, 80 or more trace minerals, mostly in parts per million, **are bound together and act as a whole.**

These nano crystal partials have a very strong electro-magnetic negative ionic charge. An energy if you will that allows it to draw positive charged ions which are some bacteria, viruses, fungi, molds, yeast, in other words the baddies.

Many of the healing properties of clay cannot be explained by scientists just as many actions of the body cannot be fully explained. Could it be because they share a common intelligence or spirituality designed by God?

IN DEFENSE OF EATING CLAY

It's an exciting time for clay. My phone has been ringing non-stop with people reporting they're seeing clay mentioned on a variety of television shows and hearing members of Hollywood's elite touting that they use clay as part of their personal health regimen. Stories of people "eating clay" have recently penetrated the mainstream media in a big way to varying degrees of understanding, and curiosity is being displayed by both the media and the public. For those of us who have spent years using this naturally occurring and incredibly safe substance, it seems only natural that it would finally be getting the praise it so much deserves. For the unacquainted, however, it's more important now than ever that quality information about the "how's and why's" of clay be made available to the public at large, so any consumer can make an educated decision for themselves about the merits of Bentonite Clay.

In the past week alone I have seen the wide distribution of a recent interview with actress and eco-advocate Shailene Woodley's use of Bentonite for internal detox, culminating with her appearance on The Late Show with David Letterman where she explains her "strange health practices." Additionally, alternative health educator and advocate extraordinaire Karen

Atkins was seen on Good Morning America discussing the benefits of taking Calcium Bentonite Clay for digestive health and its ability to cleanse toxins from the body.

As the author of *Calcium Bentonite Clay Nature's Pathway to Healing*, I continue to play an active role in the introduction of this vital substance to the world through books, blogs, articles, seminars and interviews. Since my introduction to Calcium Bentonite Clay in 1995, I began educating myself about the uses of clays in order to better understand how they work. My most important lessons learned have been that all clays are not created equal and that it is important to know your clays. Like any natural resource, taking water for example, it can vary in both quality and purity. Just because one source of water could make someone sick, it doesn't stand to reason that everyone should stop drinking it. Likewise, while Ms. Woodley may not have been able to make the strongest case for clay, she was right on the track when she said, "you should obviously be careful about your source."

My greatest revelations on the endless potential of this amazing substance come from first-hand testimonials and success stories from clay users. However, it would be short-sighted not to recognize the presence of scientific research on the subject. For those curious about how Calcium Bentonite Clay is capable of Detoxification, Stimulation, and Alkalization to the human body, I would suggest the following resources:

1. Books: This ancient remedy has been the subject of numerous texts. I am proud to say that one of the most read on the subject was written by me and can be found by visiting WWW.BentoniteClayInfo.com. Other books include [13] and [7]

2. Research: The benefits of Calcium Bentonite Clay have been considered by the scientific community. While many of these studies have not been circulated at large, they have been published; and their findings are credible to help make a positive case for the human use of clay. The following are just a small selection of the studies that can be found: "'Healing Clays' Show Promise for Fighting Deadly MRSA Superbug Infections, Other Diseases"

3. Testimonials: Calcium Bentonite Clay has been widely used for centuries with particularly positive results. An offering of testimonials can be found at WWW.BentoniteClayInfo.com.

4. Articles: WWW.BentoniteClayInfo.com, offers a fantastic selection of published articles on the subject. I would suggest the following two as a starting point:

"Frequently Asked Questions About Calcium Bentonite" Clay"
"Criteria for Selecting a Quality Clay"

[29] According to *Huffington Post*, Dr. David L. Katz, director of the Prevention Research Center at Yale University, said, "There could conceivably be benefits, but there could certainly be harms — and a favorable benefit/harm ratio has not been established to justify recommending this." It is true that few scientific studies on the subject exist on human use, but maybe it's time for that to change. I invite scientific study and put the ball in Dr. Katz' court to prove his assertions; surely with the resources afforded at his position with Yale, he is in an optimal position to study this interesting subject. To get him started, let's investigate the numerous reports outlining how the use of Calcium Bentonite Clay has shown empirical reductions in the amount of heavy metals found in the blood stream of

children diagnosed with severe Autism. Such drastic results through an indirect action would speak to a truly powerful natural substance, would it not?

The same *Huffington Post* article warns that the clay eater is "being exposed to arsenic, lead and other toxicants that naturally occur in soil." This sort of blanket assertion is every bit as naive as Ms. Woodley's less than perfect explanation of why one would use this natural remedy. Citing a study about contamination found in soil samples in Sub-Saharan Africa certainly doesn't prove that safe, edible clays don't exist. Had the *Huffington Post* done their due diligence they would have found that, in fact, numerous Bentonite product manufacturers provide products that are not only safe but meet all federal regulatory requirements to be sold as dietary supplements, food ingredients, and even pharmaceutical components.

In conclusion, it is undeniable that a national conversation is underway about the rising popularity of this ancient natural remedy. And I believe that, with a little education, clay will continue to stand at the forefront of that conversation as we bring Calcium Bentonite Clay from the fringe into the consciousness of every consumer looking for a natural alternative to maximize their health and wellness. And yes, all clays are not alike, so know your clays.

Now, go eat some clay.

PROTECTION FROM RADIATION EXPOSURE

Right now, everyone on earth is bathed in a soup of radioactive energy. Our bodies are radiated daily. It is crucially important to counter this bombardment, to remove this radiation and the resultant damage from our bodies. There is nothing better for this purpose than using a pure, high quality, living clay daily.

Radioactive material is formed carrying a positive ionic charge. Calcium Bentonite Clay is a negatively charged ion. Simply put, Calcium Bentonite Clay adsorbs and absorbs, capturing positive charged ions. Unlike other clays, only Smectites (Bentonites) can absorb and adsorb and are characterized by their expandable properties. Radiation is a real health problem. A Living Calcium Bentonite Clay is the real solution.

Steps to Take if You're in a Fallout Zone

1. If outdoors, come inside immediately.

2. When in your home or apartment, you quickly close all windows and doors.

3. Turn off any outside air source. You may leave on air conditioning or heat if it can be set to utilize re-circulated air from

inside the home.

Note: The benefit of steps 1-3 is to close your home to possible contamination from the air outside. It could be only seconds before the blast contamination is at your doorstep.

4. Go immediately to an area of your home set aside for such an emergency. Strip off all of your clothing. Secure your clothes and shoes in a plastic bag and put them outside until you can wash them with clay.

5. Using prepared hydrated Calcium Bentonite Clay: Get in the shower and dip your hands into it. Quickly apply the clay over every inch of your body (except for in your eyes). Cover your hair and all nooks and crannies. Scrub your body thoroughly with the clay. Leave it on for 10 minutes. Next, wash off, while continuing to scrub.

6. After drying off, apply another thin film coating of clay and stand with your arms away from your sides and feet slightly apart. In 5-15 minutes, the clay will dry on your body.

7. After the clay has dried, put on a disposable pull-on garment, a surgical-type face mask, and disposable shoe covers on your bare feet.

8. Take a prepared liquid Calcium Bentonite Clay and a jar of potassium iodide (KI) into the kitchen and set them on the counter by the sink. Drink 4 ounces of the liquid Calcium Bentonite Clay and take 2 potassium iodide (KI) tablets or as directed on the label. Periodically every 2-3 hours drink another 2 ounces of liquid clay.

9. If service is available stay tuned to your TV or radio to stay

informed.

Note: Get as comfortable as possible because this will be your repetitive treatment and mode of dress for several days to come. You will sleep well knowing you are being protected from radiation.

10. Take a clay bath daily using 1-2 cups of dry clay until danger has passed. You can also give your pets a clay bath.

11. Wash your clothes by adding ¼ cup liquid clay per load.

12. Rinse fresh vegetables in clay water.

If you are not in a direct fallout area drink 2 ounces of clay twice daily, take 1 Potassium Iodide tablet every morning and take a weekly clay bath. These are precautionary maintenance doses that are healthy for all of us.

STOP NEEDLESS AMPUTATIONS

Amputations, especially from diabetes, are on the rise.

What if there were a simple solution that would reduce the number of amputations by 50% or more; something simple, safe and inexpensive? This article is intended to open the doorway and shed the light on stopping needless amputations. It is intended to challenge insurance companies to encourage research that will satisfy the reluctances of the medical profession. It is intended to save limbs and significantly lower health care related costs from needless amputations.

More than 60% of nontraumatic lower-limb amputations occur in people with diabetes.

In 2004, about 71,000 nontraumatic lower-limb amputations were performed in people with diabetes.

The rate of amputation for people with diabetes is 10 times higher than for people without diabetes. [3] The increasing rate of diabetes diagnoses in the United States is cause for alarm. Related healthcare costs are staggering, as data shows the total annual cost of diabetes treatment in 2002 (including direct and indirect costs) was estimated at $132 billion, or one out of every 10 healthcare dollars spent in the United States. Other studies have suggested that diabetes-related amputations cost approximately three billion dollars per year ($38,077 per amputation procedure). [3]

So, what is this simple solution? It is a topical treatment with Bentonite Clay. A clay strong enough to draw, bind with and pull infections, gangrene and diseased tissue from the body and stimulate blood flow and oxygen to the area for the rebuilding of healthy tissue.

The potential of this clay as a healing catalyst has been so remarkable that more and more people are turning to this natural alternative and away from traditional western medicine. The rise in public awareness to this safe alternative is quickly spreading by word of mouth. The beat goes on as successful story after successful story are shared with friends and relatives.

It is time for clay to be taken seriously and recognized as a major healing agent and be recommended by doctors! It is time to put the spotlight on Clay, more specifically on Calcium Bentonite Clay.

Used internally or externally, clay's strong ability to draw and bind with toxins, viruses, and pathogens make it a healing catalyst that works with the whole organism to heal itself. It cuts healing time in half at a minimum. Clays are not new as a healing agent. Even the Bible references clay for healing. Animals in the wild instinctively are drawn to Clay Wallows and Clay Licks when sick and for minerals their body needs. Charles A. Munn, Ph.D., Chairman of the Board, Tropical Nature, documented the Macaw Parrots of South America eating clay from cliffs to detoxify from their diet of poison seeds.

So, what is it about this "dirt" that makes miracles? First, it is far from dirt. It is highly negative charged trace minerals, tightly bound together, acting as whole. These electromagnetic nanocrystals were formed from volcanic ash that landed in inland seas, lake beds and rivers and streams. In short, the thermodynamic heat from the volcano burnt out all impurities leaving super charged, tightly bound, inert trace minerals. Over millions of years, it evolved into veins of clay with super charged electromagnetic negative ionic charged particles with an alkaline pH. In the rock or powder form clay is dormant. Clay is a sleeping giant with great healing properties and benefits. When clay absorbs water, it takes on a life force energy.

This electromagnetic energy stimulates circulation and blood flow thereby revitalizing dormant cell energy and speeding up the healing process.

There are seven different clay families depending on the mineral makeup, location and the maturity of the clay. All clay deposits are different. Some are strictly for industrial use. Bentonite clays are rapidly and widely being recognized as safe and effective detox, cleansing and healing agents in the alternative health care field. The green Bentonite clays from the Smectite Family of clays are considered the most popular healing clays. These Smectites can absorb as well as adsorb. It is the absorption that sets them apart from other clays. The Smectites have an extremely large specific surface area, cation exchange capacity with an affinity to absorb water. [4] They form reactive clays also referred to as Living Clay. Living Clay or reactive clays can transform through interactive exchanges of elements and energy.

"When Bentonite clay absorbs water and swells, it is stretched open like a highly porous sponge; the toxins are drawn into these spaces by electrical attraction and bound fast. In fact Bentonites can absorb pathogenic viruses, aflatoxin (a mold), and pesticides and herbicides including Paraquat and Roundup. The clay is eventually eliminated from the body with the toxins bound to its multiple surfaces." Canadian Journal of Microbiology [5]

Though clays have been used successfully by indigenous tribes around the world for centuries, modern day doctors are slow to accept putting "dirt" in a wound or taking clay internally for gastrointestinal disorders. A pure vein of clay is far from dirt. Dirt decomposes whereas clay is inert trace minerals. Bentonites are listed as FDA GRAS (Generally Recognized as Safe). Under sections 201(s) and 409 of the Federal Food, Drug, and Cosmetic Act, any substance that is intentionally added to food is a food additive, that is subject to premarket review and approval by FDA, unless the substance is generally recognized, among qualified experts, as having been adequately shown to be safe under the conditions of its intended use, or unless the use of the substance is otherwise excluded from the definition of a food additive. [57]

It is important to do your due diligence when selecting your clay. Going back even 1,000 years ago clays we were not exposed to modern day environmental elements, industrial toxins, acid rain, agents of nuclear warfare, pesticides and the chemical sprays that contribute to the pollution of our earth's soils.

The time has come for clay therapy to be taken seriously and recognized as a major healing alternative to be recommended by doctors.

Clay therapy is safe, inexpensive and it works. It helps the body by detoxing, cleansing and balancing the pH to support a strong immune system. Reduce your need for expensive health care. Cut doctor visits and trips to the pharmacy to a minimum. Return to your natural state of wellbeing with a little help from Mother Earth's clay. Put the spotlight on clay therapy and stop needless amputations and other unnecessary medical procedures. To sum it up, Bentonite clay is the simple solution to stopping needless amputations. [2]

WHAT IS LIVING CLAY?

> "From the good earth one regenerates ones health"
>
> Louis Kervan, Biological Transmutations

I'll begin with the most basic fact of all – clay is volcanic ash, the core of mother earth with all the impurities burnt out from the tremendous heat of a volcanic eruption. The clay particle is made up of 60-80 trace minerals, fused together by volcanic heat and charged with a powerful electromagnetic energy and a strong negative ionic charge. When a volcano erupts and the lava flows down the side of the volcanic cone, the ash is blown high, oftentimes miles, high into the sky. Slowly it settles to the ground, sometimes nearby, sometimes hundreds of miles away, and in extreme cases it can circumvent the globe. Volcanic ash landing in inland lakes and seas evolves over millions of years into various stages of clay maturity and types.

Clay is a catalyst that assists the body in returning to and maintaining a state of balance and well-being. A catalyst is an agent that provokes or speeds significant change or action. For any process to occur, energy, known as activation energy, is required. Without the help of a catalyst the amount of energy needed to spark a particular reaction is high. When the catalyst is present the energy activation is lowered, making the reaction happen more efficiently. The catalyst generally works by either changing the structure of a molecule or by bonding to reactant molecules causing them to combine, react and release a product or energy. Unlike other reagents that participate in the chemical reaction, a catalyst is not consumed by the reaction itself.

The Smectite family of clays are called 'Living Clays' because of their ability to make changes. A living clay is one capable of change through balancing, transformation, stimulation and interactive exchange of elements and energy. On the other hand, a rock is incapable of transforming itself from within. It can only change from outside influences including weathering by heat, wind and water.

WHAT CLAY DOES:

The short version is Calcium Bentonite clay is a Pac man gobbling up the baddies (detoxification). It has a life force electro-magnetic energy to take it where it needs to go to clean house and revitalize our bodies. Like a cork bobbing on top of the water clays alkaline ph allows the body to maintain balance and equilibrium to stay afloat. Used topically it stimulates by drawing blood flow and oxygen to the skin surface to promote healing.

I really like keeping things simple...easy to understand. My intent is to reduce some relatively complicated scientific explanations into everyday language using analogies we can all understand. However, the fact is because of clay's multifaceted nature, understanding the mechanics of clay is still a mystery to researchers, biologists, chemists, physicists and healers. The indigenous tribes had a very simplified explanation. They believed that clay had a wisdom of its own and it knew where to go and what to do. Raymond Dextreit, French naturopath and fore runner in herbal healing states, "Clay is effective through a dynamic presence far more significant than a mere consideration of the substances it contains. It is a catalyst rather than an agent in itself. This is possible because clay is alive –'living earth'. We cannot always penetrate Nature's secrets; we must merely acknowledge and use them."

There are many factors that contribute to clay assisting the body in returning to a state of wellness. These attributes of clay work independently and synergistically.

In a nutshell this is what clay does:

Detoxifies –Both internally and externally. Its strong negatively charged ions pull, holds and captures positively charged ions, which are toxins, viruses, mold, yeast, heavy metals, and radiation made possible by its ability to adsorb and absorb.

1. Cleanses – Internally it pulls old build ups of mucoid plaque and putrefied fecal matter and parasites that are lodged in the crevasses of the colon out with the feces making better absorption of supplements and nutrients. Externally it draws out impurities and infections through the pores of the skin.

2. Balances - Clay is homeostatic. It brings the body into balance. A body in equilibrium can heal itself.

3. Alkalizes – It has a high alkaline pH in the 8.5-to-10-point range. Reduces over acidity in the body.

4. Stimulates - It draws blood flow and oxygen stimulating circulation that is needed for cellular revitalization and repair.

5. Energizes - It has an electromagnetic energy that resonates with the life force energy of the body to propels it to a higher state of well being.

Never underestimate what clay can do in supporting well being. The simple version is clay knows where to go and what to do to improve the well-being of the body.

Every cell in our body excretes waste material, which becomes toxic and poisonous to our bodies if it is allowed to build up faster than it can be eliminated or filtered out of the body. The most common symptoms of toxic buildup within the body are mental dullness, aching-stiff joints, gas and bloat, high acidity, digestive problems with the stomach and colon, acid reflux and fatigue. Therefore, it is imperative to naturally detox to rid yourself of the deleterious effects of impurities and toxins. There is a lot of popular sharing of results of clay users suggesting that Calcium Bentonite Clay therapy may be an ideal detoxification treatment because it is safe and effective. Take control of your body by detoxing to help regain and achieve the pinnacle of your health!

Internally, Calcium Bentonite clay provides a very effective detoxing and cleansing capability. It captures freshly ingested toxins before they are absorbed into the body. This is ultimate protection and prevention.

The Living Clay particle maintains its molecular integrity. It does not break down and assimilate into the body as the individual mineral components. In addition, the size of the clay particle is too large to pass through the colon wall. Remember these trace minerals were fused together by the heat of the volcano creating a negatively charged cage like structure. By maintaining its molecular whole, it passes through the body acting like a little vacuum cleaner, sucking up positively charged cations,' the baddies', capturing them and carrying them out of the body. Since Living Clay is not digested and assimilated as it passes through the alimentary canal, the clay and the absorbed positively charged cations are both eliminated together.

Do not be alarmed by the presence of heavy metals in clays. First, they are in minute amount measured as ppm (parts per million) and as said they are not absorbed and used by the body. They are now a new substance. They were baked into a Clay Particle by the tremendous volcanic heat.

Now imagine you are baking a cake from scratch, and you have many ingredients. There is sugar, flour, salt, baking powder, eggs, oil, water, spices, flavorings etc. After the cake is baked you can no longer separate the ingredients back in their individual piles. Due to baking they are now fused together into a new element- a cake. The same thing happens with clay. The minerals are baked by the tremendous heat of the volcano and now form a new element we know as a Clay Particle. The minerals in the particle are tightly bonded together with a new purpose. They now become a magnetic cage or jail house capturing and holding the toxins and eliminating them from the body.

In addition, taken internally, it cleanses the colon of built up mucous like plaque and old putrefied fecal matter stuck in the crevasses, allowing the nutrients and supplements to be more readily absorbed into the body. But that's not all. It balances the body pH levels, reducing over acidity, the cause of most digestive problems and it removes parasites. No wonder people feel so much better after taking clay.

Externally it detoxes by pulling toxins, lodged deeply in the body, through the pores of the skin when applied topically and in clay baths. When used this way, the clay literally pulls the positively charged cations, the toxins and infections through the pores of skin into its cage-like structure not to be re-released. Clay baths are becoming increasingly popular as a safe modality for detoxifying due to their extreme effectiveness in riding the body of long stored heavy metals and stimulating the lymphatic system.

Dr. Robert T. Martin, PhD, Cornell University, and Mineralogist, MIT, in his research helps us understand the true power of clay. He determined that one gram of Bentonite Clay has a surface area of over 800 square meters. That is one fourth of a football field. The greater the surface area, the greater the negative charges and in turn the greater its power to attract positively charged particles/molecules, the bad things.

Dr. Martin further reports in the same study that Calcium Bentonite Clay gives no evidence that it has any chemical effect on the body. Its action is purely physical, due to its huge surface area and strong negative charge. Is there any wonder that clay is so safe?

Raymond Dextreit commented, "One marvels at what Clay can do. For something that is merely an inert matter, it gives quite a performance. The same teaspoon of clay can cure an obstinate carbuncle and tenacious anemia equally well.

Curing the carbuncle is easily explained by clay's absorbent power...but anemia!" Its mineral composition is not sufficient to explain its rebuilding action of red blood cells, but that it produces results is easily confirmed by a red cell recount. Dextreit theorizes it is because there are substances which do not destroy themselves in action; they are the diastases and enzymes. Clay is particularly rich in these. Some of these diastases, the 'oxidase', have the power of fixing free oxygen, which explains the purifying and enriching action of clay in the blood.

We must accept the facts even if we do not understand their origin that clay does act with wisdom – it goes to the unhealthy spot. Used internally, whether absorbed orally, anally or vaginally, clay goes to the place where harm is. There it lodges, perhaps for several days, until finally it draws out the toxins, disease, etc., with its evacuation.

From helping to prevent the proliferation of pathogenic germs and parasites to aiding with rebuilding of healthy tissues and cells, clay is a 'living' cure.

[13] In *Earth Cures*, Raymond Dextreit says it this way, "Clay acts on all organs of the body – on the whole organism. Everything unhealthy and emitting positive cations are irresistibly attracted to clay and become subject to immediate elimination.

Wherever there is a deficiency, clay seems to supply the needed substance regardless of whether the clay itself is rich in that substance. Clay does not merely remedy deficiency. It goes further and stimulates the deficient organ and helps the restoration of the failing function. Are you beginning to have a new respect for this simple clump of 'dirt'. Scientists have long given up trying to replicate clay given its composition of minerals. Clay is a product of Mother Nature, God's Pharmacy.

[Louis Kervran formulated the biological transmutation hypothesis. "A biological transmutation is defined as a nuclear transmutation occurring in a living organism. Such transmutations are strongly believed not to occur according to mainstream physics, chemistry and biology; however proponents of the hypothesis claim to have empirical evidence that they do." [30] C. Louis Kervran 1966)

His theory is explained in this story from his book, *Biological Transmutations*, about the Niphargus shrimp, gives credence to the deficiency theory.

It has been known for a long time that living organisms inhabit clay while having no organic supply from the outside. This fact has intrigued research workers, and an important study was made in a laboratory installed in the cave of Moulis, France. Let us note the case of Niphargus shrimp, a small shrimp half an inch in length that lives in the clay caves. If a shrimp is given organic matter (meat, etc.) it vegetates and dies. It also dies if it is not kept in humid clay. Experiments have shown that it grows normally in pure clay to which nothing has been added. Research workers therefore thought the shrimp lived on clay and nothing but clay, impossibility according to the laws of biochemistry. Actually, it cannot live thus in clay alone, but this clay contains microorganisms which work for the shrimp, making vitamins and various mineral products, nitrogen, phosphorus, and calcium, etc.

An amazing quality of Calcium Bentonite Clay is it acts so gently and subtly you are not aware of the healing actions until you see or feel the positive results. It just works. And that is the simple answer. I really do like keeping things simple.

WHY CALCIUM BENTONITE CLAYS ARE SAFE TO INGEST

It is a known fact that because of Bentonites' volcanic origins, they will have small trace amounts of metal oxide trace elements, primarily aluminum but also lead, mercury and even arsenic. On average, clays contain 70-90 trace minerals in parts per million (ppm). These heavy metal trace minerals in Bentonite clays are safe because they are not bioavailable to the body. They serve another purpose. Their purpose is in the structure of the clay particle, contributing to the clay's negative ionic charge. In addition, the clay particle is too large to pass through the colon into the bloodstream. Bentonites are from the Smectite family of clays having a dioctahedral 2:1 structure. Smectite clays are a super stable compound, and the minerals are tightly bound by covalent O and OH (hydroxide) bonds. OH is an oxygen atom covalently bonded to a hydrogen atom, each providing an electron to form the covalent bond. Like a chain link fence these bonds hold the atoms tightly together, forming the structure of the clay particle. [7]

The only minerals bio-available in Bentonites are small amounts of calcium, magnesium, potassium and sodium. [2] These are in the adsorption layer and are the variable charge which is located on the edges of clay particles. Only these minerals can be released and absorbed by the body.

The other minerals in clays are bonded together by covalent bonding and fixed as a permanent part of the clay particle. They form the large surface area of negative charges that are found between these microscopically thin layers of clay. They act as a strong magnetic pole for capturing and removing, viruses, yeasts, molds, toxins and heavy metals found in the body. [6]

The charge distribution of positive edges and negative faces is as shown below.

Below see the clay mineral structure of a dioctahedral 2:1 structured clay; it has two tetrahedral sheets, with the unshared vertexes of each sheet pointing toward each other and forming each side of the octahedral sheet in between them.

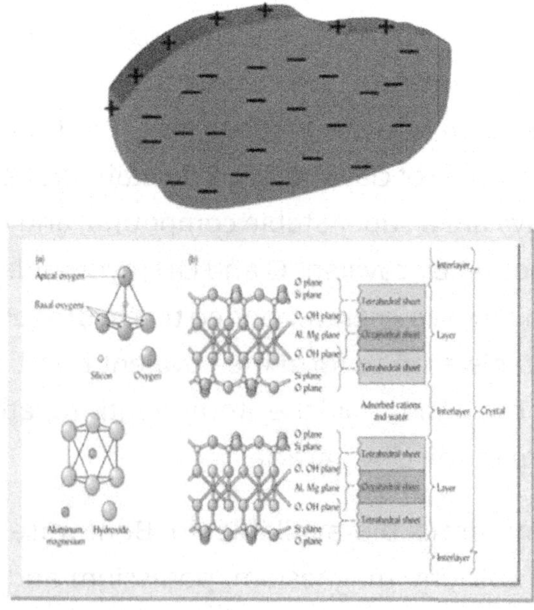

Toxins and heavy metals accumulated and stored in the body carry a positive ionic charge. The strong negative ionic charge on the large surface area of clays magnetizes these elements and removes them from the body in two ways: internally, by grabbing any toxins present in the alimentary canal from the mouth south and eliminating them from the body; and externally, removing toxins stored in the body by pulling the toxins out through the pores of the skin through the actions of clay detox baths. They become tightly bound to the clay particles.

For a chemical analysis to be performed to break these individual trace heavy metal elements out takes 600-1000 degrees Celsius or a very strong acid, much stronger than the body can produce. [7]

The clay removes toxins while staying intact and exits the body without being broken down into its trace elements. This miraculous ability is possible because clays are catalysts. A catalyst provides activation energy to the body. A catalyst is an agent that provokes or speeds significant change or action. Unlike other reagents, substances that produce a chemical reaction, catalysts, are not consumed by the reaction itself.

As a catalyst, enzymes in the body attach to the clay particles and together they become co-creators. These pairings are capable of making amino acids (building blocks of protein), proteins, peptide chains and minerals the body may be deficient in that the clay does not even contain. They are magnificent co-creators. The clay molecule itself is not changed by this process. [5]

A large proportion of our cells, muscles and tissue are made up of amino acids, meaning they carry out many important bodily functions, such as giving cells their structure. They also play a key role in the transport and the storage of nutrients. Amino acids have an influence on the function of organs, glands, tendons and arteries. They are furthermore essential for healing wounds and repairing tissue, especially in the muscles, bones, skin and hair as well as for the removal of all kinds of waste deposits produced in connection with metabolism.

Smectite clays should not be evaluated like other foods and supplements because of the body's inability to metabolize and otherwise break down the individual trace minerals in the clay. As you will come to understand, clays are a horse of a different color and because of their unique abilities, they do not fit the normal standards for FDA testing and regulations.

It is important to know your clays. Some clays are acidic, some gritty, some high sodium content, and some not mined with care. Each clay deposit is different in its mineral composition.

A company who chooses to provide a Quality Control Report, is assuring that their clay meets the specifications set by the U.S. Food and Drug Administration.

Chapter Six

CLAY TIPS

Clay Tip- Bentonite Clay for Allergy Eyes

For itchy allergy eyes make an eye wash solution. In a glass jar put 1 tablespoon of dry clay and gently add 4 ounces of Eye Wash Solution. Gently swirl. Allow it to stand without mixing for 12 hours. Pour the clear water on top off into a clean bottle to use in an eye cup or as drops as needed.

Be sure to get Eye Wash and not Lens Cleaner Some references are:

Bausch & Lomb Advanced Eye Relief Eye Wash

Collyrium for Fresh Eyes- Eye Wash

Combine this treatment with a hydrated clay mask applied over a cotton round cleanser pad over closed eyelids for 15-30 minutes. Lay a cold wet wash rag over the eyes to keep the clay moist. Repeat this 2-3 times a day. -Perry A~

Clay Tip- Clay in Coffee

I add ½ teaspoon in my coffee cup before adding the hot coffee, give it a stir and it dissolves easily. I like to add a spoonful of coconut oil last. My husband and I like it better than plain coffee. -Kelly R.

Clay Tip- Cleans Dry Erase Board

Have found that the clay powder that I bought is great for getting off leftover Sharpie ink from the dry-erase boards. Sometimes, the color ink just won't give and come completely off and renders the board useless after that.

The clay is gritty enough to mix with a little water and everything comes clean!!!!!! -Stephanie A.

Clay Tip- for Cleaning Bathroom

Every time I wash out a clear glass that had clay water in it, I notice how sparkly clean it is! That gave me an idea ... to clean my bathroom sink and toilet with clay this morning. Both are now spotless and far shinier than any chemical I've ever used! Now I no longer have to worry about what toxins my skin or lungs I might pick up from chemical cleansers when I clean. Thank you, Calcium Bentonite! -Claudia C.

Clay Tip – Foot Baths

If I can't do a clay bath for whatever reason? Take a Foot Bath to detox. Regular clay foot baths are the most relaxing and help to remove toxins. You can use a square plastic tub with a lid to soak in while watching TV. It feels so good! In the beginning your feet might feel a bit tingly when you're done, but that is a sign that it is stimulating circulation and working. This seems to improve the more you do the foot soaks.

I like to use about 1/2 cup of powdered clay mixed with hot water in a blender well. Fill it half with hot water add clay and blend well blend and add more hot water to about 1 inch from the top. Again, blend well and add to the tub. If not deep enough make another batch.

And another thing that I do to get the most out of the clay and to save money is to use the same foot bath about 3 or 4 times before throwing out that water. Just put a lid on the top and set it aside until your next foot bath. The clay still works and has drawing action throughout those multiple foot soaks. When I'm ready to do my next foot soak I carefully skim the clear water off the top and heat it in a pan on the stove. Then pour it back into your clay water and you've got a nice hot foot bath ready.

Somewhere on the wwwBentoniteClayInfo.com website there is a scientific article that explains (in detail) some lab testing that was done on clay. It's very interesting. But one of the main things that I got out of that article was that there was good clay left over after it had soaked up the virus, fungus, bacteria and toxins from the test tube. It read something like this.... After 90 min. they measured that over 90% of the bacteria was soaked up into the clay and it had used only about 25% of the clay to do that. That tells me that there was still about 75% of good clay left in there waiting to do some more work.

When you're done, pour the left-over clay water on your alkaline-loving plants. They love it. -H. Gage

P. S. Corns and calluses will loosen and come off as well.

Clay Tip- Maple Syrup

I've been adding Maple Syrup to the Internal-use clay drink and it's like a small, and very delicious, vegan milkshake. Hayes R.

Clay Tip for Wet Cell Phone

I dropped my phone into the toilet. It sunk to the bottom. I got on the internet for a solution. It said to put the phone in a bag of rice for 48 hours. Being a clay user, I added clay to the rice. Covered the phone completely. After 48 hours I charged the phone, and it works great. The phone company was amazed it worked after being COMPLETELY submersed in water. Yea Clay. -Claudia C.

Clay Tip- Emergency Supply of Clay in my Car

I Keep a small jar of powdered clay and hydrated clay in our car. If anyone ever was to get cut, sprinkle the clay directly on the wound and it will stop the bleeding. Use the hydrated for bites, wounds, sore muscles. One never knows what you will encounter when you are out and about! - Carol. R.

Clay Tip- Lymph Node Cleaning with Clay Mask

Once a week I put a glob of hydrated clay under my arms for about 30 minutes before I shower to keep the lymph nodes healthy. I feel so clean and purified after doing the underarm clay treatment. Gladys M.

Clay Tip- Moist Facial Mask & Hair Conditioner

I do (1) hydrated clay mask a week, but I also found it a bit drying until I mixed the hydrated clay equally with plain unflavored yogurt. I leave it on for about a half hour and the results are wonderful. My skin is soft and smooth, and the mask is not drying anymore. Once a month I add a tablespoon of pure honey to the mix. I usually put the remainder of the mix on my hair as a deep conditioning treatment at the same time and find it works very well...doesn't make the hair too dry either. Yogurt has anti-fungal/anti-yeast properties. Georgene

Clay Tips for Gardening-Tomato Plants

I've actually done a foot clay bath about a month ago and poured all the used water in my veggie garden. The tomato plants look really strong and healthy like I've never seen before. Sash U.

Clay Tip- Sinus Congestion and Sore Throat

If you have nasal congestion, I put maybe 1/8" thick poultice on my nose and sinuses and let dry. It will open the sinuses.

For sore throat, if somebody already feels the pain and scratchy throat, drink slowly the clay water. At bedtime put a teaspoon of the hydrated clay on the back of the tongue and gradually let it slide down your throat. For me it stopped the pain within minutes. -Sandi P.

Clay Tip- Summer Uses

Keep clay Mask on hand for fireworks, family games and outings, burns, insect bites, too much sun, sore muscles, cuts and injuries. You'll be glad you did. Going to the beach remember to use on Jelly fish stings. Takes the pain away immediately. Summertime calls for clay protection.

Clay Tip- Travel Tips

I have been using the little 2 oz. maple syrup bottles from Cracker Barrel to keep my liquid clay in for taking during the day if I am away from home. It fits perfectly in the pocketbook. Also use these bottles by the bedside to drink in the middle of the night when you have to get up. It's already mixed and in the right dose. The bottles are perfect as they are glass and have a plastic top. This might make it more convenient for some of you. Tina C.

Clay Tip- Tricky Way to Get Cats to Eat Clay

I've found an easy way to get my cats to take clay. If I take a small amount of the 'mud' clay and put it on their paw, they will lick it right off. Works like a charm. My cats are picky and wouldn't eat it in their food, so I'm glad I found this method. –Cora S.

Chapter Seven

DETOXIFICATION

Before discussing various ailments, it is important to understand the detoxification process. There is no single treatment of more value to the human body than a complete, full-body detoxification protocol using a Calcium Bentonite Clay as the cleansing agent and carrier for toxin removal.

The great majority of articles on detox and colon cleansing should be classified as colon cleansers themselves, because they will most certainly scare the poo out of you! They explain how substances that are toxic to our bodies come at us from all directions: the air we breathe, the food we eat, the water we drink, the cleaning products we use, and the metabolic waste produced inside us. Studies have discovered various chemicals from our foods and environment that indicate man contributes 700,000 tons of pollutants into the air every day, ranging from everyday household cleaners to cosmetics and hair sprays. That's just the air! Add to that the pesticides and toxins that are found in our water. Don't forget the chemicals that are routinely fed to the animals we eat and the sprayed, preserved and genetically altered plants we consume. And that doesn't even factor in the heavy metal poisoning that's occurring at a truly alarming rate — from the lead in our paint to the mercury in the fish we eat and the fillings in our teeth, and everything in between. It's truly frightening. The reports are everywhere.

You can spend weeks reading article after article, complete with pictures, that will keep you awake at night. I, however, want you to rest easy. I have chosen to concentrate on the benefits of detox — to emphasize the positive instead of beating you over the head with the all too prevalent negative. Granted, what we've done to our bodies and our environment is truly frightening. The state of our digestive systems has suffered and consequently our health in general is nightmarish. But, enough said, here's the good stuff!

THE BENEFITS OF DETOXIFICATION

Science has shown that the effects of detoxification on our body's cells are nothing short of miraculous. The following is an excerpt from Natasha Lee's article "Could Detoxification Be the Fountain of Youth?" [33]

Dr. Alexis Carrel, performed an amazing experiment in the early 1900's. He managed to sustain the life of cells from a chicken embryo by immersing the cells in a solution containing all the nutrients necessary for life and changing the solution daily. The cells took up nutrients from the nutrient-rich broth and excreted their waste into the same solution. The only thing Dr. Carrel did each day was discard the old solution and replace it with fresh nutrient solution. The chicken cells lived for 29 years until one night Dr. Carrel's assistant forgot to change the polluted solution! We do not know how much longer the cell's life could have been maintained.

[9] Dr. Carrel concluded at the end of his experiment that the cell is actually immortal. It is merely the fluid in which it floats which degenerates. He is quoted saying, "The cell is immortal, renew this fluid at intervals, give the cell something on which to feed and, so far as we know, the pulsation of life may go on forever." The average chicken lives about 7 years. His detoxified, properly nourished chicken cell lived for 29 years.

It may be hard to believe that the body could live indefinitely; however, a similar level of vibrant health and life extension can be created in humans by following the obvious similar principle.

Every cell in our body excretes waste material, which becomes toxic and poisonous to our bodies if we allow it to build up faster than we renew the fluid in which it floats. According to the above experiment, this is the cause of aging and degeneration. Factors such as "time" and ideas such as "that's just life" fade from the picture, with new data in view. The fact is, every 7 years we have a completely new set of bones, teeth, skin and hair. Logically, a person should be able to look and feel better than they did 7 years ago by changing and improving the way they take care of their own body as Dr. Carrel took care of his chicken cell.

Time alone is not a disease or poison. It is the toxins that accumulate with time that the body cannot withstand and that deteriorate health. In other words, time alone is not the cause of death.

So, logically and from the above data, by detoxifying your cells a person can freshen up and grow healthier and younger than they once were by practicing this principle. Periodically detoxifying the body, drinking lots of fresh water and staying smart on nutrition can appear to work miracles. Dr. Carrel, however, proved these amazing results are not miracles, just good science.

Another advocate and leading expert of detoxification and dietary healing is Kathryn Alexander. Alexander succinctly states the importance of dietary cleansing and the current state of our food supply: "The legacy of 50 years' exposure to persistent man-made chemicals combined with the denigration of the food chain has increased our susceptibility to chronic degenerative disease and cancer. Reversal can only come about by resolving these primary causes of disease. By releasing the toxic burden of the body and restoring its nutritional status, we can change our internal environment and achieve good health." [2]

The most common symptom of autointoxication (self-poisoning caused by endogenous microorganisms, metabolic wastes, or other toxins produced within the body) is mental dullness and fatigue. Other common symptoms are headache, constipation, diarrhea, colds, general aches and pains particularly up and down the spine and especially in the low back, skin problems, common infections (due to lowered immuno-competence), morning sluggishness, gas, bad breath, foul-smelling stool, allergies, intolerance to fatty foods, premenstrual tension, breast soreness and tendency to repeated vaginal infections. The good news: Detoxification can relieve these symptoms!

USING CALCIUM BENTONITE CLAY TO DETOX

So, how do we go about this detox business? The answer is

simple — CLAY! Not just any clay, but Calcium Bentonite Clay, a living clay.

Ran Knishinsky is an advocate of eating or drinking clay daily. In his book, he states some of the benefits reported by people using liquid clay for a period of two to four weeks include: improved intestinal regularity; relief from chronic constipation, diarrhea, indigestion and ulcers; a surge in physical energy; clearer complexion; brighter, whiter eyes; enhanced alertness; emotional uplift; improved tissue and gum repair; and increased resistance to infections. Calcium Bentonite Clay works on the entire organism. No part of the body is left untouched by its healing energies. [32]

Wendell Hoffman, through his own research, found that clean, natural Calcium Bentonite Clay used in a bath could draw out toxic chemicals through the pores of the skin. After many experiments, he concluded that optimum results are obtained by immersing oneself in a tub of very warm to hot water mixed with a clean, natural Calcium Bentonite Clay for exactly 20 minutes! Not just any clay will do. It is crucial to use "clean clay." [23]

Extreme amounts of clay used in a bath have been known to help the body detox from severe heavy metal poisoning. A detox clay bath, twice a week using 2 cups of detox clay powder for three months, is sufficient to draw out the toxins. Healing clays have been used for detoxification purposes for centuries and, due to several key factors, are irreplaceable as a part of a cleansing protocol.

One of the most amazing effects of clay baths is the ability of the clay to stimulate the lymphatic system. The more clay that is used in the therapy, the more powerful the response. I know of people who take clay baths in pits containing a thick mud of heated Calcium Bentonite Clay.

HEALING CRISIS

As part of the healing process, the body will begin to discard toxic residues that have built up in the body over the years. During the initial phase of cleansing, as your body begins to detoxify and your vital energy begins to repair and rebuild internal organs, you may experience a healing crisis.

You may feel worse before you feel better. As you continue to improve, you may begin a process called retracing. For example, if you used to get skin rashes, the rashes may reappear or get worse for a while as your body eliminates toxins through the skin. You may also experience an initial increase in urination, or you may feel more nervous. You are not getting worse; you are getting better. Soon, usually in one to three days, you will reach a plateau of better health.

For example, a varicose ulcer will at first enlarge itself as the dead flesh of the periphery will fall off the surface, and pus or blood can appear. Pain may even increase for some time, but it will decrease later and finally disappear with a definite closing of the ulcer and rebuilding of healthy tissues. We must not be afraid of these reactions; on the contrary, they are desirable, for they are signs that the body is responding to this intervention.

Sometimes an obstacle arises in clay treatment that can hinder its continuation, such as the appearance of red patches or eruptions accompanied by unbearable itching. The explanation is that perhaps acid substances flowing from internal regions pass through the tissues attracted by clay. If the itching stops after clay applications are discontinued, that will confirm this hypothesis.

During the healing crisis, it is important not to suppress these temporary symptoms with drugs because they may interrupt the process. Use common sense and listen to your body. It might be advisable to slow down on the amounts you are using and let the body detox gradually.

One of the beauties of Calcium Bentonite Clay treatments is that it is not an exacting science. Simply get the clay in you and on you in any fashion you choose. Remember, it is difficult to use clay wrong!

For ailment listings, please see the alphabetical index, which can be found at the back of the book.

Now, go play in some clay and heal thyself!

Chapter Eight

HOW TO USE CLAY

Unfortunately, with clay, one size does not fit all. What gets amazing results for one person may get minimal results for another. Our systems are at different stages, and the clay adapts and meets your body where it is. Therefore, it behooves me to say, play around with the suggested protocols and find your own unique "clay happy place." The beauty of clay is you can experiment with the amounts without harm. Just listen to your body. If you are not getting the results you want, the rule of thumb is to kick it up a notch. If you get a headache or hives or if you become lethargic, then you are succeeding in detoxing faster than the body can release toxins, so slow down a bit and build up gradually, and drink lots of water during the day. If you experience constipation, then you may actually be succeeding in pulling out old, dried, putrefied fecal matter and mucoid plaque that has been lodged in the colon. This is the cleansing action. If this is the case, keep drinking the clay and take whatever you use to keep your system working until the colon is cleaned out. Over-the-counter magnesium oxide tablets (250 mg) are a gentle solution. Some who experience diarrhea may need to bulk up with fiber or psyllium husk. On top of that, there are numerous ways to use and take clay.

PRECAUTIONS IF TAKING MEDICATIONS

Check with your pharmacist to determine whether clay will interfere with any medications. Ask your pharmacist how long it takes for the body to absorb the medication. Then allow that time to pass between taking your medication and the clay.

TAKING CLAY INTERNALLY

Suggestions for Using Liquid Clay Internally

A clean, properly functioning digestive tract is paramount to our well-being. For internal cleansing and daily detoxing, take clay daily. Doing so will get your intestines clean and keep them that way. It is important to take clay in liquid form rather than in a tablet or capsule. Liquefied Calcium Bentonite may be purchased or made from the clay powder. Clay begins working in the mouth, and the life force energy of the clay will resonate with all the cells of the body immediately. By taking it in capsule or pill form, you will miss the benefits to the mouth, gums and esophagus. In addition, it will take fluids from the body to fully hydrate the clay. In a liquid or fully hydrated form, it is activated and ready to work immediately.

Common Measurements and Conversions

When deciding the amount of liquid clay to make, keep in mind the following:

1 ounce (oz.) = 2 tablespoons (Tbsp.)

2 ounces (oz.) = ¼ cup

1 tablespoon (Tbsp.) = 3 teaspoons (tsp.)

1 cup (C) = 8 ounces

Many want to know what a single serving is. It can vary with what you are trying to accomplish. Different clays will have different mixing instructions, and you should always follow the instructions provided. But if no guidance is provided, I have found the following instructions work well for triple swelling Calcium Bentonites.

HOW TO MAKE YOUR OWN LIQUID CLAY

For a Single Serving

Mix a rounded teaspoon of clay powder in 2 ounces of water.

Shake well. Do Not Stir.

For Multiple Servings:

In a blender put 4 cups of water and add l/2 cup Detox Powder Clay.

Blend on high for 30 seconds.

Pour into a quart a glass or food grade plastic bottle with a plastic lid.

Wash blender blades of clay residue.

Liquid clay does not need to be refrigerated and will keep for many months. Take the suggest amount for your needs.

Protocols For Internal Use

A Single Serving = 2 oz. of liquid clay

General Detox

The protocol most frequently suggested by practitioners is:

Drink 2 oz. of liquid clay 3 times a day for 21 days, preferably on an empty stomach if you want the best cleansing effects.

After 21 days find your maintenance level.

After the initial cleansing the clay may be taken anytime with or without food.

One size does not fit all.

If you have serious digestive issues, you can gradually increase your amounts up to 8 oz 3 times a day if needed.

Always consult professional medical advice for specific conditions.

ADVANCE DETOX

To remove parasites, heavy metals and for more serious digestive issues, a slightly higher dose is recommended: Drink 2 ounces of liquid clay 3 times a day, increasing the dosage by 1 ounce daily to ultimately consume anywhere from 3 to 4 ounces 3 times a day, preferably on a empty stomach, away from oral medications as needed until better. As always, if you are not getting the results you want, take more. Some take 4 to 8 oz. throughout the day for serious digestive conditions.

MAINTENANCE REGIMEN

To support the body's immune system, to stay toxin free and to balance your pH level, drinking 2 ounces of liquid clay daily is suggested thereafter. More may be taken if desired. A sip of liquid clay before meals and snacks is highly recommended to capture toxins and radiation that may be in foods.

FOR CHILDREN

Infants ¼ to ½ teaspoon of the pre mixed liquid clay added to juice or water.

Toddlers to 5 years 2 teaspoons of the pre mixed liquid clay added to juice or water.

6-12 years 1 tablespoon of the pre mixed liquid clay added to juice or water.

Precaution If Taking Medications

Check with your pharmacist to determine if clay will interfere with any medications. Ask how long it takes for the body to absorb the medication, allow that time to pass between taking your medication and the clay.

Should Constipation Occur

It is not understood what gives most people three good bowel movements a day and others get constipated and some even have diarrhea. If constipation occurs, you need to keep drinking the clay and take whatever you use to keep your janitorial services working until the colon is cleaned out. Taking over-the-counter magnesium tablets of 250 mg is a gentle solution. For diarrhea you may need to bulk up with fiber or psyllium husk. After being on the psyllium for a week, take a good probiotic to rebuild the gut flora.

Suggestions for Using Clay Externally

The skin is the largest organ of your body and can be considered the outward reflection of what's happening inside. Used topically, Calcium Bentonite Clay pulls out excess oils and impurities, infections, stimulates circulation, promotes cellular revitalization and detoxifies. Whichever method you select, your skin will thank you for it!

Benefits Of Clay Baths

Because the body detoxifies through the skin, clay baths are becoming increasingly popular for drawing out toxins and cleansing the skin. Clay baths are beneficial in removing toxic buildup of heavy metals, chemicals, radiation and toxins stored in the body. They also relieve sore muscles and body aches and stimulate lymphatic action and circulation. They are very relaxing and can promote a good night's sleep. Children with autism are reported to be calmer, to maintain longer eye contact and exhibit improved communication skills after a single clay bath. However, please don't overdo it! If you stay too long in a very hot bath, you could dehydrate and experience what is known as a cleansing reaction and feel fatigue or headaches, or a burst of energy and an increase in pulse rate. Be aware of your body's response to the first detox bath. Be sure to drink water or an electrolyte drink to keep from getting dehydrated.

HOW TO PREPARE A CLAY DETOX BATH

In a blender to 3 cups of water, add 1-2 cups of dry clay, cover with more water until within an inch of the top.

Blend on high for 30 seconds.

Pour the mixture into the bathtub and rinse the blender with water.

Before getting into the bath wash the blades of your blender.

Soak for 20-30 minutes submerging as much of the body as possible. Keep the water circulating by stirring.

Relax and enjoy.

No need to rinse off, just dry off and notice how soft your skin feels.

Baths in the evening are preferred for a good night's sleep.

If the clay is dissolved adequately (no lumps), it is safe for drains and septic tanks.

Protocol for Clay Baths

To detox from heavy metals, chemicals or radiation, use 2 cups of clay powder per bath, 2 times a week for 6 weeks or longer, depending on the degree of toxicity.

Can be done more often.

For a maintenance bath to relieve sore muscles and for total relaxation, use 1 cup of clay powder as needed.

For infants, add ½ cup of liquid clay to bath water.

For small children, ¾ to 1 cup of clay per bath mixed per directions is suggested.

Another detox method is to cover yourself in the clay mask and get in an infrared sauna and allow the dry heat to open the skin pores.

Detox Clay Foot Baths

When clay baths are not possible, prepare a foot soak.

Mix the clay at a ratio of 1 cup clay powder sandwiched with 6 cups of water in a blender and blend well until it is lump free.

Pour the mix into a plastic food grade container with warm water and soak your feet for 1-hour intervals.

The mix may be used several times.

Cover it with an air-tight lid between uses.

Suggestions for Using A Clay Mask Topically

There are a variety of ways to use clay topically. In addition to facials and full-body wraps, the clay mask can be applied topically to help relieve acne, arthritis, eczema, psoriasis, poison oak and ivy, shingles, broken bones, burns, cuts, pressure wounds, scrapes, blisters, insect bites, warts and toenail fungus, just to name a few. Relief comes from the fact that the clay detoxes, alkalizes, balances and draws circulation and blood flow to the skin and affected areas. Bentonite Clay for topical application may be purchased premixed or made from clay powder.

How To Make A Clay Mask

Combine clay powder with water at a ratio of ¼ cup of clay powder to ¾ cup of water in a glass, ceramic, or food-grade plastic container with a non-metal, air-tight lid.

Cover and shake vigorously for about a minute or until all lumps are gone. For larger amounts, mix in a blender. However, take care to immediately wash any clay residue off of the metal blades.

Allow the mixture to stand for 15 minutes with lid slightly loosened to vent and allow for expansion.

Suggested amounts are:

1 cup of clay powder to 2 1/2 cups of water in the blender.

Always put the water in first then add clay. For best results sandwich the clay between the water. In other words, some water on the bottom add clay and the rest of the water on top.

This can be used for a clay mask, magma or mud, also referred to as hydrated clay, about the consistency of sour cream or pudding. Keep your clay tightly covered so it will not dry out. If kept out of direct sunlight and heat, your clay will last a long time. You will want to keep a portion of this clay with you all the time for emergencies.

Suggestions for Applying a Topical Clay Mask

Apply a thin to medium coating of clay mask to the face and neck area.

Allow 15 to 20 minutes to dry.

Rehydrate the clay and wash off.

Pat face dry.

You will notice how tight your face feels. You might notice a warmth or flush to your face immediately after removing the clay mask. Notice how smooth and soft your face feels. Weekly applications will have you looking years younger and will chase away acne. The clay mask will pull out excess oils and impurities in the skin. It is acne's worst nightmare.

Suggestions for a Full-Body Wrap

A full-body wrap is a clay mask applied to the whole body. At a spa you will be charged $150 to $300 for this service. Below are instructions on how to give yourself one at home.

Cover the body with a thin coating 1/8th of an inch of warm clay mud.

Wrap up in a Mylar sheet and lie down.

Cover up in an electric blanket.

General wrap time is 30 minutes.

You may need help applying the clay on this one. Another alternative is to put on a bathing suit and cover yourself with the clay mask and dry in the sunshine. Going to the beach to do this and washing off in the salt water is a great way to detox. As the clay starts drying, you may find some itchy spots as it tightens and pulls. Take a spray bottle of water to moisten these tender areas. During the winter do it in your bathroom.

CLAY POULTICES

A poultice is a thick application of topical clay mask to an area for things such as open wounds, burns, rashes, broken bones, and arthritic joints, back pain due to slipped disks, pinched nerves, toenail fungus, eye irritations, boils, sprains, migraine headaches and problems with body organs. It is held in place with a plastic wrap. Clay poultices should be ½ to ¾ of an inch thick. In most cases a poultice can be left on for 2 to 4 hours or all night. If used to stimulate a body organ, leave on for to an hour the first time increase by several hours each day until leaving it on all night. In some cases, such as sinus infections, toenail fungus, sprains or bruises, apply the clay and leave it uncovered to dry.

Some areas of the body are difficult to wrap. Glad Press 'n' Seal works well on these cases. It is in the grocery store next to the

Saran wrap and foils. Cut a square or strip of Glad Press 'n' Seal larger than the area you want to put it on. On the sticky side put an ample amount of the clay mask. In some cases, you may want to warm the clay lightly in a Ziploc bag in warm water. Put the clay directly over the problem area and press the dry edges of the sticky side to the skin to hold in place.

For a spinal injury, cut a long diagonal strip of Glad Press 'n Seal and apply as directed above. These may be worn under your clothes.

Apply the clay mask thickly over a circular cotton pad and apply it to the closed eyelid. If you should get some in your eye just wash it out. Leave in place for 15 to 20 minutes.

For minor irritations, pour the liquid clay on the pad and apply.

This is very soothing and will relieve itching and reduce swelling from allergic reactions. This is an excellent treatment for black eyes.

To make a clay eye wash solution: In a glass jar add 1 tablespoon of liquid clay with 4 ounces of eye wash solution and blend.

Pour the solution into a clean bottle to use in an eye cup or as eye drops daily as needed.

Be sure to get eye wash and not lens cleaner.

Some references are:

Busch & Lomb Advanced Eye Relief Eye Wash

Collyrium for Fresh Eyes- Eye Wash

Walgreen's Soothing Eye Wash

Clay Suppositories

Clay suppositories are made from thick clay, for exmple, 1 part clay to 1 part water or less.

You want to be able to mold it like sculpting clay.

Take little balls of the clay and roll them one at a time in your hands into a bullet shape.

Set them on wax paper to dry.

When you are ready to use them, lubricate the pointed end and insert and leave it in the rectum.

It will work its magic, dissolve and come out on its own.

Suppositories are beneficial for hemorrhoids, colon inflammation and prostrate conditions.

Women can use them vaginally for fibroid tumors, inflammation and yeast infections.

Clay for Enemas and Douches

Add 2 ounces of the liquid clay to a pint of water.

Clay Packs

Clay packs are direct applications of thick clay mask put directly on an area such as over the sinuses, closed eyes, tooth aches on the jaw and headaches on the forehead, temples, broken bones or at the neck. They are cool and soothing.

You may put a wet wash rag over the clay to keep it moist.

Leave clay packs on for 15 minutes or longer.

DRY POWDER APPLICATION

The dry powder Calcium Bentonite Clay application is the most basic. Simply apply dry powder by hand in the amount indicated by the treatment modality. Dry powder clay is excellent for open, bleeding wounds and oozing rashes. Packing a wound with the dry powder will help stop the bleeding and keep it from becoming infected. It is also beneficial for treating gums, tooth problems and for brushing teeth.

PROPER HANDLING AND STORAGE OF CLAY

Follow these simple rules to keep your clay clean, effective and active:

Store clay away from extreme heat and direct sunlight.

Liquid clay should be stored in a food-grade plastic or glass bottle with a non-metallic lid. The clay does not require refrigeration.

Always use clean non-metal utensils when scooping the clay out of the container.

Never leave the clay in direct contact with metals for prolong periods of time. For example, don't leave the clay in a metal bowl. The clay's electromagnetic charge will act on deteriorating metals, will cause the metal to prematurely rust, and will limit the clay's ability to draw when applied to the skin.

Keep out of close proximity to chemicals and strong odors.

TAKING CLAY OVER TIME

Most clays work best when taken over a long period. Clay does not offer instant cures for all ailments, but history shows it can encourage the body to put up a better fight when taken over time. Avoid high-sodium clays and acidic clays for internal use, especially over a prolonged time. Follow directions from the clay source supplier regarding its particular brand of clay.

When clay is taken for indefinite periods, it has no addictive qualities. One can quit taking clay at any time. There are no withdrawal symptoms, and you will never need to enter a withdrawal program. Many people ask whether clay is something they have to take for the rest of their lives. The answer to the question of course is, no, they don't have to; there is no danger in discontinuing its use. However, why not take something that is beneficial and will help cleanse and support the immune system? Especially in today's highly polluted world, the liver and kidneys are so overworked they never have a chance to rest. Taking Calcium Bentonite Clay every day helps keep the body functioning in tip-top condition. To maintain a healthy system, take clay daily.

However, remember that all clays are not created equal. Again, avoid high-sodium clays, acidic clays and impure clays. Quality-tested, pure clays are the dependable safe clays. Pure means clean with nothing added and not processed.

The regular intake of liquid clay can produce other benefits including parasite removal from the intestines, allergy and hay fever relief, and elimination of anemia and acne. For example, it reduces discomfort from allergies by quickly neutralizing allergens that would otherwise produce allergic reactions, and it reduces heartburn and indigestion by absorbing excess stomach acids.

Now what are you waiting for? Go mix some clay!

Disclaimer: This educational information is meant to supplement and not be a substitute for professional medical care or treatment. This information has not been evaluated by the FDA.

Chapter Nine

TREATING 180 AILMENTS NATURALLY

Calcium Bentonite Clay and water. Often those two lifelines are all you will need to return your body to a state of optimal health. This chapter will give you information on how to treat over 180 ailments.

The most important thing to understand is that one size does not fit all. There are varying stages of dis-ease, so know that adjustments to amounts should be made accordingly. The more serious the situation, the more clay is needed. If you have serious digestive issues, you may need to increase your amounts for optimal results. Remember, with clay, what goes in the mouth comes out south.

Although we will focus on modalities using only Calcium Bentonite Clay and water, many people use clay in conjunction with other natural products such as herbs, nutrients, cleanses or oils, all of which can be effective in their own right.

Though some of these additions can work together without harm, sometimes the actions contradict each other, weakening the effectiveness of both. It is my opinion that clay is most effective when used as a stand-alone. Oils are designed to be absorbed into the body, and clay's job is to pull out. Clay will let you know when she rejects a partner with an odor or release of gases. Here are some important reminders to review when following a protocol:

The instructions for making Liquid Clay, Clay Baths, Detox Foot Baths, Clay Mask, Full Body Wraps, Poultices, Eye Poultices, Eye Drops, Suppositories, Enemas and Douches are in Chapter 8 – How to Use Clay

When directed to take the clay internally or drink the clay, I am referring to the amount of premixed liquid clay in ounces that you drink.

If a protocol instructs you to take internal clay, be sure to take it several hours away from oral medication. Ask your pharmacist how long it takes for your medicines to be absorbed.

When mixing clay, never stir. Shake or mix in a blender. Do not leave the clay in any form in prolonged contact with metals.

Constipation: Most people have three regular bowel movements a day when taking the liquid clay. A few people may experience constipation from the clay pulling out putrid fecal matter that is old, hard and dry. In this case take whatever you need to keep your system running smoothly or try over-the-counter magnesium oxide tablets 250 mg from the grocery store.

Clay Baths: The purpose of the hot bath is to open the pores of the skin for better detoxing. With a hot bath, you only stay in 15-20 minutes and drink water or an electrolyte drink so you do not become dehydrated. Not all protocols call for a hot bath.

Drink LOTS of water during the day. It is important to flush the body of toxins. Wait 30 minutes after taking the liquid clay to start your water regime.

Disclaimer: This educational information is meant to supplement and not be a substitute for professional medical care or treatment. This information has not been evaluated by the FDA.

PROTOCOLS FOR SPECIFIC AILMENTS:

ABRASIONS

For major or minor abrasions—scratches, cuts, nicks or general boo-boos—treat topically as needed. If the abrasion is bleeding, sprinkle some dry powder Calcium Bentonite Clay directly onto the bleeding area. This will speed the clotting process and protect the wound from infection.

After the bleeding has stopped, apply a layer of clay mask to the affected area and the area surrounding the abrasion, and cover with Saran wrap or Glad Press 'n Seal to keep the wet clay in place. Pain should subside in minutes, and healing time will be cut in half.

Apply 2 to 3 times a day; the abrasion should be rinsed with water and a new application of clay applied. If clay particles stick to the wound, add more clay over the area. When clay is working, it holds on to the area until it is ready to let go. Use until healed.

ABSCESSED TEETH

Treat an abscessed tooth both internally and topically.

Drink 2 ounces of liquid clay twice daily for the duration of the toothache.

Pack dry powder clay all over the tooth and affected gums. The saliva will hold the clay to the tooth. Refresh 3 times a day and sleep with it in overnight.

Apply a poultice or clay mask to the outside of your cheek, jaw or chin, directly over the toothache area. Leave on for 45 to 60 minutes. Repeat 3 to 5 times daily or until pain/infection is gone.

ACID REFLUX

Acid reflux is easily treated with daily ingestion of liquid Calcium Bentonite Clay.

Start by drinking 2 ounces of liquid clay 3 times a day. You may also drink an additional ounce just before and after any meals that is causing discomfort.

From this point forward, simply maintain the 1-2 ounces twice daily or as needed to remove acid reflux from your life. Calcium Bentonite Clay diminishes acid reflux so quickly that many consider it nothing short of a miracle.

ACIDIC SYSTEM

Drink liquid clay to change the pH of your body from acid to alkaline. Calcium Bentonite Clay has a favorable effect on every function of your body.

Start by drinking 2 ounces of liquid clay 3 times a day, increasing the dosage by 1 ounce daily to ultimately consume 4 ounces 3 times a day. Remember to take clay away from oral medications.

Take a clay enema daily or as needed, adding 2 ounces of liquid clay to 1 pint of water.

Take a weekly clay bath for 15 to 20 minutes using 1 cup of clay powder per bath to maintain a balanced skin pH level.

There are some acid clays, so always ask the manufacturer the pH of the clay you are using.

Test your pH with easy-to-use saliva or urine test strips. Adjust the amount of Calcium Bentonite Clay needed to fine-tune your body's pH level.

ACNE

Start by drinking 2 ounces of liquid clay 3 times a day, increasing the dosage by 1 ounce daily to ultimately consume 3 ounces 3 times a day, away from oral medications as needed.

Treat the affected areas topically by using hydrated clay as a mask as needed to deep-clean the oil glands.

Take a clay bath for 15 to 20 minutes using 1 cup of clay powder once a week to maintain a balanced skin pH level.

You may also treat those severe blemishes and postulates topically by applying "spot" treatments. Just dab some clay mask onto any persistent or infected acne blemishes and "wear" all day.

A thin facial mask may also be allowed to dry and left on overnight at any time. Simply rehydrate and wash off in the morning.

To effectively deal with any problem, you must first understand and eliminate the root cause of the problem. Acne is a sebaceous (below the surface of the skin) problem and therefore must be attacked from the inside out as well as topically. We must also understand what causes acne.

Primary causes of acne:

Excessive sebum can break down cellular walls in your pores, causing bacteria to grow.

The androgenic hormones, particularly testosterone, that increase at puberty, and the surge of premenstrual hormones trigger increased production of sebum.

Makeup clogs the pores.
Sweat
Diet
Stress and overproduction of acidity
Hygiene
Heredity—Susceptibility to acne can also be genetic.

It's essential to battle the acne at its source, which is INSIDE the body. Dr. James Meschino writes: "To understand the relationship between detoxification, intestinal cleansing and prevention of acne, we must first understand the relationship between our skin, the digestive system and excretory system."

"Every cell in the body can be affected by toxins, and many forms of sickness can result from it, including acne and other skin eruptions. Detoxification is a normal body process of eliminating or neutralizing toxins through the colon, liver, kidneys, lungs, lymph and skin." [39] Bibliography

AGE SPOTS – See LIPOFUSCIN ABNORMALITIES

AGENT ORANGE DETOXIFICATION - See DETOXIFICATION

AIDS – HUMAN IMMUNODEFICIENCY VIRUS

AIDS, which is caused by the human immunodeficiency virus (HIV), attacks and quickly damages the immune system, stripping the body of its defenses. Once the damage is done, it appears to be irreversible.

There are no known studies showing that clay removes HIV. However, clay can help the body in achieving a state of balance. It is known to cleanse acidity in the blood, enrich the blood cells, increase T-cell counts and reduce free radicals. Clay also detoxifies the body internally to help lighten the load on the internal filtering systems: the liver, kidneys and lymphatic system. The clay will balance the body, reducing acidity (acid provides a breeding ground for diseases and infection).

As with all major life-threatening ailments, we encourage you to consult with your doctor before altering any treatment program you are on. Your condition may be so dependent on your current treatment regimen that you could do further harm by altering your current treatment. Supplementing treatment with Calcium Bentonite Clay includes a four-prong approach with full-body immersion baths, full-body wraps, clay poultices and ingestion of liquid clay. Throughout this period, we ask you to monitor T-cell counts and viral antibody counts weekly so you can see your results and improvement.

Start by drinking 2 ounces of liquid clay 3 times a day, increasing the dosage by 1 ounce daily to ultimately consume 5 ounces 3 times a day, away from oral medications as needed.

Take a clay enema daily or as needed by adding 2 ounces of liquid clay to 1 pint of water.

Prepare a weekly full-body clay mask and wrap yourself head to toe. Leave the mask on for 30 minutes, then shower off.

Additionally, take a clay bath twice a week for 15 to 20 minutes using 2 cups of clay powder per bath. Continue the baths for 8 weeks.

Apply a 1-inch-thick clay poultice about 10 inches in diameter to your liver twice daily for one hour. After 3 days it may be applied overnight as needed. After eight weeks check your T-cell levels for progress. Depending on progress, continue the regimen or go to a maintenance level of 2 ounces of liquid clay 2 twice daily and 1 clay bath for 15 to 20 minutes a week using 1 cup of clay powder as needed.

Monitor your progress and watch your T-cell counts.

ALCOHOLISM

Alcoholism takes a toll on the entire body – both physically and emotionally. It is a disease that harms every major organ in the body. The benefit of using Calcium Bentonite Clay when tackling a body racked by alcoholism is, first, in its function of cleansing and detoxing the entire body. Second, it sets the stage for the body to begin the healing process.

Start by drinking 2 ounces of liquid clay 3 times a day, increasing the dosage by 1 ounce daily to ultimately consume 4 ounces 3 times a day, away from oral medications as needed.

Take a clay bath twice a week for 15 to 20 minutes using 1 cup of clay powder per bath. If baths are not available, do a full-body clay mask wrap or a clay foot bath.

Apply a clay poultice to the back of the neck and/or forehead, ½ inch thick and 3-by-6 inches in size. This will reduce headaches.

Apply a 1-inch-thick clay poultice about 10 inches in diameter to your liver twice daily for one hour. After 3 days it may be applied overnight. Do this daily. The poultice will aid the liver to detox and rejuvenate itself.

ALLERGIES

Allergy protocols with Calcium Bentonite Clay may be needed seasonally or on an ongoing basis.

Drink 2 ounces of liquid clay 3 times a day.

If you suffer from drainage and stuffiness, apply a clay poultice to the sinuses for 20 minutes daily.

Apply a daily clay poultice to the liver for one hour.

For itchy eyes, apply a cotton pad soaked in liquid clay over the eyes for 15 minutes or longer. Also, follow the instructions for a Clay Eye Wash Solution such as an eye drop or an eye wash.

Take a clay bath twice a week for 15 to 20 minutes using 1 cup of clay powder per bath.

Allergies and hay fever are caused by the release of histamines. Clay will help if the allergies are due to clogged detoxification channels (liver, kidney, lung, large intestine). The liver becomes plugged up with toxins and fatty tissue and therefore cannot produce the necessary antihistamines to neutralize the allergic reactions. The first thing to do is clean and rebuild the liver. Once that is done, allergies and hay fever may disappear.

If your allergies are part true histamine response and part clogged detox channels, clay should help reduce the severity of the reaction. However, clay does not stop a histamine reaction. Some people, after taking the clay, notice an immediate improvement in their conditions.

Sometimes allergies and hay fever disappear altogether. Others see no sudden improvement and must keep taking the clay for a while before they obtain relief.

AMALGAM FILLINGS

Start by drinking 2 ounces of liquid clay 3 times a day, increasing the dosage by 1 ounce daily to ultimately consume 4 ounces 3 times a day, away from oral medications.

Pack your gums at night with the dry clay and leave until the next morning. Brush your teeth with clay powder as well.

Swish with liquid clay daily as needed.

If the amalgams are leaking, drink 1 ounce of liquid clay before eating to capture the leakage aggravated by chewing.

Apply a 1-inch-thick clay poultice about 10 inches in diameter to your liver daily for one hour. After 3 days it may be applied overnight as needed.

Take a hot clay bath 3 times a week for 15 to 20 minutes using 1 to 2 cups of clay powder per bath depending on the severity of the condition.

Drink water or an electrolyte drink during the bath. At three months, have your toxicity level checked.

In the past few years, we have learned about mercury poisoning from old amalgam fillings. No matter what type of metal poisoning or from what source the toxicity is derived, the treatment is the same. Take regular pH and metal-level tests as your benchmarks for progress and to know when all toxic metals have been removed from your body.

AMPUTATIONS

Give clay a try for 4 to 5 days before scheduling surgery. Generously apply clay masks to the diseased area and cover with a plastic wrap. Change 3 times a day with fresh poultice for overnight. Clay will pull out gangrene and blood poison and stimulate circulation for cellular repair and healing.

Drink 2 ounces of liquid clay 3 times a day, increasing the dosage by 1 ounce daily to ultimately consume 4 ounces 3 times a day, away from oral medications as needed.

For infected feet, take a Detox Foot Bath using a 1 to 6 ratio of clay to water prepared in a blender. Soak for 1 hour 3 times a day as needed. You may reuse the mixture several times. Cover the container between uses.

ANEMIA

Calcium Bentonite Clay is frequently used to stop anemia indirectly by increasing red blood cell count. The following treatment is recommended for anemia:

When your blood count is below normal: Start by drinking 2 ounces of liquid clay 3 times a day, increasing the dosage by 1 ounce daily to ultimately consume 4 ounces 3 times a day, away from oral medications as needed.

Apply a 1-inch-thick clay poultice about 10 inches in diameter to your liver twice daily for 1 hour. After 3 days it may be applied overnight as needed.

When your blood count is normal, but you have a history of anemia, continue the following regimen for maintenance.

Drink 2 ounces of liquid clay 2 times a day and apply a liver poultice as needed.

ANOREXIA

Anorexia is an eating disorder that prevents people from receiving necessary nutrients and vitamins. It is caused by an emotional disturbance that creates physical symptoms replicating starvation. Although psychological counseling lies at the core of correcting the behaviors associated with this emotional disease, Calcium Bentonite Clay greatly aids the body in its recovery and restoration process. To aid the body in coming back into balance, I recommend the following:

Start by drinking 2 ounces of liquid clay 3 times a day, increasing the dosage by 1 ounce daily to ultimately consume 4 ounces 3 times a day, away from oral medications as needed.

Apply a 1-inch-thick clay poultice about 10 inches in diameter to the liver twice daily for 1 hour. After 3 days it may be applied overnight.

Take a clay bath twice a week for 15 to 20 minutes using 1 cup of clay powder per bath.

ARTHRITIS

During presence of arthritic conditions:

Start by drinking 2 ounces of liquid clay 3 times a day, increasing the dosage by 1 ounce daily to ultimately consume 4 ounces 3 times a day, away from oral medications as needed.

Apply clay poultice to the area of concern. Allow it to dry or wrap with a plastic wrap. It can be left all night. Use during the day as needed.

a clay bath twice weekly for 15 to 20 minutes using 1 to 2 cups of clay powder per bath.

At bedtime, put a thin film of clay mask on the affected areas, let dry and leave overnight.

For maintenance after arthritis has cleared up:

Drink at least 2 ounces of liquid clay daily.

Use the clay mask topically as needed.

Take an occasional clay bath for 15 to 20 minutes using 1 cup of clay as needed.

Most arthritic conditions are due to an accumulation of waste matter and toxic byproducts that have settled in specific areas of the body such as the hands, knees, lower back, etc.

Sometimes uric acid is the culprit and will attack the cartilage of the joints, the tendons, the ligaments or other tissues, causing them to swell because of inflammation and toxic fluid buildup. The clay's action is indirect in that it acts as an analgesic to reduce pain, an absorber of excess fluid buildup and a cleanser of toxicity. In turn, the symptoms of arthritis disappear.

Calcium Bentonite Clay will relieve the pain, reduce swelling and stiffness, and increase joint motion and range.

AUTISM

For small children, and toddlers: Drink 1 to 2 teaspoons of liquid clay twice daily.

For children 50 pounds and heavier: Drink 1 ounce of liquid clay twice daily. It may be given in juice, a smoothie or apple sauce.

Give the child a warm clay bath twice weekly for 15 to 20 minutes using 1 cup of clay powder per bath. Continue the baths for 3 months to detox. Additional clay baths can be given as needed. Note: For small children, use ½ cup of clay powder per bath.

Using Calcium Bentonite Clay baths, autism symptoms among children have noticeably improved. Some expected results are calmness, more eye contact and improved verbal communication.

It is believed that some of the varied contributory factors to autism include aberrant brain wave transmission through the cerebral cortex, food and environmental allergens, and metal toxicity. Dr. Miriam Jang has seen many of her young autistic patients improving so much on the clay that she goes as far as to say that the clay works even better than the TD DMPS (transdermal dimercaptopropane sulfonate) in chelation. "So far, I have put a huge number of patients on these clay baths, and the levels of the heavy metals — mercury, lead, arsenic, aluminum and cadmium — have come down dramatically. I follow the progress with 6-hour DMSA challenge urine test from Doctor's Data. One patient had very high levels of mercury and levels of lead that were off the charts. In 3 months of twice weekly clay baths, the lead came down dramatically, and the mercury disappeared. The muscle weakness associated with high lead levels improved dramatically. Another 5 months of these clay baths showed even lower levels of lead, but the mercury reappeared. This supports the theory that mercury is sequestered in different areas of our body and it takes time to get it all out." [27]

BACK PROBLEMS

Drink 2 ounces of liquid clay twice daily, away from oral medications as needed.

Take a daily hot clay bath for 15 to 20 minutes using 1 to 2 cups of clay powder per bath.

Drink water or an electrolyte drink during the bath.

Apply thick clay poultice on the spine or affected area and hold in place with a strip of Glad Press 'n Seal. Replace with a new poultice day and night until better.

BAD BREATH

For bad breath, brush your teeth and tongue with clay mask twice daily.

Drink 2 ounces of liquid clay 3 times daily, away from oral medications as needed.

Swish with liquid clay for 15 minutes a.m. and p.m.

Taking clay daily will help to relieve the digestive tract, support elimination and bind the toxins that may be the cause of the unpleasant breath.

BEE STINGS - See INSECT STINGS & BITES

BELL'S PALSY

Drink 2 ounces of liquid clay twice daily, increasing by 1 ounce daily, to 3 to 4 ounces 2 times a day, away from oral medications as needed.

Apply generous amounts of clay masks to the affected area day and night until it clears up. It may take 15 to 30 days of intensive applications.

BIRTHMARK - See LIPOFUSCIN ABNORMALITIES

BLACKHEADS

Treat affected areas topically by using the clay mask as a facial mask, leaving it on for 15 to 20 minutes. Do this daily for 3 days, morning and evening, then use as needed.

Drink 2 ounces of liquid clay twice daily, away from oral medications as needed.

You may also treat those severe blemishes and postulates topically by applying spot treatments. Just dab some clay mask onto any persistent or infected acne blemishes and wear them all day. A thin facial mask may also be left on overnight.

BLISTERS

All raised, fluid-filled blisters are treated in the same fashion.

The goal is threefold: To stop the pain, to remove the fluid without breaking the blister and to leave no scar.

Apply a thick gob of clay mask to the blister and surrounding

2 inches of skin.

Cover that with plastic wrap. Change twice a day if necessary. Pain should subside almost immediately. All of the fluid should be gone in 12 to 24 hours.

And the healing process should be completed in 24 to 48 hours with no skin breakage or additional recovery time. On a foot or hand, cover the affected area with clay and plastic wrap at night and pull on a piece of clothing such as a sock or glove before going to sleep. Clean and redress in the morning if necessary.

BLOOD PRESSURE

For high blood pressure, apply a generous clay poultice on the inside of the upper arms from the elbow to the armpit and wrap with plastic wrap daily. Apply fresh poultice at night. After it is under control, maintain with thin applications, allow to dry and leave on day and night as needed.

Drink 2 ounces of liquid clay twice daily, away from oral medications as needed.

When you feel the need to relax, take a warm clay bath for 15 to 20 minutes using 1 cup of clay powder per bath.

BOILS

Calcium Bentonite Clay is quite effective in healing boils.

Prepare a poultice ¼ inch thick and 4 inches in diameter to apply to the affected area for 1 hour.

Repeat process throughout the day as needed.

Drink 2 ounces of liquid clay twice daily, away from oral medications as needed.

Results and relief are usually quite fast depending on how quickly you apply the clay.

BREAST HEALTH

For cysts and benign tumors, apply thick applications of clay masks to the area 3 times a day.

The clay mask can be secured with a plastic wrap or a square of Glad Press ’n Seal.

At bedtime cover it with a thin layer of clay and let it dry. Leave it on all night.

After a mammogram or X-ray, apply clay mask to the area 2 times a day to remove excess radiation.

Start by drinking 2 ounces of liquid clay 3 times a day, increasing the dosage by 1 ounce daily to ultimately consume 5 ounces 3 times a day, away from oral medications as needed.

Take a clay bath twice a week for 15 to 20 minutes using 1 cup of clay powder per bath.

BROKEN BONES

Calcium Bentonite Clay speeds the healing time of broken bones to half of the normal required time. It also reduces swelling, acts as a pain reducer and brings circulation to the affected area.

The clay protocol for broken bones is internal and topical.

Drink 2 ounces of liquid clay twice daily, away from oral medications as needed.

In cases of a splint, apply thick applications of clay mask all around the break and cover with plastic wrap and secure the splint. Change and reapply morning and night until healed.

If you wear a cast, make warm clay poultice packs in large 1-gallon Ziploc bags. Lay these on the outside of the cast as often as possible. These may be reheated in a bowl of hot water and reused.

Repeat until the cast is removed or the bone is healed.

After the cast is removed, apply topical applications of clay mask to remove odor and dead skin cells and to bring circulation to the area.

BROWN RECLUSE SPIDER BITE - See SPIDER BITES

BRUISES

Calcium Bentonite Clay is effective on any size bruise on any part of the body. Living Clay reduces the pain, removes the old fluid from the bruised area and restores healthy circulation to the area.

For bruises, apply a poultice about ¼ inch thick on the skin in an area a little larger in diameter than the bruise.

Cover with a plastic wrap. Leave on all day if possible. Repeat as needed. May take several days to reabsorb the blood.

BUNIONS

First, remove what caused the problem in the first place, such as shoes that are too tight.

Drink 2 ounces of liquid clay twice daily, away from oral medications as needed.

Prepare a small poultice clay mask to completely cover the area.

Cover with plastic wrap. Change this poultice 3 to 4 times daily and leave over night.

After the bunion is gone, continue to drink 2 ounces of liquid clay twice daily as a lifetime practice.

BURNS – CHEMICAL, SEVERE OR MINOR

Apply clay mask in thick poultices to the entire burn area immediately and cover with a plastic wrap.

Reapply wet poultices until tenderness is gone. Generally, relief from the pain is noticeable within seconds depending on the degree of the burn.

Throughout the burn healing process, drink 2 ounces of liquid clay 2 times daily.

Renew the poultice applications day and night, changing them every 6 hours. The poultices may be left on all night. Repeat the protocols until the tissues are rebuilt.

For large area burns, it is advisable to coat the whole area with clay mask and cover to keep moist.

Drink 2 ounces of liquid clay twice a day.

Clay reduces risks of infection and absorbs all the impurities and foreign bodies apt to be found in the burn. It also eliminates the destroyed cells, enabling cellular rebuilding.

CALLUSES

Drink 2 ounces of liquid clay twice a day, away from oral medications as needed.

An ideal method for calluses on the feet is to soak in a warm clay foot bath daily for as long and as often as possible. Between soaks use a good lotion or coconut oil.

Corns and calluses tend to peel off. This hard-to-treat problem is often solved in as little as 3 to 4 days.

At night cover the area with a thick application of clay mask, cover with plastic wrap and leave on all night, covered with a sock.

CANCER

In many cases Calcium Bentonite Clay has helped in discarding dead cells from the body after chemo and radiation treatments. Ideally, daily ingestion of Calcium Bentonite Clay is a helpful preventative measure for cancers, as acidic environments are breeding grounds for the rapid reproduction of cancer cells. Calcium Bentonite Clay's high pH helps bring the body into balance and reduces acidic conditions. In some cases, clay can assist the body in restoring health by eliminating highly toxic conditions.

As with all life-threatening ailments, we encourage you to consult with your doctor before altering any treatment program you are now on. Your condition may be so advanced that you may do further harm by altering your current treatment.

No statement we make or information we offer should be construed as a claim for a cure, treatment or prevention of any disease. Clay merely supports the immune system in returning to a state of well being. Below is an outline on how to use Calcium Bentonite Clay as a supportive aid in dealing with various cancers.

Start by drinking 2 ounces of liquid clay 3 times a day, increasing the dosage by 1 ounce daily to ultimately consume 6-8 ounces 3 times a day, away from oral medications as needed.

Continue this practice for 4 to 8 weeks or as needed.

Then maintain a regimen of 2 ounces of liquid clay twice a day as lifetime practice. This will help your body stay in pH balance and prevent it from becoming overly acidic.

Take a clay enema daily or as needed, adding 2 ounces of liquid clay to 1 pint of water.

Detox Clay Baths - Taking a clay bath twice a week for 20 minutes using 1-2 cups of clay powder per bath. Continue these baths for 6 weeks after chemo or radiation to help the body detox the cell die-off and excess radiation. Clay baths help people relax and sleep better.

There is no limit to how many clay baths can be taken.

Clay Poultices - If you have a localized tumor, cancerous lumps or mass, or localized skin cancer, use poultices on a regular basis away from radiation treatments, before any surgery. The clay will help to draw the cancer to the point of origin, so it is easier for the surgeon to get all the cancer. A poultice can be a ¼ inch to 1 inch thick and 2 to 10 inches in diameter. Place the clay mask directly over the area. Cover with a plastic wrap or a square of Glad Press 'n Seal to hold the clay in place. Leave on for 1 to 2 hours. Repeat this process several times a day, using a new batch of clay for each poultice.

Sometimes chemo can make the colon raw, and a clay douche or enema will be helpful. Use 2 ounces of liquid clay per pint of water for a douche or enema.

Clay Submersion Detox Baths – A Calcium Bentonite Clay immersion pit is very effective for detoxing from the cell die-off after chemo and radiation. Make your own with a kiddie pool. Mix large quantities of hydrated clay at a 1 to 5 ratio of clay to water in a blender and fill up the pool. Submerge and soak for as long as possible (hours). The clay can be reused 10 times. Cover the pool between uses. To discard the clay, add more water and pour the mixture on the lawn and water it in. A full-body clay wrap may also be used to remove cell die-off. Cover yourself with a warm clay mask from head to toe – everything but the whites of your eyes and ear canals.

After applying the warm clay, stand in open air until it dries, then bathe or shower.

Remember, cancers thrive in an acidic environment. Most Calcium Bentonite Clays have a high alkaline pH. Request a clay with an 9.5 pH or higher. Calcium Bentonite Clay balances the body's pH, removes positively charged ions, and cleanses and detoxifies as it does its work. A well-balanced raw food diet and supplements will allow the body to focus its energy on healing. As always, take clay away from prescription medications. After medications are absorbed into the blood stream, it is safe to take clay internally.

CANDIDA

Start by drinking 2 ounces of liquid clay 3 times a day, increasing the dosage by 1 ounce daily to ultimately consume 6 to 8 ounces 3 times a day, away from medications.

Take a clay bath twice a week for 15 to 20 minutes using 1 to 2 cups of clay powder per bath.

For a vaginal douche or enema, mix 2 ounces of liquid clay per pint of water.

Apply a 1-inch-thick clay poultice about 10 inches in diameter to your liver twice daily for one hour. After 3 days it may be applied overnight.

If you have a history of Candida reoccurrences, maintain a regimen as follows:

Drink 3 ounces of liquid clay 3 times a day. Douche twice weekly. It is also extremely important to maintain a Candida suggested diet and take a good probiotic.

CARPEL TUNNEL SYNDROME

Clay for carpel tunnel syndrome is a simple process, and relief occurs in as little as a day.

Drink 2 ounces of liquid clay twice daily, away from oral medications as needed.

Prepare a ½-inch-thick hydrated clay mask and apply the mask completely around the wrists. Cover your wrist with a plastic wrap and leave overnight. In the most severe cases I've seen, full motor control is usually regained within three weeks of continued treatment. In two people that I've seen, the pain began to return two months later, and one treatment of clay relieved all newly occurring pain.

How can clay accomplish this? The answer is as simple as it is mysterious. In his article "True Carpal Tunnel Syndrome," Paul R. Martin writes, "Anything which will promote circulation, helps to relieve inflammation, aids in removal of local toxins, and soothes irritated muscles and tendons will help Carpal Tunnel Syndrome." [37]

CATARACTS

Follow the instructions in Chapter 7 for a clay eye wash solution and an eye poultice.

Use the eye wash solution daily in an eye cup or as eye drops. Combine this treatment with hydrated clay mask applied thickly over a circular cotton pad and apply to the closed eyelid. Leave in place for 20 minutes twice a day. For minor irritations, pour the liquid clay on the pad and apply over the closed eyelids for 15 to 30 minutes. Repeat this daily or as needed.

Drink 2 ounces of liquid clay twice daily.

CELIAC – See Gluten Intolerance

CELLULITE

Drink 2 ounces of liquid clay twice daily.

Ideally, do a full-body application with warm topical clay, and get into an infrared sauna.

The combination of clay and dry heat will pull the excess fluids from the body and tighten the skin.

Drink water or an electrolyte drink before or during sauna treatment to avoid dehydration.

Do not have a meal for approximately 2 hours before sauna session. Pay attention to your body condition while taking a sauna. Check your pulse. If it is too high, cease the sauna session. Stop taking a sauna if you stop sweating or do not feel well. You might have red splotches afterward where the clay has pulled circulation and blood flow to the surface of the skin. This is a temporary response and a sign that the clay is working.

If you do not have a sauna, do full-body or partial body wraps daily with warm clay as instructed in Chapter 8.

CHAPPED HANDS

For dry, chapped, rough hands, partially fill surgical gloves with the clay mask, insert hands, tape the wrists and leave on all night. During the day rub coconut oil on the hands.

CHEMICAL SENSITIVITIES – See MULTIPLE CHEMICAL SENSITIVITIES

CHEMOTHERAPY DETOXIFICATION

After the chemo and radiation treatments are finished, the critical convalescing period begins, and it is time to help the body discard the cell die-off, remove excess radiation, re-alkalize and heal.

Start by drinking 2 ounces of liquid clay 3 times a day, increasing the dosage by 1 ounce daily to ultimately consume 5 ounces 3 times a day, away from oral medications as needed.

This is good for settling and balancing toxicity, internal ulcers, mouth ulcers, nauseous stomach, acid reflux, and for stopping diarrhea.

Take a clay bath twice a week for 15 to 20 minutes using 2 cups of clay powder per bath. The baths will allow the body to detox from the cell die-off and excess radiation from treatments.

Mix 2 ounces of liquid clay per pint of water for a vaginal douche or enema.

Take a clay enema daily or as needed, adding 2 ounces of liquid clay to 1 pint of water.

Apply 1-inch clay poultice about 10 inches in diameter to your liver twice daily for 1 hour. After 3 days it maybe applied overnight. Do this daily as needed.

It should be noted that Calcium Bentonite Clay might allow some patients who would otherwise withdraw before completion to finish their chemotherapy treatments. This is where the clay goes head-on against the debilitating side effects of chemotherapy.

Examples of this detox/healing process will start with oral hygiene: Apply clay powder to gums, mouth sores, tongue or lips, and gargle the liquid clay for a raw or sore throat. External conditions will be the obvious skin problems: infections, rashes and boils. Topical applications of the clay mask will help heal sores and lesions.

CHRONIC FATIGUE SYNDROME (CFS)

Start by drinking 2 ounces of liquid clay 3 times a day, increasing the dosage by 1 ounce daily to ultimately consume 6 to 8 ounces 3 times a day, away from oral medications as needed.

Take a daily clay bath for 15 to 20 minutes using 1 cup of clay per bath.

Apply a 1-inch-thick clay poultice about 10 inches in diameter to liver twice daily for 1 hour. After 3 days it may be applied overnight. Do this daily as needed.

Chronic fatigue syndrome (CFS) is a complicated disorder characterized by extreme fatigue that can't be explained by any underlying medical condition. The cause of chronic fatigue syndrome is unknown. Some experts believe chronic fatigue syndrome might be triggered by a combination of factors. Detoxification is obviously needed. Calcium Bentonite Clay should be taken daily to adsorb bodily toxins and ensure intestinal health.

Often several viruses and fungi are activated in cases of CFS. For instance, many people who come down with CFS are diagnosed with Candida in the gut. According to an article in the Canadian Journal of Microbiology, clay has the capacity to adsorb, absorb and eliminate viruses. (Steven M. Lipson and G. Stolzky. "Specificity of Virus to Adsorption to Clay Minerals." Canadian Journal of Microbiology 31, 1985)

Taking Calcium Bentonite Clay internally has many advantages, one being its ability to act as a catalyst for the formation of long peptide chains. The ability to form peptide chains is one of the keys to increasing the effectiveness of the body's immune system, which lies at the crux of the cause of CFS.

Ridding your body of CFS can be an extended process. Symptomatic relief can be experienced in as little as 3 to 5 days, but complete remission of the ailment may take 2 to 3 months.

CIRRHOSIS OF THE LIVER

Start by drinking 2 ounces of liquid clay 3 times a day, increasing the dosage by 1 ounce daily to ultimately consume 8 ounces 3 times daily, away from oral medications.

Apply a 1-inch-thick clay poultice about 10 inches in diameter to the liver twice daily for 1 hour. After 3 days it may be applied overnight. Do this daily.

Take a daily clay bath for 15 to 20 minutes using 1 cup of clay powder per bath.

COLD SORES

On first onset apply a thick application of hydrated clay mask to the area. Reapply every hour with fresh clay.

Drink 2 ounces of liquid clay 3 times a day, away from oral medications as needed.

COLON CLEANSE

General Detox:

The protocol most frequently suggested by practitioners is:

Drink 2 ounces of liquid clay 3 times a day, away from oral medications, preferably on an empty stomach, for 21 days.

After 21 days you may take the clay at any time with or without food.

Advanced Detox:

To remove parasites, heavy metals and for more serious issues, a higher dose is recommended.

Start by drinking 2 ounces of liquid clay 3 times a day, increasing the dosage by 1 ounce daily to ultimately consume 4 to 6 ounces 3 times a day, away from oral medications and preferably on an empty stomach for 21 days. As always if you are not getting the results you want, take more. Some take 8 ounces throughout the day for serious conditions.

Maintenance Regimen:

To support the body's immune system, staying toxin free, and to balance your pH level, drink 2 ounces of liquid clay daily thereafter. More may be taken if desired. A sip of liquid clay before meals and snacks is highly recommended to capture toxins and radiation that may be in our foods.

If constipation occurs, take over-the-counter magnesium tablets (250 mg) or whatever you need to keep your janitorial services functioning.

Apply a 1-inch-thick clay poultice about 10 inches in diameter to your lower stomach twice daily for one hour. Do not use poultice for an hour before and after eating.

"A clean, properly functioning bowel is paramount to our well-being. Every cell and tissue in the body is fed by the bloodstream, which is supplied through the bowel. When the bowel is dirty, the blood is dirty and so are the organs and tissues. It is the bowel that must be cared for first before any effective healing can take place." (Bernard Jensen. [28]

"So, how do you know the state of your bowels? How do you

know if you need to do an internal cleanse? My answer is quite simple... After consulting with over 20,000 patients, I can honestly state that I have never worked with an individual that did not directly benefit from detoxifying his or her body. In this day and age, we ALL need to cleanse!" (Duncan, Lindsey, ND, CN, Nutrionalist)

COLON POLYPS

Clay can shrink the polyps and remove inflammation.

Take a clay enema daily or as needed using 2 ounces of liquid clay to 1 pint of water.

Start by drinking 2 ounces of liquid clay 3 times a day, increasing the dosage by 1 ounce daily to ultimately consume 6 to 8 ounces 3 times a day, away from oral medications, preferably on an empty stomach as needed.

Apply a 1-inch-thick clay poultice about 10 inches in diameter to your liver twice daily for one hour. After three days, apply the poultice at night, cover with Saran wrap and leave all night.

For maintenance to support the body's immune system, to stay toxin free and to balance your pH level, drink 2 ounces of liquid clay twice daily. More may be taken if desired.

CONSTIPATION

When the bowels do not move properly, the reasons are usually improper diet, lack of fiber, lack of water and faulty digestion. The first thing to do is drink lots of water – no other liquids, just water. That prepares the Calcium Bentonite Clay to work and get the system normalized.

Drink 2 ounces of liquid clay 2 to 3 times a day until regular. If you experience constipation after first taking clay, it is likely to pull the 5 to 10 pounds of putrefied matter lodged in the crevasses of the colon. This hard, dried stinky stuff may need help with evacuation. Do whatever you do to keep your janitorial services working.

Taking a 250 mg over-the-counter magnesium tablet works well, and it is not a laxative. These may be taken morning and evening depending on your need.

Apply a 1-inch-thick clay poultice about 10 inches in diameter to your lower stomach twice daily for 1 hour.

After three days, apply the poultice at night, cover with Saran wrap and leave all night.

CORNS – See BUNIONS

CRACKED HEELS

The important thing for dry, cracked heels is to moisturize, soften and bring new circulation to the affected area.

Drink 2 ounces of liquid clay twice daily.

Soak the feet in a warm clay bath by blending 1 cup of clay powder with 5 cups of warm water mixed in a blender until smooth. Soak the foot for 30 minutes to an hour. Repeat daily. The clay soak mixture may be covered and used 8 times. Use a pumice stone after soaking when applicable.

For severely cracked and bleeding heels: Apply a relatively thick coating of clay mask. Cover with a large piece of plastic wrap such as Glad Press 'n Seal. Then pull a sock over the wrap and leave on overnight. During the day rub coconut oil onto the heels.

CRADLE CAP

Apply the clay mask to the baby's head and wash gently using circular motions for 5 minutes, then rinse out.

CRAMPS – See Muscle Soreness

CROHN'S DISEASE

Start by drinking 2 ounces of liquid clay 3 times a day, increasing the dosage by 1 ounce daily to ultimately consume 6 to 8 ounces 3 times a day, away from oral medications as needed.

Apply a 1-inch-thick clay poultice about 10 inches in diameter to your lower stomach daily for 1 hour. After 3 days you can do an overnight poultice.

On opposite days apply a poultice over your liver.

Take a clay bath daily for 15-20 minutes using 1 cup of clay per bath as needed.

Take a clay enema daily or as needed using 2 ounces of liquid clay to 1 pint of water.

CUTS

For treatment of a bleeding cut, pack clay powder directly into the wound to stop the bleeding. After bleeding has clotted or stopped, rinse the cut with cool water, pat dry and apply a clay mask poultice. Cover the area to keep clean and keep the clay moist.

Change the poultice 2 to 3 times a day depending on the severity of the cut. Use fresh poultice for overnight. Repeat until all tenderness is gone and the cut is closed.

If the existence of foreign bodies in the wound is feared, continue the clay poultices until there is no more doubt. All the foreign substances will be adsorbed and pulled from the body by the clay. There have been many cases in which foreign bodies that were difficult to extract surgically have been drawn out by the clay.

Keep the wound covered in hydrated clay mask and covered with Saran wrap to keep moist. Cuts heal from the inside out in half the time when using clay as the healing agent. Clay also greatly reduces the possibility of scarring after healing has occurred.

CYSTS

Apply a thick poultice over the cyst and cover with plastic wrap. Change the poultice twice a day and leave on overnight.

Drink 2 ounces of liquid clay 2 times a day.

Repeat until the cyst has dissolved. You will notice it is getting smaller. The length of time will depend on the size of the cyst.

DANDRUFF

Dandruff is easily managed with daily use of Calcium Bentonite Clay. Use as follows:

Drink 2 ounces of liquid clay 2 times a day.

"Shampoo" hair with the clay mask. Apply to all of the head as you would a shampoo.

Massage in and leave in for 5 to 10 minutes. Rinse off thoroughly.

After dandruff is gone and no traces remain, continue a daily lifetime practice of drinking 1ounce of liquid clay and shampooing hair with clay mask as necessary.

Follow with a conditioner if desired.

DEPRESSION

Cleansing and detoxing your body is a great first step to battle depression. Additionally, clay baths are the ultimate way to detox and relax. For a good night's sleep, take your clay bath before going to bed.

Start by drinking 2 ounces of liquid clay 3 times a day, increasing the dosage by 1 ounce daily to ultimately consuming 4 ounces twice daily, away from oral medications.

Apply a 1-inch-thick clay poultice approximately 10 inches in diameter to your liver daily for 1 hour. After 3 days, apply the poultice at night, cover with Saran wrap and leave all night.

Take clay baths when needed for 15 to 20 minutes using 1 to 2 cups of clay powder per bath.

DETOXIFICATION – FULL BODY

To remove parasites, heavy metals and for more serious digestive issues, a higher dose is recommended:

Start by drinking 2 ounces of liquid clay 3 times a day, increasing the dosage by 1 ounce daily to ultimately consume 4 to 8 ounces 3 times a day, away from oral medications as needed.

When the body is free of high levels of toxins, to support the body's immune system, to stay toxin free and to balance your pH level, drink 2 ounces of liquid clay twice daily. More may be taken if desired. A sip of liquid clay before meals and snacks is highly recommended to capture toxins and radiation that may be in our foods.

Apply a 1-inch-thick clay poultice approximately 10 inches in diameter to your liver daily for 1 hour. After 3 days it may be applied overnight as needed.

Take a hot clay bath twice a week for 15 to 20 minutes using 2 cups of clay powder per bath, for 3 months or longer depending on the degree of toxicity. Retest for heavy metals after 3 months.

Drink water or an electrolyte drink during the bath.

For a maintenance bath to relieve sore muscles and for total relaxation, use 1 cup of clay powder per bath weekly or as needed.

If a bath is not available, follow the instructions for a full-body wrap outlined in Chapter 8.

DIABETES - Type II

Treating diabetes is a fine balancing act. Clay will help the body maintain equilibrium and balance, which will help the body heal itself.

Drink 2 ounces of liquid clay 3 times daily away from oral medication.

Take a clay bath twice a week for 15 to 20 minutes using 1 to

2 cups of clay powder per bath. Continue these baths for 2 months.

Monitor your blood sugar 2 to 3 times daily. After completing your detox, make sure that your dietary practices are appropriate. Continue drinking 2 ounces of liquid clay as a daily lifetime practice. Of course, diet, exercise and weight maintenance are very important to the process.

DIABETIC ULCERS - WOUND CARE

For diabetic ulcers and sores that won't heal, apply the clay mask thickly over the wound and cover with Saran wrap. Change twice a day and sleep with one at night. Most people notice a significant improvement within 3 to 4 days.

Drink 2 ounces of liquid clay 3 times a day, away from oral medications as needed.

DIAPER RASH

Simply sprinkle the dry powder Calcium Bentonite Clay mixed with equal parts of arrowroot and cornstarch on your baby's behind as you would powder. If any raw rash or spots are present, generously apply some clay mask over the area and close the diaper. Be prepared to be amazed at how quickly it heals. Continue to use mask as needed. Use the clay dry powder mix as your regular baby powder to avoid future diaper rash.

DIARRHEA

The condition responds better to quick, continued treatment. After each loose stool drink 1 ounce of liquid clay and continue throughout the day as needed. When the symptoms disappear, stay on a maintenance dose of 2 ounces twice a day, away from oral medications as needed.

For infants who suffer from diarrhea, add ¼ to ½ teaspoon of liquid clay to their juice, milk or water bottle and shake. The liquid clay will mix with the solution, and the infant won't even know it's there.

Clay is recognized worldwide as a treatment for diarrhea and cholera. Clay has also been used as an adsorbent in the symptomatic treatment of various forms of enteritis, including ulcerative colitis.

According to Dr. Frederic Damrau, Bentonite is "safe and highly effective" in treating acute diarrhea. (Frederic Damrau, M.D., Medical Annals of the District of Columbia, 1961)

DIVERTICULOSIS

When the colon is not properly emptied, the walls of the intestines form balloons, or diverticula. Soon, undigested food creeps into the pouches and may cause inflammation. The condition, known as diverticulitis, is mainly due to constipation. The clay may be taken frequently to prevent this. Fasting is recommended to speed the healing process.

Start by drinking 2 ounces of liquid clay 3 times a day, increasing the dosage by 1 ounce daily to ultimately consume 6 to 8 ounces 3 times a day, away from oral medications as needed. Liquid clay may be taken with a juice or water fast.

Drinking clay will also help to form soft stools, which relieve the need to strain. Be sure to drink lots of water during the day. Keep your bowels moving smoothly.

Apply clay mask topically over the lower gut area and cover

and leave for 2 hours daily as needed.

Take a clay enema daily, adding 2 ounces of liquid clay to 1 pint of water or as needed.

DRUG ADDICTION

When changing an addictive lifestyle, the process can be eased by cleansing and detoxing your body. Any serious addiction problems should be supervised by health care professionals.

Advanced Detox:

To remove parasites, heavy metals and for more serious digestive issues, a slightly higher dose is recommended.

Start by drinking 2 ounces of liquid clay 3 times a day, increasing the dosage by 1 ounce daily to ultimately consume 4 to 6 ounces 3 times a day, away from medications. More may be taken if desired.

Apply a 1-inch-thick clay poultice approximately 10 inches in diameter to your liver daily for 1 hour. After 3 days it may be applied overnight as needed.

Additionally follow the protocols for clay baths and full-body wraps in the Detoxification - Full Body section above.

Maintenance Regimen:

To support the body's immune system, to stay toxin free and to balance your pH level, drink 2 ounces of liquid clay 3 times a day away from oral medications. A sip of liquid clay before meals and snacks is highly recommended to capture toxins and radiation that may be in our foods.

DRY SKIN

The skin is the largest organ and a means of eliminating waste; each day waste passes through the pores of the skin. Everything that affects the body in turn affects the skin. When the body is full of toxic waste and cannot eliminate them properly, various skin ailments may result. The only effective way to get rid of these conditions is by cleansing the body inside and out.

Drink 2 ounces of liquid clay twice daily away from oral medication as needed.

Apply a 1-inch-thick clay poultice approximately 10 inches in diameter to your liver daily for 1 hour. After 3 days it may be applied overnight.

Take a daily warm clay bath for 15 to 20 minutes using 1 cup of clay powder per bath.

Do a full body wrap with the clay mask or apply to the affected areas and leave on for 20 minutes, twice weekly.

EARACHE

Drink 2 ounces of liquid clay 2 times a day away from oral medication as needed.

Apply clay mask on the front and back of the ear, under the jaw and over the cheek close to the ear, changing every 2 hours as needed. At night apply a thin coat and let it dry and sleep with it on.

ECHINOCOCCUS – See TAPEWORMS

ECZEMA AND PSORIASIS

For eczema and psoriasis, the protocol is the same. They are the most common inflammatory diseases of the skin and affect millions of adults and children worldwide.

Although it is not uncommon for adults to suffer from eczema, the disease often appears during childhood or even during infancy. Eczema is a general term for any type of dermatitis or inflammation and itching of the skin, characterized by red, dry scaly skin. Atopic dermatitis is the most common and severe form of eczema, so the general term eczema is often specifically applied to atopic dermatitis. Eczema is caused by an excessive response of the body's immune system to allergens.

Psoriasis is a persistent, long-lasting (chronic) disease of the immune system. It causes cells to build up rapidly on the surface of the skin.

For severe cases, start by drinking 2 ounces of liquid clay 3 times a day, increasing the dosage by 1 ounce daily to ultimately consume 4-6 ounces of liquid clay 3 times a day away from oral medication.

Cover the areas with the clay mask and sit for 15 minutes, then step into a hot clay bath.

Take a daily hot clay bath for 15 to 20 minutes using 2 to 3 cups of clay powder per bath.

Drink water or an electrolyte drink during thc bath.

Apply a 1-inch-thick clay poultice approximately 10 inches in diameter to your liver daily for 1 hour. After 3 days it may be applied overnight as needed.

For children, drink 1 teaspoon to 1 tablespoon twice a day

away from oral medication.

Give children, a warm bath using ½ to ¾ cup of clay powder per bath.

After the bath, cover the areas with extra virgin organic coconut oil and wrap up in a towel and lie down for 30 minutes.

Repeat this process until better. Then repeat once a week for 4 weeks.

For adults, reduce liquid clay intake to 2 ounces 2 times a day after it clears up.

In the beginning the condition may appear to look red and worsen as dead skin flakes off and circulation is pulled to the area, but this is temporary.

Most report almost immediate relief from itching and discomfort. Incorporate Calcium Bentonite Clay as a daily lifetime practice for long-term relief from eczema and psoriasis.

EPSTEIN-BARR VIRUS

Also called human herpes virus 4 (HHV-4), Epstein-Barr is a virus of the herpes family and is one of the most common viruses in humans, often referred to as mononucleosis.

Start by drinking 2 ounces of liquid clay 3 times a day, increasing the dosage by 1 ounce daily to ultimately consume 5 ounces 3 times a day, away from oral medications as needed.

Gargle with liquid clay for sore throat as needed.

Apply a 1-inch-thick clay poultice about 10 inches in diameter to your liver twice daily for 1 hour. After 3 days it may be applied overnight.

Take a clay bath twice a week for 15 to 20 minutes using 2 cups of clay powder per bath.

EYES –ALLERGY IRRITATIONS (Also see CATARACTS)

Apply clay mask thickly over a circular cotton pad and apply to the closed eyelid. Leave in place for 15 to 20 minutes. For minor irritations pour the liquid clay on the pad and apply.

Drink 2 ounces of liquid clay twice a day.

This is very soothing and will relieve itching and reduce swelling from allergic reactions. Excellent as a treatment for black eye. May repeat 2 to 3 times a day.

FIBROID TUMORS

Clay is an amazing remedy for fibrous tumors.

Start by drinking 2 ounces of liquid clay 3 times a day, increasing the dosage by 1 ounce daily to ultimately consume 4 ounces 3 times a day, away from oral medications as needed.

Take a clay bath twice a week for 15 to 20 minutes using 2 cups of clay powder per bath.

Take a daily douche using 2 ounces of liquid clay to a pint of water.

For the first month apply a ½-inch-thick poultice a day on the lower abdomen, interrupting it only at the period of menstruation. The poultices must remain in place for at least 2 hours. It can remain overnight if applied just before going to bed.

It should be made clear that usually it takes months to be rid of them completely.

Raymond Dextreit tells of a woman with a fibrous tumor in her uterus that caused serious hemorrhaging during menstruation, which was treated with clay. She drank it and applied poultices on her abdomen. After 3 months of treatment, an examination in a hospital produced this conclusion: "uterus is in the condition of a person of twenty." The patient was 50 years old. (Raymond Dextreit. [13]

FIBROMYALGIA

Start by drinking 2 ounces of liquid clay 3 times a day, increasing the dosage by 1 ounce daily to ultimately consume 4-6 ounces 3 times a day, away from oral medications as needed.

Take a clay bath 3 times a week for 15 to 20 minutes using 1 to 2 cups of clay powder. One of the most amazing effects of clay baths is the clay's ability to stimulate the lymphatic system. The more clay that is used in the therapy, the more powerful the response.

Apply a 1-inch-thick clay poultice about 10 inches in diameter to your liver daily for 1 hour. After 3 days it may be applied overnight as needed.

After symptoms improve you may reduce liquid clay intake to 2 ounces twice a day.

FINGERNAIL FUNGUS

Fungus is normally found under the toenails and fingernails. It is a systemic blood-borne pathogen and quite difficult to successfully cure using traditional medicine. Fortunately, Calcium Bentonite Clay offers a quick, all-natural cure for even the worst cases of nail fungus. Use as follows:

Drink 2 ounces of liquid clay twice a day, away from oral medications as needed.

Pack clay mask thickly under and on the affected nails and leave on for about an hour. At night smother the nail thickly with the hydrated clay mask. Cover with Saran wrap and leave it on all night. It will take a while for the nail to grow out enough for the difference to be noticeable. Keep applying as long as the skin around the nail is thick and tough.

FIRE ANT BITES

Treatment for any type of insect sting or bite is the same.

Immediately dab on a finger full of clay mask. Cover the bite area and about another inch all around the bite area. Leave on to dry or cover with plastic wrap.

Repeat this process until pain, swelling and redness have passed.

FLATULENCE

Drink 2 ounces of liquid clay 3 times a day, away from oral medications as needed. It may take 2 weeks to balance the gut flora, and then the gas should no longer be a problem. Then find your maintenance level, w

hich is generally 1 to 2 ounces of liquid clay twice a day.

Apply clay mask topically over the bloated area and cover and leave for 2 hours daily. Avoid eating acidic foods.

Take a clay bath twice a week for 15 to 20 minutes using 1 cup of clay powder per bath.

FLU –INFLUENZA

Flu is a viral infection and consists of positively charged ions. Calcium Bentonite Clay is extremely effective in removing many flu viral molecules from your body. In some cases of flu, clay helps balance the pH, settling nausea and diarrhea.

Start by drinking 2 ounces of liquid clay 3 times a day, increasing the dosage by 1 ounce daily to ultimately consume 4 ounces 3 times a day, away from oral medications.

Gargle with liquid Calcium Bentonite Clay as needed.

Apply a 1-inch-thick clay poultice about 10 inches in diameter to your liver daily for 1 hour. After 3 days it may be applied over night as needed.

Take a daily clay bath for 15 to 20 minutes using 1 cup of clay powder per bath.

FOOD POISONING (also E-COLI, SHIGELLA, SALMONELLA AND KLEBSIELLA)

Clay has proved beneficial in the relief of nausea and vomiting caused by food poisoning. It is an excellent treatment for morning sickness. In India, clay was found useful in the treatment of acute bacterial food poisonings in the British army.

If nausea is especially severe, drink 1 tablespoon of liquid clay every 10 minutes, away from oral medications as needed. Usually, 4 tablespoons is enough to halt the symptoms; typically, the nausea will cease within one hour. Thereafter, you can follow up with one dose every four hours until bedtime. This will help to further relieve the gastrointestinal tract and take a heavy burden off the liver.

Drink plenty of water during the day to help the clay absorb/adsorb the toxins, bacteria or viruses that are causing nausea.

Apply a 1-inch-thick clay poultice approximately 10 inches in diameter to your liver daily for 1 hour. After 3 days it may be applied overnight as needed.

In addition, clay is a preferred treatment for any gastrointestinal infections caused by E-coli, Shigella, Salmonella and Klebsiella. Take in the same dosages as given above.

FRACTURES

Calcium Bentonite Clay can speed the healing time of broken bones to half of the normal course of events. It also reduces inflammation and swelling, acts as a pain reducer and brings circulation to the affected area.

Protocol for broken bones is internal and topical:

Drink 2 ounces of liquid clay 3 times a day.

In cases of a splint, apply thick applications of clay mask all around the break and cover with plastic wrap and secure the splint. Change and reapply morning and night until healed. Healing time is generally cut in half.

With a cast, another option is to make warm clay masks in large 1-gallon Ziploc bags. Lay these on the outside of the cast over the break for as long as possible. These may be reused many times. They can be warmed in a sink of hot water for reuse.

Apply a thin coating of clay mask topically after the cast is removed to assist with cleansing the area, rebuilding tissue and strengthening the bones.

FROST BITE

Cover the affected area thickly with the clay mask as soon as possible. Cover with a plastic wrap to keep the wet clay in place. Leave on the affected area for 6 hours and repeat. Leave on all night. Watch for circulation and feeling to return.

Drink 2 ounces of liquid clay twice daily.

FUNGUS

Fungus is normally found under the toenails and fingernails but also can be in the skin. It is a systemic blood-borne pathogen and quite difficult to successfully cure using traditional medicine. Use as follows:

Drink 2 ounces of liquid clay 3 times a day away from medication.

Pack clay mask on the affected area and leave for 4 hours. You may cover it with a plastic wrap or leave uncovered to dry. Repeat this process 2 to 3 times daily and leave a thin coat overnight.

Take a clay bath twice a week for 15 to 20 minutes using 1 to 2 cups of clay powder per bath.

If treating a foot fungus, keep shoes disinfected.

GANGLION CYSTS

Apply a thick poultice over the cyst and cover with plastic wrap. Change the poultice twice a day and leave overnight.

Drink 2 ounces of liquid clay 3 times a day, away from oral medications as needed.

Take a clay bath twice a week for 15 to 20 minutes using 1 cup of clay powder per bath.

Repeat until the cyst has dissolved. You will notice it is getting smaller. The length of time will depend on the size of the cyst.

GANGRENE – See Infections

GAS – See FLATULENCE

GINGIVITIS

For severe bleeding, go to a doctor and get a blood test. It could be a sign of a serious condition.

The clay treatments for gingivitis and pyorrhea are the same (gingivitis will develop into pyorrhea if left untreated). The first line of action involves brushing the teeth daily with Calcium Bentonite Clay. Use clay powder. The clay is absorbent, and it helps harden the enamel while it aids gum tissue repair. Furthermore, if used regularly, it helps to prevent gum recession.

At bedtime pack your gums with clay powder. Do this by loading the toothbrush handle or a popsicle stick with powdered clay and gently depositing it between the teeth and gums.

Your saliva will stick the clay to your teeth and gums. Leave overnight. As a preventative measure, swish liquid clay in your mouth 2 times a day. These actions will pull out bacteria lodged in your gums and tighten the gum pockets to your teeth.

Drink 2 ounces of liquid clay twice daily, away from oal medications as needed.

GLUTEN INTOLERANCE – CELIAC

Celiac disease is an autoimmune disorder that can occur in genetically predisposed people in which the ingestion of gluten leads to damage in the small intestine.

Drink 2 ounces of liquid clay 3 times a day, increasing the dosage by 1 ounce daily to ultimately consume 4 to 6 ounces of liquid clay 3 times a day, away from oral medications as needed

Take a clay enema daily, adding 2 ounces of liquid clay to 1 pint of water or as needed.

Drink 1 ounce of the liquid clay before eating any gluten meals.

GRAVES' DISEASE – See HYPERTHYROIDISM

GULF WAR SYNDROME

GWS is a wide range of acute and chronic symptoms including fatigue, musculoskeletal pain, cognitive problems, skin rashes and diarrhea mostly from exposure to toxins and chemicals. Start by drinking 2 ounces of liquid clay 3 times a day, increasing the dosage by 1 ounce daily to ultimately consume 6 to 8 ounces of liquid clay 3 times a day, away from oral medications as needed.

Then drink 2 ounces of liquid clay twice a day to support the body's immune system, to stay toxin free and to balance your pH level. More may be taken if desired. An ounce of liquid clay before meals and snacks is highly recommended to capture toxins and radiation that may be in our foods.

Apply a 1-inch-thick clay poultice approximately 10 inches in diameter to your liver daily for 1 hour. After 3 days it may be applied overnight as needed.

Take a hot clay bath twice a week for 15 to 20 minutes using 1 to 2 cups of clay powder per bath.

Take a clay enema daily, adding 2 ounces of liquid clay to 1 pint of water or as needed.

Drink water or an electrolyte drink during the bath.

Take additional maintenance baths a few times a month for relaxation, to relieve sore muscles and to stay toxin free.

Another detox method is to cover yourself in clay mask for 30 minutes and shower off or get in an infrared sauna and allow the dry heat to open the skin pores.

GUM DISEASE – See GINGIVITIS

HAIR LOSS

If the hair follicle is still alive, the clay will stimulate new hair growth. This is especially beneficial for hair regrowth after chemo treatments.

Use clay mask daily, parting the hair and massaging into the scalp. Leave on for 15 minutes, then rinse off.

For course, thick hair, follow with a shampoo and conditioner.

Many have reported new hair growth in as few as 2 to 3 weeks.

Drink 2 ounces of liquid clay twice a day, away from oral medications as needed.

Apply a 1-inch-thick clay poultice approximately 10 inches in diameter to your liver daily for one hour. After 3 days it may be applied overnight as needed.

HANGOVER

Clay is excellent for hangover relief. Drink 2 ounces of liquid clay before and after overindulging, away from oral medications as needed.

Repeat in the morning if necessary.

Apply a 1-inch-thick clay poultice about 10 inches in diameter to your liver for 1 hour daily as needed.

Take a clay bath for 15 to 20 minutes using 1 to 2 cups of clay powder as needed.

HAY FEVER – See ALLERGIES

HEADACHES –MIGRAINES

Upon onset of the headache, drink 2 ounces of liquid clay 3 times daily, away from oral medications as needed.

Apply clay poultice across the nape of the neck, sinuses or forehead as needed for about 30 minutes. Repeat this process as often as you like until the pain dissipates.

Take a 15-to-20-minute clay bath using 1 to 2 cups of clay powder in the bath.

Clay baths are known to diminish migraine headaches in 15 to 20 minutes. If headaches are frequent and recurring, follow the instructions in the Detoxification-Full Body section and continue drinking 2 ounces of liquid clay twice daily, away from medications as a life practice. Headaches have a variety of causes, so the treatment approach must be broad. If the cause of the headaches is due in part to chemical sensitivities, food allergies, or circulation of toxins in the body, the Calcium Bentonite Clay will enable the body to detoxify more efficiently and use nutrients more effectively. The treatment is the same whether the headache/migraine is due to muscle tension, chemical imbalance, analgesic rebound or other causes.

HEART HEALTH

Calcium Bentonite Clay is rich in diastases (enzymes), which accounts for its ability to fix free oxygen and purify and enrich the blood. Free radicals are atoms whose electrons have been stripped. A certain number of them are necessary to stave off invading bacteria, but too many can attack the body, causing cellular breakdown. Clay contributes to an improved blood supply. High levels of blood risk factors, such as too many free radicals, help to explain the breakdown of the cardiovascular system in the form of strokes or heart attacks. If the body continues to pump dirty blood to the heart, heart disease is sure to follow. The vessel walls are eventually weakened by weak blood, which cannot carry the nutrients needed for blood vessel reinforcement. Clay's cleansing action may prevent this. As part of a "healthy heart" plan following heart surgery or a heart attack, the following is recommended:

Start by drinking 2 ounces of liquid clay 3 times a day, increasing the dosage by 1 ounce daily to ultimately consume 4 ounces of liquid clay 3 times a day, away from oral medications as needed.

Take a warm clay bath for 15 to 20 minutes using 1 cup of clay powder per bath as needed for relaxation.

Apply a 1-inch-thick clay poultice approximately 10 inches in diameter to your liver for 1 hour as needed.

For both low and high blood pressure, apply clay poultice on the inside of the upper arms and wrap with a plastic wrap at least once a day and once at night. (Anjou Musafir and Pascal Chazot. Clay Cures, 2006)

As a lifestyle practice, drink 1 ounce of liquid clay twice daily and take weekly clay baths as needed.

HEMORRHOIDS

Hemorrhoids are varicose veins in the anus and colon, possibly resulting from pushing and straining when having bowel movements. They can become quite painful. Treat with clay as follows:

Drink 2 ounces liquid clay 3 times daily, away from oral medications as needed.

Take a clay enema adding 2 ounces of liquid clay to a pint of water.

Insert clay mask in and around the anus in the morning and evening.

Take a clay bath twice a week for 15 to 20 minutes using 1 cup of clay powder per bath.

Drink water or an electrolyte drink during the bath.

At bedtime insert a lubricated clay suppository if needed.

HEPATITIS – HEP C

Hepatitis directly affects the liver but is systemic in nature.

Start by drinking 2 ounces of liquid clay 3 times a day, increasing the dosage by 1 ounce daily to ultimately consume 6 to 8 ounces of liquid clay 3 times a day, away from oral medications as needed.

Take a clay bath 3 times a week for 15 to 20 minutes using 2 cups of clay powder per bath until conditions clear up.

Apply a 1-inch-thick clay poultice approximately 10 inches in diameter to your liver daily for 1 hour. After 3 days it may be applied overnight.

After 3 months of the protocol, get retested. If necessary, continue the protocol.

HERPES

Apply clay masks directly over sores or blisters. Cover or allow to dry. Repeat the process as needed.

Start by drinking 2 ounces of liquid clay 3 times a day, increasing the dosage by 1 ounce daily to ultimately consume 4 ounces of liquid clay 3 times a day, away from oral medications as needed.

Take a weekly clay bath for 15 to 20 minutes using 1 cup of clay powder per bath until conditions clear up.

Apply a 1-inch-thick clay poultice approximately 10 inches in diameter to your liver daily for 1 hour. After 3 days it may be applied over night as needed.

For genital outbreaks, apply clay poultices or clay mask to the affected area.

HIVES

Hives are a skin rash that is typically due to an allergic reaction.

Apply topical applications of clay mask on areas of any hives.

Drink 2

of liquid clay twice daily, away from oral medications as needed.

Take a clay bath daily for 15 to 20 minutes using 1 cup of clay powder per bath until conditions clear up.

H. PYLORI – See STOMACH ULCERS

HYPERTHYROIDISM

Start by drinking 2 ounces of liquid clay 3 times a day, increasing the dosage by 1 ounce daily to ultimately consume 6 to 8 ounces of liquid clay 3 times a day, away from oral medications as needed for 4 months and be rechecked.

Apply clay poultices to the thyroid starting with an hour at a time and gradually building up to longer periods if necessary.

Take a clay bath twice a week for 15 to 20 minutes using 1 cup of clay powder per bath.

IMMUNE DEFICIENCY – See AIDS

Although AIDS is quite different from a typical immune deficiency, the treatment is the same.

IMPETIGO

Apply the clay mask topically to areas of concern. Repeat as often as needed.

INDIGESTION

Indigestion is one of the easiest maladies to alleviate using Calcium Bentonite Clay. Complete relief often comes in minutes after ingestion!

Drink 2 to 3 ounces of liquid clay 3 times daily and at any time indigestion occurs. Continue this practice for 2 to 3 days or until full relief is present.

As a daily maintenance dose, drink 1 to 2 ounces of liquid clay twice daily and at any time indigestion occurs.

For severe cases, take 4 ounces of liquid clay as needed.

INFECTIONS – STAPH, GANGRENE, ETC.

Most of these infections are systemic and blood borne, with localized skin sores. The protocol for treating an infection is both full body and localized on the open wounds or skin sores.

Start by drinking 2 ounces of liquid clay 3 times a day, increasing the dosage by 1 ounce daily to ultimately consuming 5 ounces of liquid clay 3 times a day, away from oral medications as needed.

Apply a 1-inch-thick clay poultice approximately 10 inches in diameter to your liver daily for 1 hour. After 3 days it may be applied overnight.

Cover any open wounds with a 1-inch-thick application of clay mask. Cover with plastic wrap for five hours and repeat twice daily.

Apply fresh applications at night and leave on all night. Repeat this until the wound is healed. The clay will slough off any dead tissue and rebuild healthy tissue from the inside out.

Take a clay bath three times a week for 15 to 20 minutes using 1 cup of clay powder per bath. Continue until infection is completely gone.

INGROWN HAIRS

Apply the clay mask topically as needed. Clay will pull out the hair and inflammation. Use the clay mask for a close, clean shave without chaffing the skin and eliminating ingrown hairs. Make sure the razor is thoroughly washed to prevent rusting.

INSECT STINGS & BITES

Treatment for any type of insect sting or bite is the same.

Immediately dab on a generous amount of clay mask and cover the bite area. Allow to dry or cover with plastic wrap.

Repeat this process until pain, swelling and redness have passed.

Pain normally begins to leave in 30 seconds to 1 minute. Complete relief usually occurs in 3 to 5 applications over a few hours. A poultice may be left overnight.

INSOMNIA

Drink 2 ounces of liquid clay twice a day.

Take a clay bath for 15 to 20 minutes using 1 cup of clay powder per bath in the evenings. Clay baths have a relaxing and calming effect that leads to a good night's sleep. Sweet dreams.

IRRITABLE BOWEL SYNDROME - IBS

Clay is an excellent choice for this very real ailment.

Begin by doing an internal colon cleanse.

Start by drinking 2 ounces of liquid clay 3 times a day, increasing the dosage by 1 ounce daily to ultimately consume 6 to 8 ounces of liquid clay 3 times a day, away from oral medications as needed.

Apply a 1-inch-thick poultice over the lower abdomen and cover with Saran wrap for 1 to 2 hours daily. After 3 days leave the wrap on all night.

Take a clay enema using 2 ounces of liquid clay to 1 pint of water twice a week.

Take a clay bath twice a week for 15 to 20 minutes using 1 cup of clay powder per bath.

This ailment is characterized by alternating conditions of diarrhea and constipation with gas, pain and emotional ups and downs. Because the cause of irritable bowel syndrome is unknown, treating the condition with drugs can be dangerous. Even naturopathic doctors have a difficult time in controlling, managing and curing the disease.

ITCHY SCALP

For a good scalp cleaning, part the hair, massage clay mask into the scalp, leave on for 15 minutes and wash out. Repeat as needed.

Drink 1 ounce of liquid clay twice daily.

ITCHY SKIN

Itchy skin can be from dry skin or allergies.

Drink 2 ounces of liquid clay twice a day until condition clears up.

Take a clay bath for 15 to 20 minutes using 1 cup of clay powder per bath to relieve itchy skin. Apply a hydrated clay mask topically on the itchy areas.

KIDNEY STONES

Kidney stones can effectively be treated using the following protocol: complete removal of the stones may take 1 to 3 months.

Start by drinking 2 ounces of liquid clay 3 times a day, increasing the dosage by 1 ounce daily to ultimately consume 4 ounces of liquid clay 3 times a day, away from oral medications as needed.

Take a clay bath twice a week for 15 to 20 minutes using 1 to 2 cups of clay powder per bath.

Apply a clay poultice (½ inch thick by 10 inches in diameter) over each kidney for 1 hour daily.

Watch for sand like particles (the dissolving stones) in the urine. Until all traces of kidney stones are gone, drink 3 ounces of liquid clay twice daily.

Take clay baths (1 cup of clay) as needed.

LACTATION

Applying hydrated clay masks to the breast will help new mothers bring down their milk.

It is also beneficial in relieving nipple soreness when first nursing.

LEAKY GUT SYNDROME –See IRRITABLEIRRITABLE BOWEL SYNDROME

Please see the treatment regimen for irritable bowel syndrome – IBS. Although the locations along the digestive path where these two ailments occur are different, the treatment plan is the same.

LIPOFUSCIN ABNORMALITIES

Calcium Bentonite Clay works for most types of skin coloration abnormalities. Skin coloration abnormalities are caused either by an abnormal buildup of pigment (lipofuscin) or by a deficiency or absence in the nerve supply to blood vessels. Calcium Bentonite Clay strives to create a balance of pigment in any affected area. It will reduce age spots (liver spots) in 4 weeks with daily ingestion and applications. Birthmarks and other forms of skin discoloration may change but also may not go away completely.

Apply Calcium Bentonite Clay as follows:

Drink 2 ounces of liquid clay twice daily.

Take a clay bath twice a week for 15 to 20 minutes using 1 cup of clay powder per bath.

Apply the clay mask in a relatively thick coating to the discolored area. Allow to dry and leave for 45 to 60 minutes.

Wash and reapply 2 to 3 times daily. At night, apply a thin coat and leave on overnight.

Apply a poultice to the liver for 1 hour daily; after 3 days apply overnight.

Continue this treatment until skin has changed to the desired color.

LIVER CLEANSE

Start by drinking 2 ounces of liquid clay 3 times a day, increasing the dosage by 1 ounce daily to ultimately consume 6 to 8 ounces of liquid clay 3 times a day, away from oral medications as needed.

Take a clay enema using 2 ounces of liquid clay to 1 pint of water twice a week.

Take a clay bath a few times a week for 15 to 20 minutes using 1 to 3 cups of clay powder per bath.

Apply a 1-inch-thick clay poultice approximately 10 inches in diameter to your liver daily for 1 hour. After 3 days it may be applied overnight as needed.

The liver is frequently referred to as the body's detoxification pilot. It breaks down poisons or transforms them into less harmful compounds. The poisons include toxic substances found in food (nitrates, monosodium glutamate and herbicides), toxins produced by the body (ketones, indoles, phenols and aldehydes), and harmful chemicals in the environment. In addition, the liver performs a long list of other functions, including the manufacturing of bile salts, the activation of vitamin D, and the storage of glycogen, vitamin A, copper and iron. The liver, without a doubt, is vital to one's health. Calcium Bentonite Clay can be an invaluable aid to a poorly functioning liver. It works indirectly on the organ as follows: After you eat, the absorption of nutrients takes place throughout the length of the small intestine and the large intestine. From here they are transported in the bloodstream to the liver by way of the hepatic portal system (the flow of blood from the digestive organs to the liver). After their passage through the liver, they move through the heart and then enter general circulation.

If the bowels are not working right, waste matter will be continually reabsorbed into the bloodstream and carried to the liver. As a result, the liver is forced into doing extra work that might not be needed if the bowels were in good working condition. This places an unnecessary burden on the liver and the rest of the body. Consuming clay will have a positive effect on the liver by facilitating the cleansing of the gastrointestinal tract. Through absorption, many of the toxins will exit directly through the colon and bypass the liver and general circulation.

LYME DISEASE

First, confirm the diagnosis with an enzyme-linked immunosorbent assay (ELISA) test and/or a Western Blot Test. An aggressive three-prong attack is needed to make a difference.

Start by drinking 2 ounces of liquid clay 3 times a day, increasing the dosage by 1 ounce daily to ultimately consume 6 to 8 ounces 3 times a day, away from oral medications as needed.

Start by taking four clays bath a week for 15 to 20 minutes using 2 cups of clay powder per bath. Then continue taking 2 clay baths a week using 1 cup of clay powder per bath for 3 months or until well.

Apply a 1-inch-thick clay poultice about 10 inches in diameter to your liver twice daily for one hour. After 3 days it may be applied overnight as needed.

Take a clay enema using 2 ounces of liquid clay to 1 pint of water daily or as needed.

If you know where the bite site is, cover it with a wet clay poultice for 10 hours at a time. If the disease has passed through the brain barrier, massage the clay mask onto the scalp and base of the neck, cover with a shower cap and leave on for 30 minutes to an hour daily.

LYMPHATITIS – LYMPH GLANDS

Lymphatitis is treated both internally and topically. Because Lymphatitis is present throughout the body, a full-system cleanse is the requisite first step.

Take a clay bath twice a week for 15 to 20 minutes using 1 to 2 cups of clay powder per bath as needed.

Drink 2 ounces of liquid clay twice daily until the lymph glands system is back to health.

If there is any swelling or tenderness in any specific glands, such as under arms, neck, etc., apply a poultice directly to the affected glands. Leave on for 30 minutes and repeat twice daily. Continue until lymph system is again in balance.

MERCURY TOXICITY

Start by drinking 2 ounces of liquid clay 3 times a day, increasing the dosage by 1 ounce daily to ultimately consume 4 ounces 3 times a day, away from oral medications.

Apply a 1-inch-thick clay poultice about 10 inches in diameter to your liver daily for 1 hour. After 3 days it may be applied overnight as needed.

Take a hot clay bath three times a week for 15 to 20 minutes using 1 to 2 cups of clay powder per bath.

Drink water or an electrolyte drink during the bath. At three months, have your toxicity level checked.

If the cause is from leaking amalgam fillings, pack your gums at night with the dry clay and leave until the next morning. Brush your teeth with clay powder as well. Swish daily with liquid clay.

Drink 1 ounce of liquid clay before eating to capture the leakage aggravated by chewing in addition to the 3-times-a-day protocol above.

During the past few years, we have learned about mercury poisoning from old amalgam fillings. No matter what type of metal poisoning or from what source the toxicity is derived, the treatment is the same. Take regular pH and metal-level tests as your benchmarks for progress and to know when all toxic metals have been removed from your body.

MIGRAINES - See HEADACHES

MOLES

Some moles are quickly and easily removed using clay mask.

Drink 2 ounces of liquid clay twice daily.

Dab a relatively thick amount of clay mask directly onto the mole. Leave it on and allow it to dry. Repeat this process 5 to 6 times daily. At the end of the day, apply the last coating and leave on all night.

Continue the process until the mole is completely gone and smooth skin appears in its place. It could take as long as 3 to 4 months for larger moles.

Once healed, continue drinking 1 ounce of liquid clay twice daily as a lifetime practice.

MONONUCLEOSIS – See EPSTEIN-BARR VIRUS

MORNING SICKNESS – See NAUSEA

MOSQUITO BITES – See INSECT BITES

MOUTH ULCERS

Mouth ulcers are easily treated with Calcium Bentonite Clay. Because the inside of our mouths is wet, you can dab on, or sprinkle on, some dry powder clay, allowing it to stick to the ulcerated area. Allow the clay to remain in place as long as possible. As it dissolves or is washed away, simply swallow and reapply throughout the day.

Drink 2 ounces of liquid clay twice daily and swish with the liquid clay for 1 minute twice daily.

MRSA STAPH INFECTION

Drink 2 ounces of liquid clay 3 times a day, increasing by 1 ounce daily, to 6 ounces 3 times a day, away from oral medications as needed.

Take a clay bath for 15 to 20 minutes using 1 cup of clay powder 3 times weekly as needed.

Apply a clay poultice to the liver for an hour daily. After 3 days it may be applied overnight as needed.

For wounds, apply a poultice ¼ inch to 1 inch thick over the area of concern. Cover with a plastic wrap or a square of Glad Press 'n Seal to hold the clay in place. Leave for 3 hours. Repeat this process several times a day, using a new batch of clay for each poultice. Leave a fresh poultice on all night. Do this as needed.

MULTIPLE OF CHEMICAL SENSITIVITIES (MCS)

MCS includes sensitivities to many things including food, pollen, mold and scents, as well as chemicals. Build up your treatment slowly.

Start with ¼ teaspoon of the liquid clay with meals for 1 week. If tolerated, increase to ½ teaspoon of the liquid clay the second week.

Then increase to 1 teaspoon, gradually increasing until you can take 1 to 2 ounces. Go at your own pace. Gradually you will notice a decrease in your sensitivity.

MUMPS

This inflammation of the salivary and parotid glands may affect the testicles, ovaries, mammary glands, pancreas and thyroid.

Treat with liquid clay and poultices as follows:

Drink 2 ounces of liquid clay twice daily during the duration of the inflammation.

Apply poultices over the parotid glands and any inflamed areas for about 30 minutes 3 times daily.

Apply a thick poultice of the clay mask over the testicles and wrap in Saran wrap. Repeat 2 to 3 times a day. Reapply if the clay gets hot.

This will cut the normal healing time in half and better protect other organs as well.

MUSCLE SORENESS – CRAMPS

Muscle soreness and problems with muscle cramping are easily remedied with Calcium Bentonite Clay.

Take a hot clay bath for 15 to 20 minutes using 1 cup of clay powder per bath as needed for soreness.

Drink water or an electrolyte drink during the bath.

Relief should occur in less than 20 minutes. Take an additional clay bath for any remaining soreness the next day.

You may also want to treat specific areas of soreness or cramping with applications of clay mask. Simply apply the clay mask to the entire affected area thickly and cover with plastic wrap. Leave on for 1 to 2 hours, then wash off. Repeat this process 3 times daily if necessary.

Drink 2 ounces of liquid clay twice daily during the period in which you are experiencing muscle cramps or soreness.

NAUSEA – MORNING SICKNESS

First, begin sipping liquid clay until the nausea is under control.

If the nausea is especially severe, 1 tablespoon of liquid clay every 10 minutes will be helpful. Usually, 4 tablespoons is enough to halt the symptoms; typically, the nausea will cease within 1 hour. Thereafter, you can follow up with 1 ounce of liquid clay every 4 hours until bedtime. This will help to further relieve the gastrointestinal tract and take a heavy burden off the liver. Thereafter, drink 2 ounces of liquid clay twice daily for maintenance and prevention.

NUCLEAR RADIATION DETOXIFICATION

"Clay is excellent for chelating radioactive materials out of the intestines. It is best to use if there is a major exposure." (Gabriel Cousens, M.D. Remedies for Radiation, 2013)

In the event of a dirty bomb, Living Clays can be your best friend. If you are exposed to excess radiation, generously rub clay mask on scalp and body. Scrub the body and allow the clay to remain on for 10 to 15 minutes. Wash off thoroughly. Add ½ cup of clay powder to your washing machine, then wash your clothes. Follow by washing in laundry soap.

Drink 3 ounces of liquid clay 4 times a day and increase in the event of nausea and signs of radiation sickness. If in doubt, take more.

Take a daily hot clay bath for 15 to 20 minutes using 1 to 2 cups of clay powder per bath.

Drink water or an electrolyte drink during the bath.

Take a clay enema daily or as needed, adding 2 ounces of liquid clay to 1 pint of water.

Apply a 1-inch-thick clay poultice approximately 10 inches in diameter to your liver daily for 1 hour. After 3 days it may be applied overnight.

Apply poultice to the thyroid gland as needed, but do not use poultice on two body organs at the same time.

Do this daily for as long as the danger of radiation is still in the atmosphere.

Calcium Bentonite Clay was used to clean up after Chernobyl. After the disaster, soldiers passed out chocolate bars made with Bentonite clay to children to get clay in them. Additionally, the U.S. government uses Calcium Bentonite Clay as a protectant to line the walls of its nuclear fallout shelters.

OILY SKIN

Drink 2 ounces of liquid clay twice daily.

Apply a daily clay mask to the oily areas of the skin and allow to dry.

Take a weekly clay bath for 15 to 20 minutes using 1 cup of clay powder per bath.

OSTEOPRORSIS

Start by drinking 2 ounces of liquid clay 3 times a day, increasing the dosage by 1 ounce daily to ultimately consume 6 to 8 ounces 3 times a day, away from oral medications as needed.

Apply a 1-inch-thick clay poultice approximately 10 inches in diameter to cover the areas of concern for at least an hour daily. For the spine and where possible leave it on all night.

Take a clay bath for 15 to 20 minutes using 1 cup of clay powder per bath twice weekly as needed.

PARASITES

For internal parasites: Start by drinking 2 ounces of liquid clay 3 times a day, increasing the dosage by 1 ounce daily to ultimately consume 6 ounces 3 times a day, away from oral medications as needed.

Apply a 1-inch-thick clay poultice approximately 10 inches in diameter to your liver daily for 1 hour. After 3 days it may be applied overnight.

For external parasites: In addition to drinking the liquid clay, apply hydrated clay mask thickly over the lesions. It can be left to dry or covered with Saran wrap to keep it wet. Continue after lesions have cleared up for a minimum of two weeks.

Most Americans in today's society have parasites. This is something we must take very seriously. The combination of environmental toxins, unhealthy diets and parasites poses a grave danger to humans. "In fact, parasites have killed more humans than all the wars in history," reported National Geographic [44].

It is not known why every generation prior to modern times made de-worming a regular part of their lives, but our generation chooses to ignore this basic practice. According to numerous books, parasites are commonly found in people with AIDS, chronic fatigue syndrome, Candida and many other disorders.

Symptoms may include abdominal pains, diarrhea, anemia, cardiac insufficiency, nausea, perianal and perineal pruritus, dysentery, amebic hepatitis, weight loss, intestinal toxemia, colic and cirrhosis.

Ran Knishinsky writes: "While many herbs and homeopathic remedies are suggested for this condition, I believe Calcium Bentonite Clay offers the finest treatments for all types of parasites. Considerable research has shed light on the connection between clay eating and parasites." Ran Knishinsky [32]

pH BALANCE

Calcium Bentonite Clay is the great pH balancer! A healthy body maintains about a 7.0 to 7.356 pH. In an acidic environment, less than 7.356 pH, disease can flourish.

Drink a liquid clay with a pH of 8.5 to 10.0 to change the pH of your body from acid to alkaline. Calcium Bentonite Clay has a favorable effect on every function of your body.

Drink 2 ounces of liquid clay 3 times daily.

Take a weekly clay bath for 15 to 20 minutes using 1 cup of clay powder per bath.

Do one full body wrap weekly until your pH is in an acceptable range.

There are some acid clays, so always ask the manufacturer about the pH of the clay you are taking.

Test your pH with inexpensive, easy to use saliva or urine test strips. Adjust the amount of Calcium Bentonite Clay needed to fine-tune your body's pH level.

PIMPLES – See ACNE

PINK EYE - conjunctivitis

Apply clay mask thickly over a circular cotton pad and apply to the closed eyelid. Leave in place for 15 to 20 minutes. For minor irritations, pour liquid clay on the pad and apply. You may also apply the clay mask in a thin film on your eyelid and surrounding area as would be done in a facial and sleep with it on at night.

Drink 2 ounces of liquid clay twice daily until ailment is gone.

POISON

If poisoned, immediately begin drinking 1 ounce of liquid clay every 10 minutes for 4 hours.

Call the poison control center to find out whether it's better to induce vomiting or to allow it to pass through your system. Immediate attention is required in any case. Apply a 1-inch-thick clay poultice about 10 inches in diameter to your liver twice daily for 1 hour. After 3 days it may be applied overnight as needed.

Continue with the liquid clay for the next few days at the rate of 2 ounces of liquid clay 4 times daily.

The nutritionist-author Linda Clark states that "European doctor, Meyer-Camberg, recommends clay for neutralizing poisons. According to Dr. Meyer-Camberg, clay can take care of any bad poisoning, even arsenic!" "Doctors fed lethal doses of the herbicide to rats and recorded the effects. They noted that an excess of the poison caused respiratory failure, liver damage and kidney failure, which soon led to death. Several adsorbents were shown to be effective in counteracting the effects of the poison before the poison was ingested. Only one adsorbent proved successful in counteracting the toxic effects of the poison after it was ingested: Calcium Bentonite Clay."

PISON IVY OR OAK

Daily apply topical applications of clay mask on specific outbreak areas as needed for itching and to dry up the condition. Repeat as needed.

Take a warm clay bath for 15 to 20 minutes using 1 cup of clay powder per bath as needed.

Drink 2 ounces of liquid clay twice daily, away from oral medications until ailment is gone.

PREGNANCY

Before pregnancy clay is taken as a means of encouraging pregnancy and is recommended for women who are having trouble conceiving. It is good for cleansing the body and for creating a better environment to house the infant. It is long believed that the unborn infant benefits from the mother's consumption of clay during pregnancy.

Throughout pregnancy drink 2 ounces of liquid clay twice daily, away from oral medications, and take a weekly clay bath as needed. Liquid clay doses may be increased in the instance that the mother experiences heartburn and indigestion. It is also beneficial in preventing and counteracting morning sickness.

Apply the clay mask over the stomach to ease tenderness.

Eating Calcium Bentonite Clay during pregnancy is a very common practice and helps a variety of ailments that may occur during pregnancy and postpartum.

It is believed the fetus will be bigger if the mother eats clay, and it will give the fetus good bones and teeth. Calcium Bentonite Clay will calm stomach acidity and absorbs metabolic toxins such as steroidal metabolites associated with pregnancy. Women rub their breasts with the clay mask to stimulate the secretion of milk. Eating clay is a safe and suitable practice that can be maintained during pregnancy. But, as I have emphasized throughout the book, it is important to find the right clay. Not all clays are good for internal use. You want a clean, alkaline, natural, quality-tested Calcium Bentonite Clay.

PREMENSTRUAL SYNDROME – PMS

Drink 2 ounces of liquid clay 3 times a day, away from oral medications.

Drinking clay is therapeutic in cases of menstrual cramps. By drawing the metabolic waste products and improving intestinal health, clay helps prevent cramps and lessens the related symptoms (headaches, bloating, irritability). Many naturopaths agree that menstrual cramps are not only a hormonal matter but are partly due to constipation.

Apply a ½-inch-thick poultice a day on the lower abdomen, interrupting it only at the period of menstruation. The poultices must remain in place for at least 2 hours. It can remain overnight if applied just before going to bed. Interrupt the application during the menstrual period, then resume applications. Be sure to slightly warm up the poultices in order not to create a congestive state. For long-term sufferers of the emotional rollercoaster that often precedes a menstrual cycle,

I recommend drinking liquid clay as a daily lifestyle practice.

PROSTATE HEALTH

Drink 2 ounces of liquid clay 3 times a day, increasing the dosage by 1 ounce daily to ultimately consume 4 ounces 3 times a day, away from oral medications as needed.

Use a Calcium Bentonite Clay suppository or clay enema as needed.

Take a clay bath twice a week for 15 to 20 minutes using 1 cup of clay powder per bath.

Take a clay enema daily or as needed, adding 2 ounces of liquid clay to 1 pint of water.

Apply a thick clay poultice over the lower abdomen just above and around the base of the penis and cover with Saran wrap and leave on for several hours daily. Continue with the poultice as needed.

The prostate is located between the rectum and the neck of the bladder. Because of its location, its health can be directly influenced by the condition of the bowels. An impacted colon will undoubtedly affect the health of the prostate. Therefore, a clean colon is the first thing to implement in any prostate rebuilding program. Calcium Bentonite Clay will help prevent the accumulation of waste matter and feces that can clog up the rectum. This could help to diminish the possibility of any future prostate problems or remedy a current one.

PSORIASIS – See ECZEMA

PYORRHEA – See GINGIVITUS

RADIATION EXPOSURE – See NUCLEAR RADIATION

RAZOR BURN

Instead of using shaving cream, apply a thin coat of hydrated clay mask. The clay will pull the hairs up for a close shave without chafing the skin.

RINGWORM

Daily apply topical applications of clay mask on specific outbreak areas as needed for itching and to dry up the condition. Repeat as needed.

Take a warm clay bath for 15 to 20 minutes using 1 cup of clay powder per bath as needed.

Drink 2 ounces of liquid clay twice daily, away from oral medications until ailment is gone.

ROSACEA

Rosacea is the flushing (reddening) of the skin, usually localized in the face and neck area.

It is one of those gray areas with clay. Clay facials either help tremendously and quickly, or they seem to aggravate the condition, which is sometimes a detox reaction. Detoxing the body internally and through clay baths will help balance the body's pH levels and help clear symptoms even when facials don't.

Apply the clay mask to the face every other day, allow it to dry for 15 minutes and gently wash off. It may redden more after the first few applications, but you should start seeing remarkable improvement during the first week if it is going to work for you. If you feel it is working, you can put a thin coat on at night and sleep with the clay mask on.

Drink 2 ounces of liquid clay twice daily, away from oral medications.

Start by taking a clay bath twice a week for 15 to 20 minutes using 1 cup of clay powder per bath. Continue the baths for 4 weeks. Then take weekly clay baths thereafter.

Over a 4-to-8-week period, you will notice a greatly reduced number of outbreaks.

SCALD – See BURNS

SCAR REMOVAL

Scar treatment is quite successful and oftentimes quite dramatic.

Drink 2 ounces of liquid clay twice daily, away from oral medications.

Apply the clay mask to the scars or stretch marks.

Cover with plastic wrap and leave for 1 hour. Repeat 2 times daily. Leave a thin application on overnight uncovered.

Scar removal, both the knotting and keloid effect, as well as the discoloration can be remedied in a period of 1 to 4 weeks. Stretch marks such as those occurring as a result of pregnancy are a bit more difficult of an issue.

SCIATICA

Drink 2 ounces of liquid clay twice daily, away from oral medications.

Take a daily hot clay bath for 15 to 20 minutes using 1 to 2 cups of clay powder per bath.

Drink water or an electrolyte drink during the bath.

Apply a thick clay poultice on the spine or affected area and hold in place with Glad Press 'n Seal. Replace with a new poultice day and night until better.

SCRATCHES – See ABRASIONS

SEXUALLY TRANSMITTED DISEASES – STDs

STDs are usually systemic, bloodborne, and require a full-body detoxification at the outset.

Start by drinking 2 ounces of liquid clay 3 times a day, increasing the dosage by 1 ounce daily to ultimately consume 6 to 8 ounces 3 times a day, away from oral medications until symptoms disappear.

Do a full-body clay mask wrap weekly – head to toe. Leave on for 30 minutes. Shower off.

Take a hot clay bath for 15 to 20 minutes using 1 cup of clay powder 2 times a week for 4 weeks.

Drink water or an electrolyte drink during the bath.

Take a clay enema daily or as needed, adding 2 ounces of liquid clay to 1 pint of water.

Apply a 1-inch-thick clay poultice about 10 inches in diameter to your liver twice daily for 1 hour. After 3 days it may be applied overnight.

For skin lesions and sores, coat liberally with clay mask the entire affected area and 2 to 3 inches of the surrounding area. Leave on until dry or cover the area. Reapply 3 times daily.

For vaginal areas, apply the clay mask liberally to the vaginal area and wear a pantiliner. Reapply after wiping.

SHINGLES

Start by drinking 2 ounces of liquid clay 3 times a day, increasing the dosage by 1 ounce daily to ultimately consume 4 ounces 3 times a day, away from oral medications as needed.

Apply a layer of clay mask to the affected area and cover with Saran wrap or Glad Press 'n Seal to keep the wet clay in place and off of your clothes.

If the clay gets hot, it is drawing out inflammation, remove the poultice and replace with fresh one.

Take a daily hot clay bath for 15 to 20 minutes using 1 to 2 cups of clay powder per bath. Drink water or an electrolyte drink during the bath.

SINUSITIS

If you suffer from sinusitis, make a compress by saturating a hot wash rag with a hydrated clay mask. Lie down and cover your sinuses with the hot, wet compress for 15 to 20 minutes.

Repeat as often as needed.

Drink 2 ounces of liquid clay twice daily, away from oral medications.

SKIN CANCER LESIONS

Clay Poultices – If you have a localized skin cancer, use poultices on a regular basis, especially before any surgery. The clay will help to draw the cancer to the point of origin so it is easier for the surgeon to get all the cancer.

A poultice can be a ¼ inch to 1 inch thick and between 2 and 12 inches in diameter. Place the clay mask over the area of concern.

Cover with a plastic wrap or a square of Glad Press 'n Seal to hold the clay in place. Leave on for 1 to 2 hours. Repeat this process several times a day, using a new batch of clay for each poultice. For small skin lesions, apply and leave uncovered. Repeat applications several times a day.

Drink 2 ounces of liquid clay twice daily, away from oral medications, to balance your pH.

As with all life-threatening ailments, we encourage you to consult with your doctor before altering any treatment program you are currently on. Your condition may be so advanced that you may do further harm by altering your current treatment. No statement we make or information we offer should be construed as a claim for a cure, treatment or prevention of any disease.

SKIN HEALTH

The skin is the largest organ and a means of eliminating waste. Everything that affects the body effects the skin. When the body is full of toxic waste and cannot eliminate them properly, various skin ailments may result. The only effective way to get rid of these conditions is by cleansing the body inside and out. Most skin conditions are first liver conditions. Take a simple pH strip and measure your saliva. If the saliva pH is 6.5 or below, it is too acidic. Skin conditions respond extremely quickly to Calcium Bentonite Clay.

The protocol is both internal and external.

Drink 2 ounces of liquid clay 3 times daily, away from oral medications.

Apply a clay poultice to the liver for an hour daily. After 3 days it may be applied overnight.

Take a clay bath twice a week for 15 to 20 minutes using 1 cup of clay powder per bath.

Do a full-body wrap and leave on for 20 minutes twice weekly.

SNAKE BITES

Venomous snakebites require emergency measures and immediate treatment. First, apply clay mask immediately to the bite marks. If a hospital is nearby or if you have access to ambulance assistance, use these life-saving emergency services.

After medical treatment, apply a 1-inch-thick poultice 6 inches in diameter to the affected area.

Leave on for 15 minutes and apply a new poultice. Repeat process 6 to 8 times or as often as needed. It will help reduce swelling as well as help pull out the venom.

In addition, drink 2 ounces of liquid clay, away from oral medications, 3 times a day as needed.

SORE THROAT

Drink 2 ounces of liquid clay 3 times a day, away from oral medications.

Gargle with liquid clay 2 to 3 times a day.

Apply clay mask under the jaw and down the neck. Lay a hot washcloth over your throat and under the jaw area for about 15 minutes. Do this as needed.

At bedtime, apply a thin clay mask to your entire throat and neck area, allow to dry and sleep with it on. For coughing, place a teaspoon of clay mask on the back of the tongue and let it gradually slide down the throat.

SPIDER BITES

Spider bites fall into one of two categories: emergency, which are possibly life threatening, such as a brown recluse or black widow bite; and nuisance bites, the ones that may raise a small bump and itch a little.

If bitten by a known venomous spider, apply Calcium Bentonite Clay poultice thickly to the bite area and surrounding area. Seek immediate emergency treatment. Immediately drink 2 ounces of liquid clay.

Later, to reduce swelling, change the poultice every hour and continue for 2 to 4 hours of repeated treatments. Finally, apply a heavy coat of clay mask, cover with plastic wrap and leave on overnight.

For nuisance spider bites, apply a coating of clay mask and

allow it to dry. Wash and reapply every two hours or so until pain and redness go away.

SPRAINS

Treat sprains both internally and topically as follows:

Drink 2 ounces of liquid clay twice daily, away from oral medications.

Apply a ½-inch-thick poultice, enough to more than cover the area of damage. Leave it on for 2 to 3 hours. Reapply 3 to 4 times daily. As it pulls the heat out and the clay feels hot, replace it with cool, fresh poultice. At bedtime, apply fresh poultice, cover with Saran wrap and leave on overnight.

Take a clay bath for 15 to 20 minutes using 1 cup of clay powder 1 to 2 times weekly, immersing the affected area.

STAPH – See INFECTIONS

STOMACH ULCERS –H. PYLORI

In 1980, Dr. Barry Marshall proved that H. pylon bacteria cause many ulcers. [36] Calcium Bentonite Clay not only captures this bacterium but also has a very high alkaline pH. This is necessary in most over-the-counter medications used to treat heartburn by neutralizing stomach acid and coating sensitive ulcers in the stomach and upper regions of the small intestine.

In addition to changes in diet and lifestyle, we suggest drinking 1 ounce of liquid clay 3 times a day, increasing by 1 ounce daily to 5 ounces 3 times a day, away from oral medications, until symptoms disappear. It may be taken with or without food.

You will be amazed how quickly ulcers respond to Calcium

Bentonite Clay. The clay helps to alkalize an acid stomach, bringing almost instant relief. It also rebuilds the gastrointestinal wall, which has been eaten through by the acid.

STRETCH MARKS – See SCAR REMOVAL

SUNBURNS

Apply clay mask over the sunburn about ¼ of an inch thick. Cover with plastic wrap and leave for 1 hour. Gently wash off. You may repeat as often as needed.

SYPHILIS – See SEXUALLY TRANSMITTED DISEASES

TAPEWORMS – ECHINOCOCCUS

An aggressive approach is recommended for these tenacious parasites, especially if they are found in the liver.

Start by drinking 2 ounces of liquid clay 3 times a day, increasing the dosage by 1 ounce daily to ultimately consume up to 8 ounces 3 times a day, away from oral medications as needed.

Take a clay enema daily or as needed, adding 2 ounces of liquid clay to 1 pint of water.

Some of these parasites manage to make their way into the liver. Apply a 1-inch-thick clay poultice about 10 inches in diameter to your liver twice daily for 1 hour. After 3 days it may be applied overnight. Recheck for tapeworm in 4 weeks.

THYROID – See HYPERTHYROID

TOENAIL FUNGUS

Fungus is normally found under the toenails and fingernails. It is a systemic, blood-borne pathogen and difficult to cure using traditional medicine.

Fortunately, Calcium Bentonite Clay offers a quick, all-natural cure for even the worst cases of nail fungus. Use as follows:

Drink 2 ounces of liquid clay 3 times daily, away from oral medications. Pack the clay mask under and on the affected nails and leave on for about 1 hour. You may wrap in plastic wrap or allow it to dry. Repeat this process 3 times daily. Leave a thin coat on overnight for a week.

Watch for the nail to grow out and a healthy pink nail bed to replace it.

TONSILLITIS – See SORE THROAT

TOOTHACHE

Treat a toothache both internally and topically.

Drink 2 ounces of liquid clay twice daily, away from oral medications, for the duration of the toothache.

Apply dry powder clay over the tooth during the day and again at night. Leave overnight.

Apply a thick coating of clay mask or a small poultice to the outside of your cheek, jaw or chin, directly over the toothache. Leave on for 45 to 60 minutes. Repeat 3 to 5 times daily or until the pain/infection is gone.

TRAMATIC INJURIES – See WOUNDS

TUMORS - BENIGN

To begin treatment for tumors, please read the CANCER section even though not all tumors are cancerous.

Apply a thick poultice over the tumor or growth and cover with plastic wrap. Change the poultice twice a day.

Start by drinking 2 ounces of liquid clay 3 times a day, increasing the dosage by 1 ounce daily to ultimately consume up to 8 ounces 3 times a day, away from oral medications as needed.

Take a clay bath for 15 to 20 minutes using 1 cup of clay powder per bath twice a week.

Repeat these steps until the tumor has dissolved. You will notice it is getting smaller. The length of time for treatment will depend on the size and complexity of the growth.

URINARY TRACT INFECTIONS

Drink 2 ounces of liquid clay 3 times a day, increasing the dosage by 1 ounce daily to ultimately consume up to 4 ounces 3 times a day, away from oral medications as needed.

Apply the clay mask vaginally toward the urethra after each urination. Wear a pantiliner.

Take a clay douche using 2 ounces of liquid clay to a pint of water as needed.

VARICOSE VEINS

Start by drinking 2 ounces of liquid clay 3 times a day, increasing the dosage by 1 ounce daily to ultimately consume 4 ounces 3 times a day, away from oral medications as needed.

Do foot and leg applications of clay masks as needed.

Apply the clay mask thickly to the affected areas as you would a facial mask. Cover the areas with plastic wrap or allow it to dry. At night, reapply and cover.

Varicose veins are caused by a toxic blood system. The small, fine capillaries near the surface of the skin become clogged, stopping blood flow to its spider-web-looking field of even finer capillaries. These blood toxins normally settle in our lower extremities, our legs. In later years as toxins build and circulation lessens; varicose and spider veins begin appearing.

VISION

For some cases of vision loss, try the following:

Apply clay mask thickly over a circular cotton pad and apply to a closed eyelid. Leave in place for 15 to 20 minutes 3 times a day. For minor irritations, pour liquid clay on the pad and apply for the same amount of time.

You may also apply the clay mask in a thin film on your eyelid and surrounding area as would be done in a facial and sleep with it on at night. It may take as long as 6 weeks to notice an improvement.

Drink 2 ounces of liquid clay twice daily, away from oral medications as needed.

VOMITING - See NAUSEA

WARTS

Warts are usually quickly and easily removed using Calcium Bentonite Clay.

Drink 2 ounces of liquid clay twice daily, away from l medications as needed.

Dab a relatively heavy amount of clay mask directly onto the wart. Allow the mask to dry. Repeat this process 5 to 6 times daily. At the end of the day, apply the last coating, cover with a plastic wrap and leave on all night.

After 5 days you will notice small pieces of the wart beginning to flake off as you wash off the clay. Continue the process until the wart is gone and smooth skin appears in its place. It could take as long as 15 days for larger warts.

Once healed, continue drinking 1 ounce of liquid clay as a daily practice.

WASP STINGS – See INSECT BITES

WEIGHT LOSS

Start by drinking 2 ounces of liquid clay 3 times a day, increasing the dosage by 1 ounce daily to ultimately consume up to 6 ounces 3 to 4 times a day, away from oral medications as needed.

Drink lots of water throughout the day.

Take a clay bath twice a week for 15 to 20 minutes using 1 cup of clay powder per bath.

Take a clay enema daily as needed, adding 2 ounces of liquid clay to 1 pint of water.

Do one full-body clay wrap weekly.

Apply a 1-inch-thick clay poultice about 10 inches in diameter to your liver twice daily for 1 hour. After 3 days it may be applied overnight as needed.

After you have reached your desired weight, a maintenance protocol of 2 ounces of liquid clay 2 times a day is recommended.

One of the major contributing factors to obesity is toxins in our bodies. Toxin buildup in the body contributes to premature aging and chronic and degenerative diseases. Chemicals and toxins accumulate in fat tissues. To lose weight, it's imperative to get rid of these toxins. Detoxification is a key element to weight loss, and clay is a safe and effective way to detox. Nothing is better for this than clay. According to Ran Knishinsky, "The best, most natural way to internally cleanse and detoxify is with clay." (Ran Knishinsky. The Clay Cure, Healing Arts Press, 1998)

Clay will assist in the assimilation of food. The body can feel starved if the cells are not receiving their nutritional needs, which can increase a person's appetite.

One study indicates weight gain and depression are just two common manifestations of a congested, overworked liver. Restoring liver function is one of the most important and vital actions you could do for your health. When the liver gets congested and toxic, it will remain that way and get worse until it is detoxified and rejuvenated.

WORMS – See PARASITES

WOUNDS – TRAUMATIC INJURIES

Dry powder Calcium Bentonite Clay is antimicrobial and antibacterial. It is also highly absorbent and is an excellent clotting agent. If there is an open bleeding wound, simply hand cast, or pack dry powder Calcium Bentonite Clay into the wound. Use your hand as a pressure bandage and hold the wound closed until the bleeding has stopped or clotted. For smaller wounds See Diabetic Ulcers-Wound Care.

Calcium Bentonite Clay is excellent as a first-aid tool and should be available on every ambulance and emergency vehicle in the U.S. Every combat soldier should carry it. And it should be in every emergency first-aid kit on the planet. Can you tell I am passionate about this?

YEAST INFECTION – See CANDIDA

Although yeast infections and Candida have different causes, please see that section for specifics. The procedure is the same for both.

Chapter Ten

WHAT OTHERS SAY ABOUT BENTONITE CLAY

Testimonials from real people

Understanding the science behind clay's efficacy is one thing. Hearing about results from your friends or family members is quite another. Using clay and experiencing the miracle of its healing powers constitutes the highest level of "understanding."

I am including here a few of my favorite testimonials from that second tier of understanding. These are unsolicited testimonials from real people. My hope is that you will find one that will move you to that third tier of understanding – personal use and your own success story. So as not to be mistaken for advertizing the brand name of the clay used in these testimonials has been removed. For more testimonials go to www.BentoniteClayInfo.com

The testimonial below is in a category all its own.

Clay for Life

"If I could have only ONE health solution to help me through my life, it is the CLAY! I cannot do without." - Lisa C.

Disclaimer: This educational information is meant to supplement and not be a substitute for professional medical care or treatment. This information has not been evaluated by the FDA.

ARTHRITIS, BONES, JOINTS, AND BACK AND NECK PROBLEMS

Amazing Relief from Rheumatoid Arthritis

I started thinking. "I wonder could this help me with my rheumatoid arthritis." So I had my daughter cover my baby finger of my left hand and all the rest of my left hand with clay. I also had her cover my then-swollen right knee with clay. What happened next brought me to tears. Military doctors told me the deformity of my left baby finger due to rheumatoid arthritis was something I was just going to have to live with. Do you know that my finger, the first joint in it has just about gone down? I can already straighten it out! Hallelujah!!! That swelling in my right knee – gone after just three applications of the clay in Saran wrap! — Jacq P.

Ankylosing Spondylitis

Ankylosing Spondylitis (chronic inflammation of the joints in the spine.)

My ankylosing spondylitis has affected my life, general well-being and quality of life since the age of 12. However, it was not diagnosed until I was at the age of 30. The symptoms that I have experienced, is pain and stiffness in the back, all the way up to the neck, general tiredness and problems with the colon.

An Icelandic doctor confirmed that the tummy problems were related to the Ankylosing Spondylitis and that Candida were somehow linked to the onset of the disease. For many years I had painkillers and various anti-inflammatory drugs (NSAIDs) for breakfast, lunch, and dinner, or so it felt. Until one day I had had enough. That was the year 2006. From that time, I have been looking for something as an alternative to these dangerous products from the pharmaceutical industry. And I have tried almost anything, but nothing really worked until I tried the clay. I use roughly one teaspoon dissolved in water in the morning and at nighttime, as well as drinking freshly squeezed fruit or vegetable juice at lunch. The difference is vast! A feeling of well-being is something I have not experienced before (as far as I can remember), along with my colon problems having completely disappeared. Everybody compliments me on how well I look and ask how I do it. I have not tried the clay poultice, as the clay is only sold in a tiny glass jar in one place in Iceland, each jar weighing 50 grams or 1.76 oz. This is an obstacle in using the clay here in Iceland. I can't wait to buy it in bulk so that I can try the bath and poultices. I want to tell everybody about the clay and I want everyone I know to use it. I know firsthand that the clay works, even for me, and that people will want to buy it when word gets out. -Sólveig H.

Broken Wrist Healed in Three Weeks With Out a Cast

I am 55 years old and right-handed. I broke my left wrist when a horse fell with me. The break was at an angle just above the wrist joint. I live in a small town and they put a splint on it, suggesting I drive 70 miles to the nearest hospital and have a cast put on for eight weeks. Instead, I went home, wrapped it in a thick clay poultice and left it on the first day and night.

Then I did fresh poultices three times a day for four hours the first week, then went to a poultice one hour every third day. I also started drinking 2 ounces of liquid clay a day. The only pain pills I took were Ibuprofen and Tylenol. At 2½ weeks I was back riding horses, penning cattle and shifting tractor gears. At three weeks I helped trim a barrel horse's hooves when he threw a shoe before a major barrel race. It is a little stiff, but the feeling in my little finger came back, and I am using it more each day thanks to a special clay and following my gut instinct. — Steve H.

Wrist With Spiral Break

My husband Charles fell off a ladder a week ago. He went to hospital to learn of a spiral break in wrist and fingers where he caught himself. They put him in snug splint and want him return to doctor. Instead, he has been soaking his hand and wrist in clay several times a day with his hand totally immersed in clay. He canceled the doctor appointment and his hand has no more swelling and hand feeling better. It's been 8 days. Thank you and blessings. – Julie F.

Disc Bulge Problem in Back

I have a disc bulge in my lower back and sacroiliac. One day I had spent five hours in the yard raking and mulching. When I came in I could barely move. Sitting, standing and moving from either position were extremely painful. This is typical of my condition. I had clay prepared but hadn't used any yet. I took 2 ounces and 10 minutes later, the pain was GONE. I felt fine the rest of the evening. I was stiff when I woke up in the morning and took 2 more ounces. I had no pain the rest of the day. Typically pain like I had that evening would have lasted at least a week and may have even caused me to miss that following day of work. I am amazed at the power of this product. — Dawn S.

Hammer Toes

I had a toenail fungus and soaked both feet 3-5 x a week in your clay and then cut down the amount to maybe 1 or 2 x a week. A small hospital plastic basin with Berkey filtered water to cover my feet with a 1/2 cup dry mixed clay with 8oz filtered Berkey water, mixed in my magic bullet and added to the water in my basin. Then gradually added more hot water. I changed the water maybe once a week. I heated the water each time in a separate tea kettle and kept the soak water hot. I soaked my feet for 30-40 minutes.

I commented to my husband that I thought my hammertoes looked straighter as he had noticed them before also. I would not have thought anymore about it except I was listening to a past show where you said someone else had mentioned it also. I doubt you would get a podiatrist to agree but it sounds like we may "be on to something" helpful. – Joy C.

Knot in Neck - No Movement

I just wanted to share my experience from today. I woke up with a horrible knot in my neck. The was pain shooting up into my head, and I couldn't move my head side to side or even up and down without crying (literally, and I am not much of a crier). I took lots of Ibuprofen and Tylenol and even a muscle relaxer out of desperation. All of that and the only thing it did was make me sleepy. I finally took a clay bath this evening and soaked for 45 min. up to my neck. While my neck is definitely not pain free, it is tolerable, and I can move my neck about 45 degrees now! It doesn't sound like much, but I couldn't move it this morning. This is amazing! I am going to pack it on and read a book now. I don't know how it worked and at this point I don't care LOL but I must say that the clay in the bath was very noticeably black. Love this stuff. — Leah G.

Joint Pain Free, Bunion Smaller and Off Nexium in Three Weeks

I've been drinking clay for three weeks now, and none of my joints hurt including a bunion, (that is smaller now). I carry myself differently not giving in to the pain and stiffness. I use muscles haven't used well in years. This is so wonderful. I could tell a difference in my inflammation all over within 2 to 3 days, and it just gets better! Three weeks now. I haven't taken my Nexium since I started taking clay. My bunion is yet smaller, and the range of motion in and below that great toe is unbelievably improved. Also, I have lost weight, enough that people ask me and others say I just have a glow! I think I can see better. Can't see living without this clay! — Chrysanne R.

Knee and Joint Pain

I have had knee pain for over 15 years, I am 40. It's basically overuse and tendinitis. I have had issues like this with tennis elbow (still have it a little but getting better now. I think it's the clay), achilles tendinitis and carpal tunnel. But my knees have been the hardest to deal with because I like to exercise. And I have tried so many, many things to help me, but I still have constant discomfort. I am taking 6 ounces of liquid clay/day most days and put the mask on my knees 2x per day and let it dry 20 minutes and remove it. I have made a 30% improvement so far. It's been about 10 days since I started doing this. — Heidi F.

AUTISM & HEAVY METAL DETOXING, CLEANSING

Autistic Boy's Eyes Locked on Mom

Alex is doing well with the clay baths for his autism. After only his 2nd clay bath, his eyes locked onto mine for five minutes. I didn't want to look away ... he's never done that before.

He has improved tremendously with potty training and following verbal commands. I sometimes do the clay like a body mask (1 part clay, 2½ parts water) and apply it to his entire body for about 15 minutes, and then he showers. He asks for the clay at bath time sometimes! He points to the jar and says, "I want that thing." I believe he can feel the difference. We are doing a mask daily and since we started this, Alex understands the use of the potty (for #2), which had been such a challenge, and incorporating the use of clay to our daily protocol has been key to Alex's progress. Even his speech therapist, who had not seen him since mid-Dec., told me last Monday that she had the best session with Alex ever. So we will continue to use clay and see how it keeps helping Alex in this journey of recovering from autism. — Becky F.

Autistic Child Responds to Clay

I gave the 5th dose of liquid clay to Tara on 6th August. Oh gosh, a miracle, lots of changes. My heart says I am in the right direction at last.

Today she went to a play center, where a child fell while running. Since no one helped that kid, Tara went and picked her up and tried to wipe her eyes. By then her mom also came running. My husband was shocked and told me this. Tara never did this before. Every day I am seeing changes. It's slow but it's working. Also, I do want to report that clay also causes detoxes for Tara. In fact, Tara has detox now. But what I noticed is, the detox is the same like any other treatment but it goes away on its own within 3 days after the clay is ingested. For Tara her first detox symptoms were a rash all over the body, diaper rash and sleep disturbance.

I got a report from Tara's school that something major happened during the vacation...that Tara is totally a different child now. All I did was give her clay before school started. To be honest it's true that Tara was different two weeks before. I emailed her teacher that Tara was in worst shape and asked her to be prepared. Then I googled and came up with the clay and started clay exactly 1 1/2 weeks before the school started. The fun was of course Tara transformed from worst to super good. I am typing this email with tears in my eyes. – Pradmavathy G.

Autistic Son Gets Instant Results from Clay Bath

I cannot say enough about Calcium Bentonite Clay and how it has helped my son, Max. He has autism and along with some behavioral and sensory issues, has trouble with communication. The first time I tried the clay, I was afraid he wouldn't go in since the water was cloudy, but he was fine. He relaxed and seemed to enjoy himself, which in itself was a benefit. What I couldn't believe was how much he talked that night. I didn't expect improvement so soon!

The talking keeps increasing, and his overall mood is better, too. For months, he took a clay bath every day, and now he takes it once a week. Max has not regressed at all since cutting down the frequency of the baths — his language is continually improving. However, on the nights he does take a clay bath, he talks nonstop! Everyone who knows us noticed that the sudden spurt of language started with clay. I think it really gave him the boost he needed to overcome his difficulties and really kick-start his communication skills. — Diana P.

Autistic Son's Speech Improves

As a parent of a child affected by autism - I will try anything (safe) to help my son. I figured I'd give clay a try. Oh my goodness - the changes have been incredible! A few days after my son's first detox bath his teacher asked me if I gave him a "speech pill"! I'm sure you can imagine my excitement. I personally know the cost of trying to heal a child and when you find something that works, it's just an incredible feeling. Again, I'm just so thankful I was turned onto this product. Thank you for providing help to our children!!!! — Anna W.

Autism Son WIth Genetic Disorder

A few months ago I found out that he has a genetic disorder that has caused his autism. Now I know that it is not only environmental factors that have caused his autism, it's his genetic deletion. My understanding is that genetically caused autism are more difficult to "cure" than environmentally caused ones but that does not mean that I will not keep trying to help him every way I possibly can.

The clay has been amazing. He loves taking baths in it and really enjoys eating it. My husband is still hesitant when he eats it so I'm the one that supervises all his baths. The clay is so pure, I really cannot describe just how pure and pristine this clay is. I just put in a new order for 2 more gallons. Thank you with all my heart. – Chantal A.

Baby Born with Meth Addiction Makes Miraculous Recovery

This is a second-hand story because of legalities we cannot share names but needs sharing. Perry A~\A newborn baby was abandoned at a hospital. The baby was most likely born in an alley and is addicted to Fentanyl and crystal meth. The baby is well enough in 8 days to go to a caring family. The baby weighed 5 ½ lbs. when they got her. The baby screams non-stop, has tremors and her fingers and toes are gray. The next evening the caring family notices there is puss coming from all the babies nail beds. They called a nurse and was instructed to bring the baby the next day for antibiotic treatment. So, at 9 days old, this caring family put clay on the baby's hands and feet, wraps them in teething mitts with clay for the night. In the morning she takes the wraps off, the fingers are now pink with no puss. The nurse cannot believe the healing.

At 10 days old, the caring mom puts the baby in clay baths at 7.a.m., noon and 6.p.m. They made a jar of clay mask using 1 cup dry clay to 3 cups of water in a blender. They took a half cup of hydrated clay from that jar into a small baby bathtub and mixed well with 8 - 10 cups of warm water and put the baby in that for 15 to 20 mins. What happens next in those 20 minutes is a miracle. The tremors are gone, and she can sleep. The tremors stopped and the baby sleeps 14 hours that night. The clay baths have been done every day for 5 days now. The tremors always go away while the baby is in the clay bath water, and they are getting less while this poor little muffin detoxes. The baby is now gaining weight and is 6 pounds. I talked to the caring mom today and the tremors are all but gone...the baby is able to sleep and eat without agitation. The baby was 10 days old when they started 3 baths a day and continue to this day. Today she is 17 days old. The care mother said it is night and day difference now. She has been doing this kind of work for years and has never seen anything work like the clay. She has shared it with a couple other care takers, and they are also seeing the same results. So amazing!!! A Caring Nurse

California Fire Toxic Damage

These California fires are unique in that the air is additionally highly poisonous to breathe.

I'm reminded of the wonderful testimonial a woman in the Canada fires came on the Clay Cafe call to share last year. She talked about her asthma being so activated, and having such awful terrible problems breathing, constantly using her inhaler, but still challenged. By putting the Castro oil mixed into the clay mask and smothering her chest and going to bed, her breathing problems completely cleared by the next morning and she did not even have to use her inhaler anymore! And it lasted, and she was able to breathe again despite the toxic air from those Canada fires! I want to share this being able to use it on the lungs, and also to help ease the breathing in these smoke and fire infested neighborhoods in California.

The news, of course, isn't covering the level of harm done. The Vistra, the company who owns the largest Lithium Battery Plant, is silencing this and stating it's not bad. This is the 4th or 5th fire at this plant. 100 K batteries burned, and they don't have the means/knowledge on how to put these fires out. "Just let it burn out on its own," they say.

SJSU (Nearby University) has done soil testing of the slough, (where otters play & live) and the surrounding area. The soil shows its highly contaminated. It will take 2 years until planting can occur. This area provides so much produce to the United States.

People are sick, I touched an outside tarp and it irritated my skin. The clay stopped the irritation immediately. Clay baths will remove the toxins and clay poultices stop the pain for any visible burn blisters or skin irritations. -Violet S.

Editor's note: Calcium Bentonite Clay is known to reduce pain, prevent infection, and help regenerate healthy skin.

Clay Baths Detox Lead in 3-year-old

My 3-year-old son was diagnosed with high levels of lead in his blood - 7.3. The doctors wanted to put him on drugs and intravenous chelation. I had heard about Calcium Bentonite Clay for detoxing and wanted to try it first. I gave him two clay baths a week using 1 cup of clay in each bath for three months. My son calls them chocolate milk baths. Went back for the check-up in three months and the doctor came in and asked, "What have you been doing?" He said there was no sign of the lead. Wanted to know what he had been doing to get rid of the lead. I told him about the clay baths. I was giving him a little liquid clay, 1 tablespoon at night for acid reflux, and that is all we did. After a few baths my son started asking for chocolate milk baths. — Ben H.

Clay Detox of 12-Month-old Child with Lead Toxicity

I want to thank you for your clay book. The clay has been such a blessing to us. When our daughter was 12 months old, we took her to holistic practice for a checkup. They did a routine hair analysis on her and found that she had lead in her system. We immediately started to give her clay baths, 3 times a week, for 2.5 – 3 months. Additionally, we gave her 1 tsp of hydrated clay with her food, 1 time a day, every day for 2 months. We then had her blood tested. Lead levels greater than 10 micrograms/dL are considered abnormal, according to the CDC. Our daughter's test results came back at 2 mcg/dL, out of a normal range of 0 – 9. We will continue to give her the clay as we had been doing to completely remove the lead from her system, but we are very relieved her levels are getting closer to zero, and that we didn't have to go the route of intrusive chelation treatments. — Natalie M

Clay Bath Detox Results

The clay has been working so well for me that I can hardly believe the results I have gotten and quickly, too. The first clay bath I took almost did me in. I must have been very toxic. I was tired and lethargic for about 3 days after, sleeping a lot and feeling exhausted. After I recovered, I felt better than I have in a very long time. I knew this could happen and was not dismayed in the least that it did, in fact, I was thrilled because I knew something good would come of it. A side benefit to all of this claying of my body is that my skin is so soft and smooth, it's never looked healthier, and I feel so much better. — Linda W.

Cleansing Soaps

OK, we're talking soap - good soap. I've found that it is in fact worth the price. Why? It lasts nearly 2x as long as other healthy chemical free bars. Plus the added benefit of the calcium bentonite clay makes it even better. The cleaning power is remarkable, especially the face, neck, ears and body folds. One pass gets it done. Excellent feel on the skin, not dry, not oily- just natural. The different natural scents are perfect, not overwhelming. As expected, Perry formulated the soap perfectly. My wife and I enjoy and appreciate (maybe for the first time ever) using a high quality, healthy bar of soap each day - esp in the central FL summer heat, often after working in the yard. Peace of mind goes a long way, not having to wonder if we are putting chemicals and artificial dyes on our bodies. In our current environment, that means a lot - thank you Perry for turning out healthy products that help, not harm. Thank you for ALL that you do! – Tom O.

Clay Converted Pharmaceutical Representative

Testimonial: "I am a former Pharmaceutical Representative. I am fully aware of how pharmaceutical companies operate, and the negative side effects that accompany any drug consumed by an individual. As for myself, I have always looked for an all-natural and holistic approach to healing and health. I came across the Living Clay Company back around 2008 after being diagnosed with Epilepsy in 2006. I was medicated with anti-epileptic medication that was so toxic, I felt sick all the time. I began to look for something to help with the nausea which I felt all day long for over a year. I battled with my Neurologist stating "I would rather have a seizure than continue these medications."

When I discovered Bentonite Clay, I read through Perry A's

book just like I would with any Clinical Study or Clinical Trial as I did when I was a Pharmaceutical Rep. I tried to pick and tear it apart to find some lie or deceit. However, I couldn't find any. I took the chance and ordered both the powder and clay. Much to my surprise, coating my chest and shoulders with the clay took away the nausea within 15-20 minutes at most. I also suffer from Insomnia and Anxiety. Following the book's instructions, I began taking baths with the powder mixed with the water. Without delay, I immediately began sleeping without the need of sleep medications. As for my anxiety, I also noticed a radical change in my mood for the better. I found myself much calmer and more relaxed throughout the day, which many of my friends would note.

One day, I came down with the flu. As I sat there with the chills and cold sweats, I almost reached for medication but quickly thought of the Bentonite Clay. I coated my chest and shoulders once again with the clay, and within 15 minutes, I immediately noticed I was recovering from the flu. After 25 minutes, I was completely back to my normal self. That was truly my absolute full-on belief in the miraculous healing qualities of this Calcium Bentonite Clay. From that point on, I began ordering it on a regular basis and began buying it as gifts for family and friends. Of course, with anything new it was met with skepticism. However, I always included the book to go along with it. I would simply show them the many ailments that the clay would cure and/or provide relief: from helping with Autism, burns and scars, anxiety and restless sleep, not to mention what a wonder it is on the skin!

As someone who knows the pharmaceutical industry very well, I am so incredibly grateful to have found an alternative, holistic approach to dealing with so many different conditions that we as people endure everyday: Calcium Bentonite Clay. I am just one of many who can claim firsthand, this is the real deal! I stand behind it 100%. Oh, did I mention? I have PTSD. It helps with that as well. I also work with the military. Guess who's going to be getting some Bentonite Clay as gifts this year!" - Rizer W.

Migraine Headache Gone in Minutes + Energy Boost

Gone in minutes. Well, I have to tell you.... I took my first clay last night at 10 p.m. ...drank water thru the night....each time I woke up....at 6am I woke up with a horrific migraine....like USUAL....and at about 45minutes later went to the bathroom (the clay is working WOW) and my migraine was instantly GONE!! 7a.m. I'm putting on my makeup and now at 7:13 a.m. I'm emailing you with so much energy IM SOLD!!!!! EVERYONE NEEDS CLAY!!!!!! OMG I HAVE NEVER SEEN ANYTHING LIKE THIS!!!! THANK YOU. – Christi B.

Editor's note. Clay baths also work to relief Migraine Headaches. If you can't do a bath, put the wet clay on a wash rag and put it on the back of your neck or your forehead and of course drink some clay

BITES & STINGS

Cat Bite

I fixed up a streaky red, infected cat bite a while back. Made a poultice of wet clay about half an inch thick, covered with wet paper towel, then plastic wrap, then wrapped in an ace bandage. About 2 hours later the inflammation and streaks were subsided. I replaced it with new poultices twice and the arm healed right up. In a couple days it was just a scab. — Heather H.

Centipede Bite

One morning, I pulled on a pair of shorts from somewhere deep in my closet. I felt a strange tickling sensation down by my groin. I looked down and saw a baby centipede crawling out of my shorts, and before I could knock it away, it bit me. Right in the area where all those lymph nodes are located. A centipede bite is sheer fire that begins to spread through your body, and it doesn't just stay in that localized area ... it spreads far and wide. And just like scorpions, the younger the centipede, the more powerful its venom. So, one look and I knew I was in trouble.

On my way to the bathroom cabinet, I could already feel the white fire spreading throughout my body. Then I'm into the cabinet, open the clay and put a nice little dab all around the two fang puncture marks on my body.

I first noticed the coolness of the clay as it touched my skin. Then, to my amazement, I began to feel the white fire retreating and immediately dissipating. Within 30 seconds, I could no longer feel the fire. Now, all I felt was the cool of the clay doing its work. Within two minutes, I could hardly feel anything at all, and I waited a few more minutes just to be sure, but within five minutes after rinsing off the clay and looking down in that area, all I could see was the two puncture marks the centipede had left, and no red and no swelling and most importantly. ... no pain. — Dylan H.

Brown Recluse Bite - Severe

I had a huge brown recluse bite on my inner left thigh that I had started using Activated Charcoal on. (What a mess that was!!)

I was into my second week of battling this bite, when I finally remembered that I had purchased some Calcium Bentonite Clay months before, so I started using it, applying a thick paste of it to the wound, which at this point was about the size of a quarter. As soon as that dried, I would remove it, then reapply it again. The clay started working immediately! I did this for over a week, but after just one day, the wound was noticeably better. Like I said above, the dead tissue was about the size of a quarter, but the whole area that was affected was about 6 inches in diameter. I knew that if I could not stop this toxin, this whole area was going to look like the quarter size spot. I continued doing this for two weeks, and now I can hardly tell there was EVER a bite there. Very minimal scarring!! That was not the only bite I received. A couple of weeks later, I had four bites on my left arm. (Killed the little bugger this time!) I immediately applied the clay to these spots. They never progressed beyond little red bumps. I amazed family and friends when I told them how I cured these bites. I think they are now believers.

I am ABSOLUTELY satisfied with this clay. WILL NEVER BE CAUGHT WITHOUT IT AGAIN!! I also drink it every day, since we are invaded with environmental toxins everyday!! — Lori F.

Fire Ant Bites

I was cleaning the graveside and reached down to pull up tall weeds -my hands were covered with hundreds of fire ants. I received a minimum of 50 bites per hand. I had a jar of clay which is always with me. Applied 1 1/2 in of clay to both hands and put on plastic gloves. Within minutes all swelling - redness

- pain was gone. The pain had been intolerable. I left pack on for 2 hours. Totally clear when the pack was removed. I also took a dose of Apis 200c at home. Miracle!!!!! — Mary J.

Jellyfish Sting

A few days ago, my husband went out snorkeling across the street. Within a few minutes he came running into the house, dripping wet and said, "I need your help!" I rushed in to see what was wrong. He had been stung by what appeared to be a long-severed tentacle of a jellyfish all over his torso. We immediately began spreading the hydrated Clay over all the long red welts and noticed that the red streaks were already starting to blister up. He felt an instant cooling relief as the Clay was applied, and the stinging began to subside. We placed plastic strips over all the clayed areas to keep it from drying. About half an hour later, we removed the plastic and rinsed the clay off, and there was not a mark left on his body! Once again, our special clay to the rescue! — Dylan & Clover H.

Puss Caterpillar Sting

I got stung by a puss caterpillar. The stings can be vicious. But I did what I could to get the stingers out immediately, and I kept clay on the wound. Today there is still a mark, but no pain, swelling or burning, which is unusual. The Bentonite sucked all the poison out of the wound. It really did the job OVER NIGHT! — Robin S.

BURNS

Burned Hand with Boiling Water

One morning, I was boiling a cup of water in the microwave for hot tea. I reached in to pull the cup out of the microwave and the sleeve of my bathrobe caught on the door, and over half of the boiling water poured over the top of my hand. It was extremely red and hurt very much. I thought of grabbing the already mixed clay from the jar and layered it over my hand in a wet, paste-like consistency and then wrapped it in gauze for 24 hours. After 12 hours, I sprayed some water on the gauze to keep the clay moist until morning. The next morning, I removed the gauze and to my amazement, the skin was silky smooth and had no signs of being burnt except a small amount of redness. I wrapped it again and left it on another couple hours, and when I removed it the second time, it looked and felt completely normal. — Barbara H.

Burned Hand with Hydrochloric Acid

Worker's hand burned with Hydrochloric Acid. Doctors wanted to amputate part of his thumb and do a skin graft to the dark fleshy part between his thumb and forefinger.

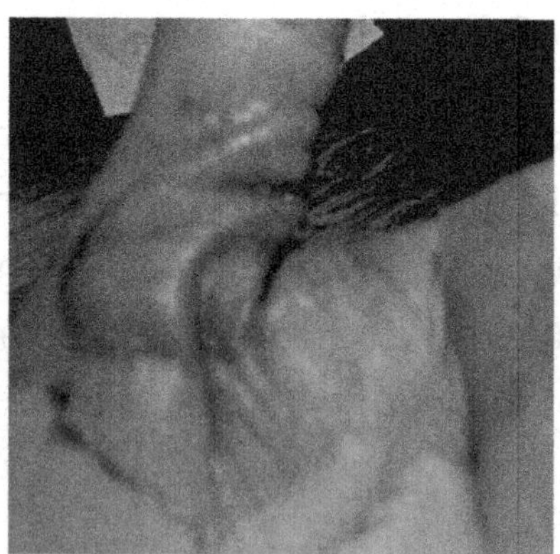

He chose clay and soaked his hand in a thick clay mask for 13 hours the first time. Prior to the clay application he had intense severe burning pain and could not move his thumb. The next morning the pain was greatly reduced and he could wiggle his thumb. He kept doing poultices for 4 more days and the clay cleaned the wound and the dead skin started peeling off. His is in no pain can move his thumb easily and new healthy pink skin is now present and no amputation or transplant needed. – Robert H.

During Healing-see below

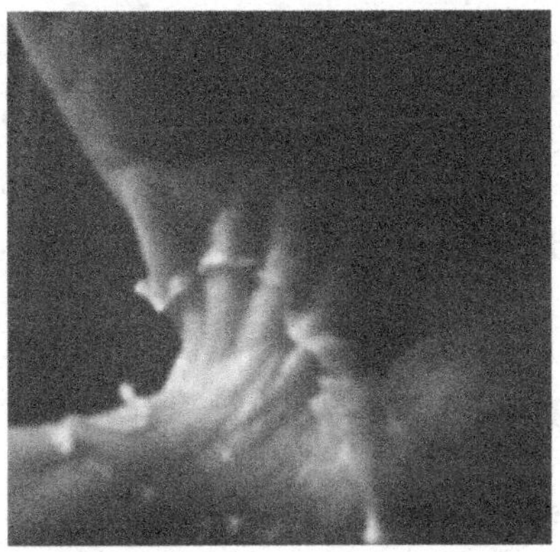

After 4 days of clay applications.

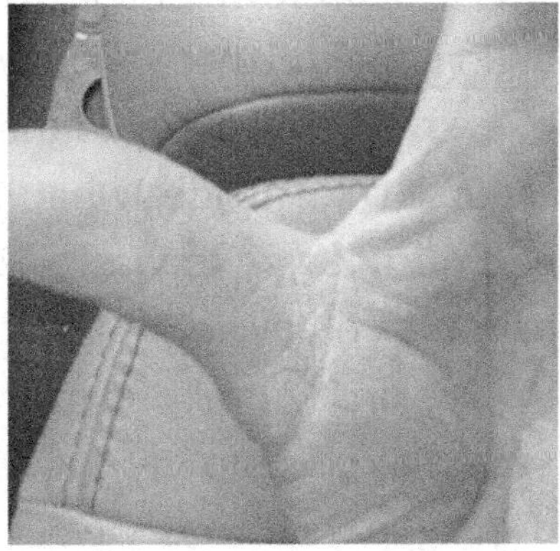

Completely healed. – Robert H.

Hot Pizza Bite –Clay to the Rescue

A few weeks ago, I had made a pizza for dinner. It smelled so good coming out of the oven! Even though I knew better, I cut a slice and took a big bite...and promptly burned the daylights out of my tongue and the roof of my mouth! I ran to the den where I keep some ready-mixed clay in a mason jar. I scooped out about two tablespoons of cool clay into my mouth and just held it there. About fifteen minutes later I chased it down with a glass of water...and the burning pain was gone! The pizza had cooled down in the meantime and I had a wonderful, pain-free dinner! What did we ever do before clay came along?! — Jamie C.

Jalapeño Face Burn

The other night while washing my face, I got jalapeño juice on my face and in my eye. It's a long story, but Cliffs Notes are: My son eats peppers all the time, and he used a face towel as a placemat while eating on the furniture, and it ended up in the towel cabinet as a clean towel. I felt my eye burning but thought I had soap in it and further wiped with the towel. My eye, my face, a lip, everywhere I dragged the towel across my face was on FIRE! At first, I had no idea what was going on, only that the water I was using to try to wash it off was making it worse! I have sensitive skin anyway. So I looked at the towel and saw the green juice on it. I grabbed my hydrated clay and used a Q-tip to place it as close to my eye as possible and all along my face and lip. Within seconds the burning stopped and after several minutes the pain and burning were completely gone! I love my clay!! — Justine F.

Motorcycle Burn

It was a typical 100-degree summer day in Texas as I straddled my motorcycle to ride to work for the day. I was in shorts, thinking more about my day of working outside than the brief ride on the bike. After parking, I went to dismount as I felt the stinging pain and literally heard the sizzle of my calf as it touched the red-hot tail pipe, resulting in a severe burn about 4 inches by 2 inches in size. Remembering a story I had heard about using clay for burns, I immediately applied a thick layer of hydrated clay over the area. The intense pain dissipated in a matter of seconds! I continued to apply fresh clay to the burn throughout the day and applied clay poultice overnight. The next morning I was relieved to see only a slightly red area but no blistering and, after a full recovery, no scarring. What an incredible gift from Nature. — Kyle J.

Sun Burn Blisters

First, I would like to tell you that the inflamed sun blisters my son got in the Norwegian alps healed very fast! He put clay poultices on for a couple of hours each evening for a week and now it looks good. Thank you! — Gunilla A.

Three Fingers Burned from a Hot Grate

I burned three fingers picking up a very hot grate on my stove. We had just boiled some water and removed the teakettle, and I noticed it needed to be cleaned underneath the grate. I dropped the grate as soon as I picked it up, and I rushed to put globs of clay on each finger. After about an hour, most of the clay had fallen off, and I had almost forgotten about the incident. When I washed the remaining clay off my fingers, I found no sign of a burn. Advice: Keep the clay "handy"! — Mary Helen K.

CUTS, WOUNDS AND INJURIES

Bruised Muscle from Fall

My 65-year-old husband, God love him, decided to ride our grandson's scooter down a ramp at a skate park this past Friday. Well, the scooter flew out from under him, and he fell hard onto the left side of his back - sort of where the kidney would be located. We are convinced it is only a bruised muscle as nothing else seems to be affected - he can still bend over and touch his toes, no blood in urine, etc.

Last night I made a poultice of Calcium Bentonite Clay, alkaline water, tea tree oil, and peppermint oil and swathed that all over the sore area and then wrapped him in saran wrap!!! This morning, we re-applied the poultice and wrap. I will keep you posted on his progress.

Day 5 Quote hubby: "I am a believer now." He feels as though he never fell last Friday. He wore poultice, wrapped in Saran, 24/7 since Monday. He works on boats, which is strenuous work and this morning he felt good as new. He is off to a shooting competition today, with his mid-section wrapped in clay and saran. LOL YAY CLAY! - Susan S.

Clay For Back Relief and Deep Cuts

It is working wonders as a clay mask when applied to my lower back for L5 S1 arthritis. It literally makes my back feel 10 to 20 years younger, no joke. I also put it on my hips and partially balding head, and I swear my hair looks thicker and has more regrowth, again no joke. Lastly, I once hit my arm on the corner of a cabinet in the kitchen and it made a pretty deep cut/gouge. I immediately put the clay mask on it to stop the bleeding and dry it which it did, but what's really strange is that it didn't even scab up and for the next week was just a light gray spot which slowly faded and is pretty much almost gone. This clay is truly some remarkable stuff. - Joe D

Clay For Kitchen Accidents

I keep a glass jar of dry clay and clay poultice on my kitchen counter. If I burn my fingers while cooking i put my finger right into the poultice - works every time -

Two weeks ago during a snow storm I sliced my finger dicing vegetables. My husband thought I should go to the ER but with the snow falling I didn't think that was a good idea! I packed the cut with dry clay and when bleeding stopped started clay poultices - within a few days the cut was completely closed and continued healing. Clay is indispensable for first aid. -Jo-Ann E. Martha's Vineyard

Cut Earlobe

I was visiting India last year and I was in a five-star hotel bathroom. I never drink so what happened is I had this freak accident where I slipped and fell and hit my ear on the marble sink and got quite a wound all the way around the middle of the earlobe. It bled a lot. My son came in and we did clean with alcohol. I said I am not going to the ER so I put clay on it and then used an Em Pulser which is an emf device for sport injuries. I did that for a few days, kept keeping it covered with clay. It is all healed up. I have a bit of disfigurement, but stitches would have left a scar too. - Roxanne B.

Cut Finger

I cut my finger pretty badly about 2 weeks ago. While attempting to clean out a glass jar, the bottom of the jar came off and the glass sliced my finger. I called you to discuss putting clay on it and that's what I did. I used dry clay to stop the bleeding and then I mixed some dry clay with water to make a "paste" with the clay which I applied to my finger and wrapped with a gauze and band aid. I changed the Band-Aid every night and after about 3

days, I noticed it starting to look better. I continued to apply the clay paste for another week, keeping a Band-Aid on my finger. It has been two weeks and now the Band-Aid is off and my finger is almost back to normal. -Linda K.

Cut Finger Bleeding Profusely

I cut my finger, and it was bleeding profusely and I stopped the bleeding with Dry Powder Clay. It formed a crusty scab, then was covered with clay mask and wrapped in plastic wrap over night to soften the crusty scab. The next day after I washed the clay off, the wound had closed and was healing nicely. -Martha J.

Deep Cut Healed in 24-36 Hours

I cannot say enough how much we LOVE our clay. Just 3 days ago I had another amazing personal clay experience. I was cooking dinner for the parents and sliced my thumb pretty good on a brand new knife. As soon as I felt the knife go through my thumb, I instantly squeezed the cut closed and said to Dylan, "I think you better grab the clay!"

We covered it in clay and taped it closed, the next day. When we untaped it 24 - 36 hours later, the cut had already sealed itself back together. And it was a deep cut! Once again, but not to our surprise, the clay has worked wonders!!! — Clover H.

Cyst Under the Knee

I have a recent knee sprain (MCL) and an MRI shows I have a small cyst of blood/fluid under the skin of my knee area. A doctor has recommended full surgery to remove this pocket of blood/fluid, as it's stopping me from bending my knee.

As you suggested, I applied a thick clay wrap over the knee and covered it with Glad Press 'n Seal to keep it in place. I've done the clay wrap for the past 3 nights and it has really helped – fluid seems to have been removed from the cyst and has drained to the side of my knee. I'll continue with this and working with a lymphatic drainage therapist. -Priscilla & Dave

Finger Saved from Amputation

Clay saved my finger from amputation and me from sepsis due to the injury. I sent you a text about the severe injury which my HMO had treated so badly, it was severely infected and not healing. Any way you called and took me through the process of packing it and it healed from the inside out (it was, 90 percent severed through the first joint pad almost through to the nail on the other side). The ER had Steris tripped it (hard to believe.) It ruptured open and was turning black. Now, I cannot even see a scar!! R. C.

Foot Injury

I injured my foot simply by squatting down for an extended period. Now my left foot is swollen, red, and very warm to the touch. It seems to get worse when I stand on it. I had not been able to wear a shoe for two weeks because the swelling was so bad. I heard your broadcast on the "Power Hour" and ordered some clay. I used clay on my foot. I could not believe the results. I made a thick paste-like texture with the clay, applied it to my foot approximately a quarter inch thick. The clay seems to have a very powerful drawing effect. Within 30 minutes the swelling was reduced by at least two-thirds. The fluid was coming out of my foot so fast that the clay kept falling off at the point of injury, and I had to keep reapplying it until most of the fluid was gone. This stuff is great! It was amazing. After three applications like the one mentioned above, my foot returned to normal with no pain whatsoever. — Joe G.

Foot Pain

Severe pain on top of left foot and huge knot: I don't know what was wrong with my foot. It just started hurting and having severe muscle cramps between my big toe and my ankle. This hurt for months. I put my foot into a clay bath and honestly, the pain was so bad I almost didn't do the foot bath. But something told me not to stop. So, I put the foot in there and the pain subsided. After the foot bath, I put on a clay poultice and left it overnight. The next morning all the pain was gone and has not returned, and it's been a week now. I can tell it is not going to come back, and the knot is gone, too. – Linda W.

Injured Quadriceps

I had an injury to my left quadriceps. I applied thick clay masks to the area. It stayed like that for hours. I walked (limped) and worked in the garden, pulling hoses around, digging, etc. I was amazed how fast the pack/poultice pulled the pain out of the muscles. It had been a rather significant strain - actually, it was the third time I'd injured it recently and this one was a doozie! — Coya S.

Lump Infection on Foot

I had a lump on the ball of my foot. I had had a tumor removed from there 15 years earlier. This area was raised or swollen and slightly irritating. Sometimes not always. Usually, I noticed discomfort. Then I decided I was going to apply clay. I put the clay on and covered it with plastic to keep on my foot. Soon, for a couple of hours there was the worse odor, and the dog kept sniffing my foot. I checked the area and didn't see anything unusual, and I left the plastic on. I could feel relief. When the smell and a little drainage were over, the area was clean and no longer bothersome. This really worked! — Janet M.

Neck Injury

I was in a car accident 20 years ago and every single day, I've experienced severe neck, shoulder and back pain. After just one clay pack on my neck, the pain is gone. I used clay packs on my shoulder and lower back once, and that pain is hugely reduced. I will continue to work on this. — Linda W.

Severe Cut to the Shin

Hi Perry A~, a long time ago I interviewed you on The Power Hour, I just want you to know how much I still appreciate you and the clay. I take it every day, twice a day, just a teaspoon with two ounces of water. I'm healthy as a horse. The other thing,...I was working and fell down, not seeing the " hole" in a trailer on the back of a truck. My shin bone was lacerated. This was 11 days ago. It went deep. Once I was able, after the hydrogen peroxide for the bacteria, and a little bit of silver solution, I slapped some clay on it then bandaged it up for five or six days. After that, I cleaned it again, the swelling around my leg was about 6 inches in diameter, it was deep. So, after the drill of hydrogen peroxide and silver solution I put more clay on. What was interesting, after that first cleaning, some of the original clay stayed put, well, after that, I gave it some sun, and the clay is still there, helping create the scab. I've also used a bit of aloe for the redness, now only about one inch on either side of the gash - and found some DMSO, which I dabbed on that redness a bit ago. Anyway, the clay is so incredible. I drink it, I use it for any type of skin wound or bite, I think it is the best thing in the world, and well, since the Creator made us out of the clay, we ought to keep using it as much as possible. – Sam S.

Shoulder Injury

My daughter Melanie introduced me to clay several months ago. Earlier this year, I sprained my right shoulder. I had been forced to take physical therapy on the same shoulder a few years earlier, so I was very concerned. Melanie came over one evening when I was in terrible pain. She prepared a clay compress, massaged my shoulder, applied the compress, and fixed a cup of tea for me. The pain decreased enough for me to sleep several hours that night. After continuing the compresses for three or four days, I had achieved almost a full range of motion. Unbelievable, compared to the weeks of therapy that it took to regain motion in my shoulder several years before. — Teddy J.

Wren Cyst Behind Ear

I had a cyst on the back of my head about 2 inches behind my left ear, just above the hairline. It had been there for a couple of years and was about the size of a pencil eraser. started drinking 1 oz of clay a day. JUST ONE DAY after starting the clay, the cyst started to swell and within 10 days was pus filled, round, flat and about the size of a quarter. I had taken my daughter to the doctor for a knee issue and asked him what it was. He told me it was a Wen cyst and would need to be surgically removed because there is a sac around the cyst that if it isn't removed, will cause the cyst to keep coming back. My mother and my grandmother both had them before, among other Aunts and Uncles on that side of the family. I continued to drink 1 oz of clay a day and then finally, after 12 days or so it ruptured. Within a few days it filled up again and then ruptured a second time. The cyst is gone and hasn't come back. That was almost 8 months ago. For the record I am 44. -Jennifer O.

DIABETES

Diabetes and Chronic Insomnia

I'm an elderly retired man who suffers from both diabetes and chronic insomnia. I've spent years taking prescription sleep aids with un-satisfactory results. My son, a naturopathic doctor, sent me 16 oz. of liquid clay and the clay book by Perry A~. I began taking the clay internally, and after two days my insomnia has all but disappeared. I've not slept this well in years! Furthermore, my average morning blood sugar readings are around 145; I've now been getting consistent readings of 75! I credit my newly found clay regime for both significant breakthroughs. It amazes me that such an affordable, natural, and effective cure has found me. I will tell everyone I know about this amazing clay. — Bob C.

Diabetic Facing Leg Amputation

My father has had diabetes for over 30 years as well as many other problems caused by diabetes. Ten years ago he lost his leg due to gangrene. He is now 73 years old. Two weeks ago, he developed gangrene on his foot. The swelling of the leg extended up to his knee. He had open wounds on his toes. The leg was in such bad condition that the only solution was to amputate it.

My father didn't want to go to the doctor. We decided to try to heal him with Calcium Bentonite Clay. We started applying clay on his foot all the way up to his knee two or three times a day. We used 2.2 pounds of clay per application. Between each application we would wash his leg in hydrogen peroxide and iodine. We kept the clay on his leg 24 hours a day. I must mention that we gave him antibiotics at the same time.

In two days, the swelling was gone and blood showed up in his wounds (which meant that it was circulating properly) and in less than a week his wounds started healing. My father said that for the first time he can feel pain in his foot. For years he couldn't feel anything in his foot due to neuropathy and poor circulation.

We are still following the same regimen of keeping a thick layer of clay on his foot/leg 24 hours a day. We plan to do that for another four to five weeks and see how it goes. — Giordona A.

Diabetic Infected Heel Ulcer

After last round of antibiotics. Doctor's only solution was to amputate her foot. Now see what clay did.

To the left: Improvement two weeks later. Swelling in ankle area down. Dried flakey skin

Day 4. of applying clay. Top black layer of gangrene infection gone. Scaly feet. Notice bottom of foot skin thick and dry. Elephant like texture. The clay will slough off the dead tissue and skin and new healthy new skin.

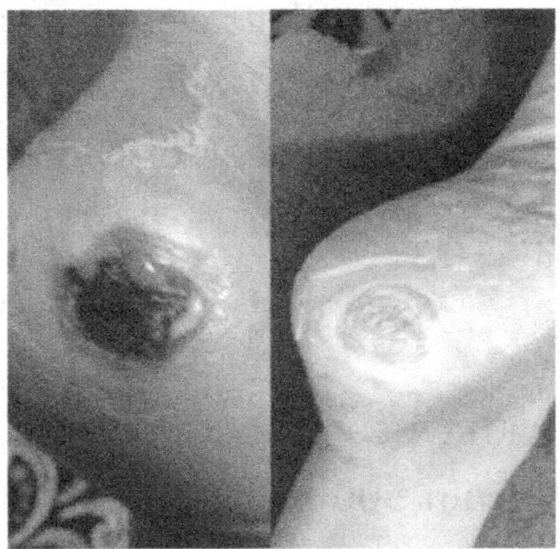

45 more day. (I stopped going to her house because of snake bite). I could not document the healing during this period.

These are pictures after she healed. I took these pictures 45 days from the day of my snake bite.

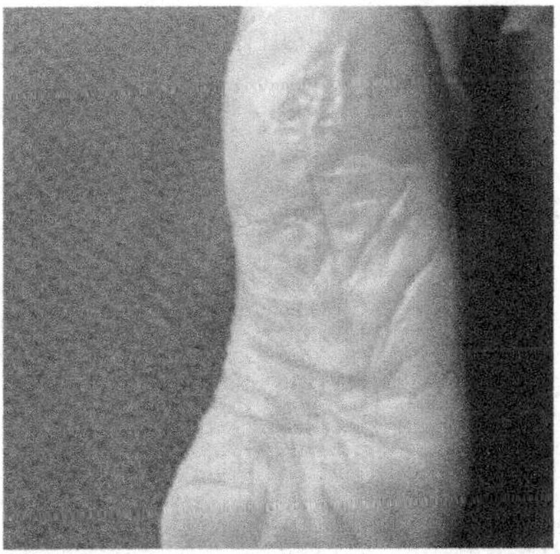

Notice new skin, new texture and skin on her sole and around ankle and sides. The clay ate the infection into a crater eating all the pus/ infection inward. Then it filled out. I wish I could have seen it filling out. – Frankie W.

Purple Legs and Numb Feet

I want to give a testimony about my 94-year-old diabetic father. Dad lives with us and usually has his pants on when sitting in his recliner. One day I went into his part of the house, and he wasn't wearing his pants. His legs were purple up to his knees and were numb. My wonderful wife packed clay around his legs twice a day with Press 'n Seal for two weeks. His legs are now white and pink. Praise the LORD! — David S.

Type II Diabetes

I was diagnosed with type 2 diabetes in May of last year. They put me on Metformin 500 mg 4 times a day. For the past few months, they have been really monitoring my progress, because the metformin was not doing what it was supposed to do. They had run several tests and said that I was going to have to go on shots. I ask them to let me try something first. I have been on the clay for 3 months now. They ran the same tests and show that my diabetes is doing better. They said that if I keep up with what I am doing I may be off the pills by the end of the year. Still working on it. — Kathy M.

Diabetic Foot Pain Stopped

Skip and I have been using the clay gel. It has removed pain from his diabetic feet and my body pain. We are gery pleased with the quick results. – Shelly K.

DIGESTIVE PROBLEMS

18 Years of Acid Reflux Stopped within 2 Days

You have heard of the song Amazing Grace, well here is my story about the amazing clay. For the past 18 or so years

I have been taking a 40 mg. daily dose of Nexium in order to control an acid reflux problem that never seemed to get better. If I missed a day the discomfort at times would be unbearable. Recently, over the last year or two the problem was exacerbating, and the doctors had no answers. Finally, at the urging of my daughter, I decided to try the clay to treat the horrible problem, as I was in the middle of a severe attack. My thought was I finally am going to need surgery to fix this. In desperation I contacted the very gracious, Perry A and she explained how to best mix and utilize the clay. After the very first dose, 1 oz. at a time, twice daily the problem almost miraculously vanished. Within 2 days I stopped the Nexium and have now been symptom free for 9 days. My daughter refers to this product as MAGICAL CLAY. Incidentally, I am 57 years old and have never before written a testimonial about anything! Amazed and thankful in Miami. — Brian S.

Bloating, Digestive Issues and Joint Pain

I LOVE CLAY!! It truly has helped to heal me. My digestive issues (severe bloating, bowel issues etc.) that have plagued me for years are so, so much improved. My joint pain, interestingly, is significantly less. I hadn't done anything new other than the clay and adding MSM (sulfur) to the diet, so I firmly believe that the clay is helping to reduce my overall inflammation in the body (which I have a ton of)...it is gentle yet so effective. It is a godsend, a miracle. I take one teaspoon in 2 oz of water every morning on an empty stomach. Thank you again for this wonderful product. It has helped me where nothing ele has been able to. — Erin S.

Clay Enemas Expel Parasites

I have done the clay enema 3 or 4 times now. Most recently, the next day I saw a lot of parasites in my stool. When I was trying to figure out what all was being released, I think I found some stones as well. Amazing! Thanks. Maura E.

Constant Diarrhea Stopped in 1 ½ Days

In October, I started to have pretty much constant diarrhea. Saw my GP (Australian name for a non- specialist MD.) and she put me on various medications with zero results.

She went on holidays and I saw another GP. She took me off all medications, to see what would happen. Went on unabated and needed a colonoscopy. Then I remembered the clay.

In early February I started to take liquid clay, 3-4 oz, 3 times a day and used hydrated clay on relevant areas.

The diarrhea stopped completely in one and a half days, never to return, and it is now April! Never had the colonoscopy.

I did however have a severe detox reaction, with beetroot red swollen glands under my armpits, so I put clay packs there as well and they too are now history.

Perry's book has become one of my most prized possessions, always within reach. -Mary C.

Colon Surgery and Chemo Recovery

Clay has been a valuable part of my personal wellness strategy as a colon cancer survivor. After multiple surgeries, a colostomy/ileostomy/takedown, chemo and radiation for stage 3 colon cancer, I was seeking ways to help my body recover from treatment. This clay became a trusted tool. My understanding was that it may draw out radiation from the body; it made great sense to me and was an easy addition to my daily routine. When colon cancer returned a year later as stage 4, I embraced a wellness plan that included juicing and raw foods, and I became much more diligent about drinking the clay every night. I chose to drink the clay each night through a second round of targeted radiation treatment in hopes of limiting additional damage to my bowels. I now take a clay bath after CT or PET scans due to the radiation exposure. Another way I like to use clay is to make a paste to brush my teeth. I will continue using clay as a part of my personal wellness strategy as a cancer survivor. — Sharon O., "Clear" Stage 4 Cancer Survivor

Colonics and Clay Cleanse

I am writing to let you know how the clay has changed my life and the lives of my clients. I have been a colon hydro therapist for six years now. I started by drinking the clay myself several days before my "spring cleansing," followed by my usual psyllium husk regimen. I went in for my cleanse and what came out was amazing — ropes of mucoid plaque. Now whenever my clients are preparing for their cleanse, I make sure they drink the clay. Everyone including myself actually just keeps drinking the clay. I am now up to 3 ounces three times per day, and I have never looked or felt better. I would recommend this product to any colon therapist that wants the best for their clients. It's the safest and most effective way to eliminate that old toxic waste. Just doing a colonic is not always enough!! Thanks again. — Vanessa G. of Cleansing Concept

Constant Diarrhea Stopped in 4 Days

I have a testimony to tell you about this clay; my sister Jacque

Carter first told me about the clay, so I bought a large container. This past June I began to have diarrhea and it wouldn't go away. It lasted a little more than two months. I felt awful, like I had a stomach bug. I ended up getting very dehydrated, so I went to the doctor and did bloodwork, and stool samples ...they couldn't find the problem, so that's when I decided to start taking the clay every day, 3-4 oz. of liquid clay, 3x a day. That's when I started noticing I wasn't going to the bathroom as much, and I could actually get some nutrients from the food I was eating. It took about four days, and I can tell you my diarrhea was gone! No more stomach pains, or nausea, or cramps. I feel like I've been completely healed from whatever it was! Thank goodness I learned about the clay. I'm taking it once a day now, just for maintenance.

Thank you for your good work to tell people about this wonderful natural substance! -Karis L.

Crohn's Disease

The clays I've had the best luck with for my Crohn's thus far are any type safe for internal use that SWELL. Now I wouldn't say this to any crohnnies out there who have stricturing in their gut, as the potential for a partial or total blockage is high. These clays work for me as I no longer have any stricturing after a surgery 8 years ago that removed a foot of strictured small intestine & cecum. Currently, I've had problems confined to the large intestine that respond quite well to clays. I believe they do a great job to remove all the excess water, mucus, and bacteria in the gut.

I hope this post helps any of you newcomers to the list with digestive issues. I'm thrilled to have found a natural product that helps to control some of the difficult symptoms of this disease. -Mike Y.

Heartburn and Rotator Cuff Pain

I have been using it for over 18 months now. It alleviated rotator cuff pain that was so bad that I could not sleep at night in just 24 hours. Not to mention eliminating heartburn so bad that I was using a 12-hour heartburn pill and eating Tums like candy after that wore off! Hoping to avoid any chance of cancer by changing my body's pH and I am thinking that it is helping things that I don't even realize. I also use it on burns, cuts, stings, sore bottom (way better than Desitin ointment.) I will be using clay for the rest of my life! — Jeffery S.

IBS-D

I have a new life because of this clay, and so does my sister. I started having IBS-D after having huge doses of antibiotics for strep in college. I am turning 60 this summer so that is a long time. I take 1 T. of liquid clay in the morning and 1 T. of liquid clay in the evening, both in kombucha. We make our own kombucha now and it is a good probiotic. I never miss a dose. I have noticed that the clay has helped me in levels. At first it slowed my system down some and made the stool more solid (sorry folks) but I was still going four times a day. Then the next level was that it did the same thing but more. I have just reached a fourth level where I only go twice a day and it is totally controllable. I have the urge but if I am in a car or it is inconvenient, I am okay.

The interesting thing was that for the first month or two my stool was smelly (sorry again). I think that even though I was going a lot - obviously the clay was sweeping out toxins, overgrowth of Candida, etc. My grandson is 11 and he spent a week in the NICU when he was born and was on high doses of antibiotics. He struggles with the same thing. I put him on clay, and he has done really well on it. vLynn, I have a new life because of Living Clay, and so does my sister. I started having IBS-D after having huge doses of antibiotics for strep in college. I am turning 60 this summer so that is a long time. I take 1 T. of living clay in the morning and 1 T. of living clay in the evening, both in kombucha. We make our own kombucha now and it is a good probiotic. I never miss a dose. I have noticed that the clay has helped me in levels. At first it slowed my system down some and made the stool more solid (sorry folks) but I was still going four times a day. Then the next level was that it did the same thing but more. I have just reached a fourth level where I only go twice a day and it is totally controllable. I have the urge but if I am in a car or it is inconvenient, I am okay. I am going to Europe this summer and it will be two weeks of planes/trains and automobiles, actually planes, buses, Metro, tube, and shuttles. I would have been in a blind panic before Living Clay. I had a mild case of the flu this winter and there were a few times where I knew if I hadn't been taking the Living Clay, the stomach flu portion of influenza would have manifested itself. The interesting thing was that for the first month or two my stool was smelly (sorry again). I think that even though I was going a lot - obviously the Living Clay was sweeping out toxins, overgrowth of Candida, etc. My grandson is 11 and he spent a week in the NICU when he was born and was on high doses of antibiotics. He struggles with the same thing. I put him on clay and he has done really well on it. I have to say that I think I have a colicky/spastic colon congenitally.

Several members of my extended and immediate family have it. I think the high doses of antibiotics triggered an acute phase of it. With the clay it soothes that down. I tell everyone I know about this clay. we swear by this clay. Since I take so much clay, I have to have the best clay. - Melissa S.

Intestinal Parasites and Diarrhea

In the past week, I had a serious bout with intestinal parasites. Have experienced this before, and I knew the signs. I was losing energy quickly. And had episodes of diarrhea, almost not getting to the bathroom in time to avoid an accident. Anyway, I began liquid clay at 1:8 parts per water, taking twice then three times daily for the past six days. After just one clay drink of 1/4 Cup, I noticed improvement in stools. I'm still on 3X /day at same ratio. Feeling confident. Also, taking psyllium husk powder and will continue with this twice daily. For now, the diarrhea has been cured, although infrequently I feel gripey and some occasional gut pain. I think you have advocated drinking clay once daily for general health purposes. I guess this will be a protocol or regimen to follow indefinitely. -Pam R.

Leaky Gut

I had a blood test and my body is not absorbing all of my supplements. I have leaky gut. I have been drinking Calcium Bentonite Clay daily for nine months. It has helped with this condition plus many more health issues that I had going on within my body. I have a very sensitive system. I had no problem with clay being added daily. Clay is a wonder, and it did balance my pH. — Diane W.

Liver, Colon and Tapeworm

In March 2012 I went to my doctor not feeling well. He got the results of my blood work and sent me to the hospital for further testing. In the hospital they ran more blood work, X-rays, ultrasounds, MRI scans and colonoscopies. They told me I had tested positive for Echinococcus, a large tapeworm in my liver, (I was #11 in Canada to ever have this) and they had pictures of it and four cysts in my liver. I had anemia and had a blocked colon. The images from my colon also had unexplained images of tiny horseshoes that were highly reflective, and I was hyperthyroid.

The doctor's plan was to hospitalize me and address the parasite in my liver first with high doses of antibiotics and vitamin K for my liver, then to get special medication to be able to biopsy my liver to figure out how to treat the parasite. Two weeks of IV and then they had to transfer me to a larger center with a liver specialist five hours away.

The antibiotic treatment is now completed, a friend got me the clay, and I started to drink it without telling the doctors while in the hospital. I worked my way up to drinking 1 cup of the mixture three times a day. After two weeks of drinking the clay in the hospital they had acquired the special pills I had to take. The pills would coat my system with a film so that if eggs escaped from the parasite into my body, I would not die from anaphylactic shock. They took me for a scan to see the location of the parasite and the cysts on the liver. All the cysts on the liver were gone and only a bit of scar tissue the size of the fingernail on your pinky finger remained. The parasite was no longer there either. They concluded the blood test and pictures for the parasite were now incorrect and could not explain how the liver healed itself that quickly. They biopsied the liver and the test results came back negative for a parasite and negative for infection.

I was allowed to go home after 30 days and then the doctors wanted to do bowel surgery. It was explained I would lose a large section of my colon and possibly have to wear a bag. I was reluctant at the time and wished to continue my clay of 1 cup at 8 a.m., 1 cup at 2 p.m. and 1 cup at 9 p.m. My mixture was 1/4 cup of clay to 2 cups of water and shake well. I was still a bit hyperthyroid, and my anemia was 50% better and still on no medication. The doctors still think I am a miracle and have no idea I am on the clay, so they let me go home and I am told that the bowel will need surgery.

I continued from April 2012 to Aug 2012 (4 months) to faithfully drink 1 cup of clay three times per day. Also I put a half-inch poultice on my belly at night with Saran wrap and slept with it on. My belly had a rash that outlined the damaged intestine. In August I felt a sharp pain in my guts, and I knew it was my spleen. It had been angry for some time, and the pain came from the area were the rash had been. I spent 45 minutes in the bathroom with a bowel movement that was the size of a baseball. (Sorry to be graphic, but it is etched in my memory.)

It is now August, and I head to the hospital, and they do my sixth colonoscopy and more scans. The doctors tell me that my intestine has opened, and my spleen has fallen into the intestine. I am hospitalized waiting for emergency surgery. I am told I will lose my spleen, and I may go septic.

Again, I was on no medication and only on the clay. Three days later they did the surgery and opened my abdominal up 9 inches and remove 8 inches of intestine. I woke up surrounded by 5 doctors all wanting to know what I had done to change my intestinal health. One asked, "How did you change your intestines from a 70-year-old to a 20-year-old in four short months?" No more colitis, ulcers, diverticulitis, polyps etc.; it was a miracle. It is then I told them about the clay.

The surgeon says it definitely is Crohn's disease, and it has that look she has seen hundreds of times. We waited for the test results to come back, and it is negative for Crohn's. I spent one week in the hospital healing from abdominal surgery. They said that was record time as well. I put poultice on the staples in my stomach and slept at night with Saran wrap over it. The doctor took my staples out in nine days, and he said it looked like a four-week post operation and there was rust on the staples.

To this day I continue to drink clay but only 5 oz. three times a day. Truly a life saver and a blessing. It is amazing when used properly.

I find people do not stay on it long enough nor do they take large enough doses. One of the biggest mistakes is they stir it instead of shaking it. At the first sign of a bit of discomfort they stop using it. I get asked a lot if the clay just sits in your colon. Well, I tell ya, after six colonoscopies in four months, if the doctors saw clay, I would have known about it. Instead, they saw unexplainable healing. — Marg L.

Long Time Digestive Problems

I had digestion problems for a long time. So I was amazed that I enjoyed immediate improvement from my very first dose of the clay. It's become a daily dose! Also, the clay has worked for me in several ways. When I had a bug bite on my hand I was awake with severe itching. I made a poultice of the clay. I applied it to my hand, wrapped it with plastic wrap and had immediate relief. The itching did not return. Next, I had relief for my dry eyes for several days when I used the poultice on a cotton pad applied to my eyes for about a half hour. Yay clay! – Patty K.

Severe Stomach Pains

I have severe stomach pain going on seven days now, the doctor has no idea what it could be, I had blood work and urine test. She checked for hernia, kidney stone everything. Still has no idea what is causing it. If you can add more details on the next part. I started the clay on February 15th it started working immediately each day I was feeling better. Today February 13th, I can say I feel 100% healed. I'm going to continue the clay for the 21 days, and maintain after. - Helen D.

Toxicity Exhausts 8-year-old

My first experience with calcium bentonite clay for healing happened back in 1978. I am now a Chiropractor and Acupuncturist, but many years ago people would ask my opinion on health issues in a purely casual manner just because I had been involved in the natural food industry and herb and spice wholesale industry for many years. I did not know much but if asked I would share my opinion. I had learned about healing clay after reading Our Earth Our Cure back in the 1970's. It spoke of the tradition of using clay in France for a multitude of therapeutic and cosmetic purposes.

Now to the story. A woman asked me about her 8-year-old son. His problem was he was very tired and sleepy most of the time. He had not always been this way. This had come on gradually and now was a genuine problem. She took him to her pediatrician because the school nurse said he had some kind of attention deficit disorder and was recommending he be put on medication. The pediatrician said he could find nothing wrong with the child after an exam and a lab workup, and it was up to her what the next step should be.

I asked what the boy's symptoms were and she said he was tired and sleepy all the time. He would sleep all night, go to school and fall asleep in class and come home from school and sleep more instead of playing with his friends. This did not sound like ADD to me or to the pediatrician, but the doctor could find nothing wrong. Back in the 1970's people were already talking about toxicity issues and all the ways to help the body cleanse itself using diet and herbs. I did not feel trained to give advice on diet or herbs, but I remembered the stories I had read about using clay externally for detoxification. This was before I learned of the internal uses of clay. In any case I told her if she wanted to try, she could do clay packs over his liver area which I thought could either do nothing or might be of help. I instructed her how to do it and where she could get some bulk green clay locally. I recommend she do one clay pack over the liver area daily for a week. To me that was enough time to see if it would help. I told her it would be very messy, but it was inexpensive and might help. She agreed. In one week of once daily clay packs over his liver for 30-60 minutes using green calcium bentonite clay powder he was his normal healthy self. No more fatigue, excess sleep or problems staying awake in school.

She called me to thank me for my suggestion. I enquired further to try to understand the situation. How could he have gotten so toxic? She said she had been thinking about that all week and something occurred to her. This all began after they had moved to right outside Corpus Christi, Texas, a city with many petrochemical processing plants. She said the water from the tap was slightly yellow in color and had a bad smell and taste so they bought and consumed bottled water for drinking and cooling. But they did bathe in that tap water. Her family did not think that was an issue if they did not drink the water. Well after her son's dramatic recovery she and her husband realized that her son, who liked to take baths had absorbed enough of the chemicals to create a significant problem which she now had the solution to. This was an important anecdotal story that I never forgot and wanted share. I hope this can be of value to others. Dr. B.

DISEASE AND INFECTIONS

13-year Illness Gone After A Month On Clay

I am turning 25 in just a few days and have been taking the clay internally three times a day for a month now. I have been sick on and off for 13 years and the traditional doctors could never find a cure for me. I had just accepted that I had a sickly body and a weak immune system. I had bald spots and began fainting at the age of 12, then at 20 I became nauseous all of the time. When I graduated from college, I was so sick that I needed to take some time off before obtaining my master's degree. I began researching different ways to detoxify my body. I started getting colonics, bought an infrared sauna, and eating raw food. But it was only when I started drinking Calcium Bentonite clay that I started feeling like a normal human being for the first time in 13 years!!! After 3 weeks, I had an energy surge. I started wanting to do things I hadn't wanted to do in a long, long time...simple things like taking a hike with my family. This clay has given me back my passion to live my life to the fullest. Before the clay, I was sick, exhausted, and depressed. Now, I feel alive! People are even saying how good my skin looks! Like I have a glow!! I will, without a doubt, be a lifelong customer. Anytime I have any questions, I just call Perry A. and she answers my calls directly and with such kindness and grace. This clay truly saved my life. — Stephanie D.

Anemia and Thyroid

My doctor told me I would have to face six months of iron injections in the butt to deal with my anemia, and that my thyroid was Graves' disease, and they would have to kill it, and I would be on meds for the rest of my life. My GP said I had done so much for myself with this clay that he would like to put it to the test. I was to report every Monday at the same time for blood work, and we would monitor it. Inside of four weeks I was no longer anemic nor was I hyper thyroid. The doctors told me that thyroids never heal themselves.

To this day I continue to drink clay but only 5 oz. three times a day. Truly a life saver and a blessing. It is amazing when used properly. — Marg L.

Breast Cancer

An Amish lady I knew put a thick clay poultice hydrated with Miracle II Soap. Hers was so advanced; she had kept it a secret. Anyway, she refused typical cancer treatments and used the

above, along with fresh burdock leaves on top. The result was so profound that even the hospice nurse claimed she had never witnessed the like. The electromagnetic properties of the hydration gel complement about any alternative method.
I am also witnessing breast cancer with another alternative modem and with my own dog's external tumor on his hind quarter.
We love clay, first and foremost! – Tracy G.

Cleared of Stage 4 Colon Cancer

"Your Calcium Bentonite Clay has been a valuable part of my personal wellness strategy as a colon cancer survivor. After multiple surgeries, a colostomy/ileostomy/takedown, chemo and radiation for stage 3 colon cancer, I was seeking ways to help my body recover from treatment. This Calcium Bentonite Clay became a trusted tool. My understanding was that it may draw out radiation from the body; it made great sense to me and was an easy addition to my daily routine. When colon cancer returned a year later as stage 4, I embraced a wellness plan that included juicing and raw foods and I became much more diligent about drinking the clay every night. I chose to drink the clay each night through a second round of targeted radiation treatment in hopes of limiting additional damage to my bowels. I now take a clay bath after CT or PET scans due to the radiation exposure. Another way I like to use the clay is to make a paste to brush my teeth. I will continue using the clay as a part of my personal wellness strategy as a cancer survivor."
Sharon O., "Clear" Stage 4 Cancer Survivor

Editor's notes: Sometimes Clay Believers make decisions on their own on how to use the clay for their specific needs on their own. Perry

Foot Fungus

Last month I got fungus/athlete's foot between a couple of my toes (feet get wet and the area doesn't dry... I called it jungle rot when I was in basic training). I used over-the-counter treatment for the first two days, but it continued to hurt and not heal up. So, on the third day I tried the clay, and the pain was gone immediately and the sore healed within 24 hours. Great stuff!! — Julie B.

Fibromyalgia and Chronic Fatigue Relief from Liver Poultices

I've been diagnosed with several health conditions including fibromyalgia, chronic fatigue, sarcoidosis and heavy metal toxicity. One of my main symptoms is severe food allergies and mal absorption of nutrients. I started taking daily clay baths and foot soaks and drinking liquid clay internally and immediately felt much better.

I've also noticed a big benefit from having liver poultices on a regular basis. As soon as I start putting the clay on my liver, I can feel my body relax significantly and something just "unwinds" internally.

It's a very interesting feeling. I usually must go to the restroom within five minutes of putting the clay on, and I feel lighter and happier and more relaxed in general after doing a half-hour- to two-hour poultice. If I feel irritated or out of sorts about something, putting liver poultice on immediately helps improve my mood. It's great! — Audrey W.

Wife's Fibromyalgia

The first thing I would like to say is "THANK YOU" for making your this clay available to the world...!!! As you know, over a year ago Linda got fed up with mainstream medicine continuously feeding her drugs, drugs, and more drugs in what an attempt was to control (not CURE) her Fibromyalgia. After hearing you speak on the Power Hour, she decided to take charge of her own life by giving up ALL her meds overnight (cold turkey) and turn to the living clay. Knowing how things work (or don't work) when it comes to the FDA, you could only say it might help. What an understatement...!!! Today, Linda has lost almost 60 pounds (without exercising) and for the past month or so has been mowing our lawn (as well as my mother's) and is basically a new person. I am not saying she is cured but the truth is, I haven't seen her this physical in 15 plus years...she even went out and bought a bicycle to ride...thank you both again for giving me my wife back!!! Dan R.

Gout

I have been drinking clay regularly, and I usually suffer from gout attacks. Since I have been drinking the clay, I have had only one minor attack. I doubt that this is a coincidence. I really believe the clay is having a cleansing effect on my body. — George B.

H Pylori

We have gotten rid of the Pylori Bacteria and the only thing we have found is the clay that would get rid of it, other than antibiotics (and not sure if the antibiotics always work) and we avoided the antibiotics. It took 2 large doses of clay, one dose a day. For adults and children adult size, we used 1/3 cup of hydrated clay, all in one setting. For the little ones (our grandson was right at 2 years old and about 26 pounds), we used 2 tablespoons of hydrated clay. If you prefer the liquid, just dilute the hydrated clay with good water and let sit long enough to make the liquid. We had to dose the whole family all the same time so for the little ones you can mix it in yogurt or something that they would like. I have found that when the little one's "need" the clay ...they gladly eat it in whatever you put it in. That has been our experience. Love my clay!!! — Dee E.

Lyme's Disease

Clay has been a life saver for me. I was dying from undiagnosed Lyme's Disease, low/slow thyroid, gall stones, tooth and gum infections...I am healed and getting better every day.

It all started in 2007. I started feeling bad and kept going downhill. I started feeling cold all the time, hair falling, body temp 94 in the a.m. I was constantly sick and felt like I was a dead woman walking. Finally, in June, 2010, my doctor decided to have me tested for Lyme's Disease. I tested positive. He put me on doxycycline for 3 weeks. I did not get better, I got worse! Believe me when I say I tried everything. Then I found out about clay and talked to Perry A~.

The bottom line, less than a month on this Life Saving Clay and I feel like a brand-new person. My gums have cleared up and all my problems have gone away. I drank Clay 2 ounces 2 times a day, ate clay cookies, took 5 foot soaks for 30 minutes in one month plus 1 clay bath. (I put a liquid clay mix of 1 part Clay to 6 parts of warm water in rubber boots up to my ankles and massaged coconut oil on feet afterwards.) The healing began WELL BEFORE a month. So, LESS than a month, I feel well again, and I am well on my way to a FULL recovery!! — Jae C.

Lyme's Disease - Chronic

It's just fabulous for anyone but especially for Chronic Lyme Disease, the root of all my health issues. People with Lyme Disease and co-infections (Borellia, Babesia, Bartinella, and Mycoplasma in my case) absolutely need to rid the body of the spirochete die-off but also parasites, heavy metals and toxicities that contribute to the total body burden. Whether by pharmaceutical or natural antibiotics, (my personal protocol includes immune support products from my brilliant father and highly antimicrobial therapeutic-grade essential oils, specifically YoungLiving - also found in nature.) once destroyed, the dead spirochetes must be removed from the body or will become neurotoxins. This is done in many ways but very simply, painlessly, and effectively with clay. I bathe in it regularly and take it internally to cleanse my body of all the nasty bugs and toxins. I must say, God knows what He is doing. In His very creation, He gave us all we need to heal and maintain health naturally. I give Him all the glory. — Carla S.

Mosquito bite to Staph Infection to MRSA

I had a mosquito bite on the back of my right leg that I scratched and got infected with what the doctor claimed as a granular staph infection. Since it was granular the 2 bouts of antibiotics had no effect on the wound. It was still necropsying so I knew I needed to find something that would pull the infection out of the wound topically. The infection was now what I believe to be MRSA. I searched the internet and eventually came upon your website among others that described the healing powers of the clays. I ordered the bentonite clay and started applying a wet paste of the clay on the wound the first week of December in 2011. There was a noticeable change of the wound within 2 days. It was not as red and "angry" as it had been prior to the clay. I would mix the clay with distilled water and apply it directly over the wound and cover it with part of a collard green leaf (I found it worked better than cellophane wrap) and wrapped the area of my leg with an ace bandage. I would change the dressing 3 times a day for the first two weeks and then reduced it back to 2 times a day after that. By mid-January (approx. 7 weeks) the "infection" was cleared. The wound is still healing from the whole that it left in my leg, but at least the necropsying has stopped, and the underlying tissue is healing. In all, it has taken about 3 months to get to this point. The clay was very soothing to the area of the wound. The pain associated with the infection was bad and within 3 weeks the soreness had subsided. I know that it sounds like a long time but with the depth of the wound and the infection involved, it certainly was faster and less evasive than the alternative of various antibiotics and possible skin grafting that I was told was to be expected.

I am glad to say that I won out on all levels! The wound is healing, and I did not have to sacrifice my bank account and relative health to achieve this outcome. If you're an outdoors person like me, this is a product that is a must for your "medicine cabinet"! — Connie M.

MRSA Infection

I used thick clay poultices 3 times a day for my 50-cent size MRSA infection/boil. I got immediate relief from the pain and the swelling that was past my wrist. I have not needed to take any ibuprofen since. I was taking 800 mg every 4 to 6 hrs. I am reluctantly taking the antibiotics but feel that it was the clay that prompted my speedy healing. I still have a rather large boil, but it is now draining. I am so excited about the clay!! Why are the doctors not using it? I am planning on telling as many people as I can about it! Now I am putting a bathtub in my backyard for mud baths!! — Denise W.

Night Sweats from Lyme's Disease

When I get night sweats from Lyme disease - I get up and drink an oz. or 2 liquid clay in water - it always helps cut the fever, then I can sleep. — Coya S.

Parkinson's Tremors

I have Parkinson's and when I drink the clay, my tremors are cut in half, and my muscles are stronger. Thanks for this product. — Carol E.

Urinary Tract Infection - Reoccurring

I have suffered from recurring urinary tract infections for several years. I have had so many that they usually go straight to the kidney and are resistant to the antibiotics that are used to treat it since I have used them so much and have developed a tolerance to them. I have undergone a cystoscopy to be sure there are no abnormalities that would cause this, and all was normal. To completely rid myself of infection I have had to use Cipro for twice as long as the usual treatment, sometimes longer. Leviquin was to be the next drug to try. In January, at Mayo Clinic, I saw an urologist and was put on Cipro as a preventative, taking one to two pills after intercourse since the infections invariably occur at these times. This has been a problem in my marriage not to mention the frequency of infection and all that goes along with that. Recently, I had the bright idea to try an experiment.... :-) You can probably guess what I did. Since most often the cultures show Ecoli, I can assume it is caused by bacteria that enter the urethra during intercourse regardless of how much I wash or clean myself before and after. So, after intercourse, I applied a little of the clay mask to the point of entry for these bacteria. Yep, you guessed it! No need for antibiotics and no infection. It was fabulous! — Anonymous

Weeping Leg Ulcer

I had been battling a 5.5-inch painful, weeping leg ulcer with antibiotics with no success when I thought to try the clay. I applied a generous amount of hydrated clay to the wound and covered it. It was cold at first and gradually became warm. When I felt the heat, I put a second poultice on. In 24 hours, my leg ulcer has dried to a scab and little flaky skin and was reduced to one-fourth of an inch in size. I am now applying a third poultice to clear up that last one-fourth inch. — Mike T.

Yeast Infection

I have been prone to yeast infections my whole life, especially in hot weather. Well, I received my first yeast infection and I took a clay bath then made a paste and applied it to the Urethra area and drank 2 oz twice a day and the itch and pain was gone when I woke up. I have never received relief like that with any medication, and I have not had a yeast infection since. — Adriana V.

EYES AND SINUSES

Clay for Dry Eyes

I'm excited to report that the Clay eye wash is helping my dry eye issue. Since I've been doing a daily rise with the eye solution my eyes are more hydrated and less irritated during the day. It's been an incredible relief. Is there any limitation to how long I can continue to use the eye wash in this manner? Also, after reading another user's report of teeth whiting from brushing with the clay. I started doing that. Now I brush daily with clay. Again, I've been amazed at the results. -Lori S.

Nasty Eye Infection - Downs/Autistic Son

A 29-year-old Downs/Autistic son COMPLETELY CURED of a nasty eye infection. He was very cooperative (Autistic people are mostly 'not comfortable' outside their comfort-zone) so it must have felt very soothing to him. It only took about 1 day of 4, 10-minute sessions. I brewed Coriander seeds in filtered water - then chilled. I made your 3-1 clay poultice recipe. Soaked cotton balls in the chilled tea, then piled the clay mask onto the cotton balls and treated both eyes, even though only one looked infected. Asked him to close his eyes and just laid the trans-dermal treatment on his lids. Just held them there and we sang together for about 10 minutes each session.

After each application, I rinsed his eyes several times with the Coriander tea using numerous cotton balls, as to not cross-contaminate. Lots of white, stringy debris removed from his eyes after each session. DAY TWO: Back to normal. He WELCOMED the treatments. — Sara R.

Pink Eye – Conjunctivitis - Clay Treatment for my 'Pink Eye'

I am 55 and a contact lens wearer of 40 YRS and have admittedly been over-using them, thus, the worst case of conjunctivitis in my personal history. My eye appeared as if it was 'bleeding' and was swollen shut. I feared for my sight in that eye. I mixed a fresh batch of the drinkable 8/1 mixture and used as an eyewash cup and rinsed as often as I could tolerate. I know that putting clay directly into the eye is not recommended, but I was desperate. In addition, I consumed additional liquid clay and time permitting, put poultice on a cosmetic pad and taped over my eye. The healing did not happen overnight. It took much due diligence, yet at the same time, and living in this get-well-quick world in which we live, the results were quite miraculous. I added another natural plant-based-product as I saw my progress, called EYEBRIGHT. I had never heard of this plant before. It really helped, after the clay healing, with resolving the lingering redness. Thanks for all your help. I have called on you before and you have never let me down, nor has THE CLAY. — Sara R.

Sinus Problems

I have had sinus problems for the past 25 years and my nose has NEVER been this cleared up. I've been on Allegra, Claritin, Singular and NONE of them ever worked. I started drinking clay on Feb, 19, 2014 and the very next day my nose was NOT stuffy anymore. I've been drinking clay for a month and a week and my sinus problems are GONE. This stuff is amazing. — Julie W.

GENERAL HEALTH

35-Year-old Bump on Nose Going Away

After listening to several clay seminars, I started putting the clay paste on a bump that had develop on the side of my nose. This thing has been there for 35+ years and just seemed to pop up, i.e. not due to any injury. It has been about 6 weeks and the bump is almost completely gone. I put the paste on and take it off several times during the day and then wear a thin smear at night. Works great! - Julie B.

Allergy Relief

Warning!! Bentonite Clay has side effects!! IT CURED MY HAY FEVER!!!

It's really refreshing to have positive side effects from a health product; unlike the negative ones we get from pharmaceuticals. Like using Bentonite clay, only to find out my 30 years of suffering from Hay Fever is now a thing of the past. I added Bentonite clay as a detox and when spring came around, I noticed no runny nose, no sneezing nothing. The TV told me we had a really bad day coming up, but when it arrived I noticed nothing again! When I searched for "Bentonite Clay allergies" I found this site, and it confirmed exactly what I was experiencing.

As a child I went to every allergy expert in the country! I went to the doctor's office weekly to take injections of allergens for my system to be more accustomed to them, but it didn't work, those so-called experts know nothing! All I needed was a bit if dirt in my diet, I wish I knew this 30 years ago, it would have prevented 30 years of suffering! I'm also glad I'm no longer contributing any more money to big pharma's antihistamine scam!!! Thanks for getting the information out there, its vitally important for people get this information. — James C.

Blood Pressure, Ganglion Cyst and Blood Work

I just wanted you to know that everything is going great. I

have cut my BP med in half, with my doctor's blessing. My ganglion cysts in my wrists have completely disappeared as well. Yesterday, I had blood work done at the doctors, and all my values are getting better, and I believe it is all due to the clay. I have not changed anything else! I'm very grateful for this product! – Tamara L.

Blood Pressure Lower and Thyroid Improvement

My husband and I have been drinking and using clay topically for over 2 1/2 years. The health benefits have been subtle, consistent lower blood pressure, my hypothyroid medication has been cut in half, no chronic sinusitis, improvements in our digestion. We are in our mid 60's feeling well and strong. Thank you for such a great product. — Noreen T.

Cesarean Scar

I had a cesarean for my twins 21 years ago (and not a young mother) and put clay on scar straight away. It became red and itchy. My doctor told me to stop using clay. I rang Dextreit and he said it was a sign that it was working pulling out some chemicals. I can't remember if I continued using it or waited a few days until I got back home. When I went for my check up the doctor was amazed how quickly my womb got back to normal and he could hardly see the scar. — Corrine M.

Drinking Calcium Bentonite Clay

I wanted to send this off because I'm amazed at how easy it is to drink this Calcium Bentonite Clay. I had been taking plain old (food grade) DE and this clay is soooo much easier to take. Plus, the DE would pick me up in the morning with energy and then I'd crash around 2 p.m. I don't have the wild ups and downs with this stuff. I'm still in the process of a lot of 'detox' symptoms but just being able to 'enjoy' drinking this is a real plus for me.

–Renee C.

Dry Eyes and Whiter Teeth

I'm excited to report that the clay eye wash solution is helping my dry eye issue. Since I've been doing a daily rise with the eye solution my eyes are more hydrated and less irritated during the day. It's been an incredible relief. Also, after reading another user's report of teeth whiting from brushing with the clay. I started doing that. Again, I've been amazed at the results. Many Thanks! — Lori S.

Feel Like a New Person

In less than a month after I start using the clay, I feel like a brand-new person. Liquid clay 2 times a day, eating the clay cookies, foot soaks (5), (1) bath with 1 cup.

My husband uses it also. His feet used to hurt, no more. He does the rubber boot foot bath too. He packed his teeth 3 nights in a row, tooth infection gone! He is 72 yrs old.

He said he feel like a new person as well. He started putting thin layer behind his ears last night as instructed regarding ringing and hearing loss.....will get back to you with results. Blessings! – Jae C.

Flu Avoidance After Exposure

Last week one of my co-workers came back to work after being out for a week with the flu. When she came back to work, she was having a relapse -- she was still sneezing violently, with total disregard to who she sneezed on, blowing her nose all over the place, and still running a fever. Her face was flushed red. She handled the phone, she handled every doorknob in the place, she ate in the kitchen, she used the same bathroom. I was so upset, because I just knew I'd caught the flu from her. I went home and put 1/4 cup of clay in a 20-ounce water bottle. I literally carried it around with me for about 3 days and drank it throughout the day. I would re-fill it as needed. And I did NOT catch the flu from her!!! I did not take any other vitamins or supplements, just the strong clay water!!! — Jan D.

Food Poisoning and Heartburn

Well, it's only been 2 days, and I have been completely cured of my first malady.

Christmas time I suffered with a terrible case of food poisoning. My stomach, digestive system, bowels had not been the same since, I was on the verge of incontinence. I thought I would have to give up my daily yoga practice as the uncomfortable gas, and heartburn was too much to struggle with daily. After taking the clay internally for 2 days I AM CURED!!!!!!!!!! and so-o-o-o-o-o happy. I have been singing the praises of this clay ever since. At 62 there are certainly other issues that I am living with and will keep you posted as progress develops. — Barbara S.

General Health

I have been using clay for almost 2 months and love the results. I use it for facials, hair mask, tooth paste and ingest it for general health. I am no longer on any meds and I feel great.

Believing & claying are the natural medications that I've needed all along. The clay is a natural healing source and natural is always better than the synthetics created by man. – Joanne G.

Getting off Zoloff and Depression Gone

My Husband Tom and I have been on the clay detox regime for 3 days now. We are both feeling so much better. I went to bed late last night and got up at 8:00, which is unusual for me since I've been getting off of Zoloft. Tom had deep depression on Sunday when he started the clay and now it's all gone. I have good energy, too. I'm ready to say, "Yes, this stuff really works!" I cannot express how glad we are that we discovered the clay, it's truly amazing. Thanks for the help and support. — Ariel M.

Gluten Intolerance

Our 13-year-old is intolerant to gluten. She takes a teaspoon of the clay mask. On a recent holiday she ate some before every gluten containing meal. And it really helped. Now we are home, she is still gluten free but if she has a little bit of gluten then she has a little clay usually prior to eating it and every night she has a bit before bed.

It works though...enough time has passed to see that the recurring behavior patterns are not apparent after gluten consumption. For a 13-year-old, she really impresses me, with how she takes the clay daily. Clay really has turned or lives around. The change to our family is massive. I can't thank you enough. — Lizzy D.

Hangover Gone with Clay

Hi! I don't recommend anyone make a habit of this, but I went to a party on Saturday and decided to have a little more wine than I knew was going to be good for me and just pay the price. But, when I got home, I took some clay before I went to bed, along with a good amount of water. When I woke up the next morning, I was better than I expected to be, and took some more clay, and felt pretty darn good all day! — Mary Beth D.

Health Crisis

I was in a health crisis. I was throwing up daily from other medical treatment and meds. I was wasting away and didn't know how to stop it. Not keeping food down was starting to make me feel a little crazy. I have been drinking a small dose of one teaspoon hydrated clay on the 1 to 3 ratio with lots of water three times a day. If really sick, I sip on a bottle of water and clay. I have been doing this for about one week, it is changing my life. Thank you so much for providing me with a tool to save myself. It feels so good to keep food down. I am slowing and starting to feel like myself and feel peaceful again. I asked again and I received my solution-clay!!! — Tiffany K.

Heartfelt Gratitude for Calcium Bentonite Clay Uses

Thank you, Miss Perry, for the opportunity to express from my heart how I feel about this product, your Specific Calcium Bentonite Clay. I have been an organic nut/ health nut sense 1971. The supplements did a good job at helping me maintain a good status of what I would call good health, such as four minor head colds from 1971 to 2015. In June 2014 I lost my wife of 57 years, so I would classify myself as somewhat lost for a period of time. I had a double bypass in January 2015 which if I had known of the benefits of this remarkable clay, I would have leaned very heavy on getting healed by natural means. I consider medical doctors and pharmaceutical medicine as alternative medicine and natural products as the proven method of healing along with the Word of God. I started taking this clay the 20th of March along with the attitude that I will walk in perfect health as long as I have breath. At first, I went through a period of weakness and was a little depressed. I now know that the clay was removing products from my body and the body was fighting back but it lost and I have never felt so good and full of energy in my life. Everything your book says, I find to be so very true and this clay has corrected everything I know of that was not functioning the way it was designed to function. I desire to experiment with this clay on livestock and in my garden. I am a physicist, so this kind of thing comes natural with me. I am writing a book titled "Ranching With Jesus" because I have applied co-laboring with my Lord in a major way and have seen the results which is quite like the good results of applying clay internally and externally to your body, it works. I was skeptical when I first heard of this product because I get so many handouts written by a professional writer indicating this product will do this or that and your money is guaranteed to be returned if you are not satisfied with its performance. This is a marketing concept which I don't care for. It is a hungry greedy world. I am recommending your book and this clay to everyone I know and some I don't know, because I don't know of anyone that doesn't need to detox. Thank you, so much dear lady, for helping so many people, actually, coming to their rescue as you did me. Charley L.

Hormones, Heavy Bleeding and Loss of Libido

Regarding my hormones: I was experiencing heavy bleedings and loss of libido for many months. I tried the medical route but didn't help, then I tried Traditional Chinese Medicine and helped a bit, but I was still not happy. One day I heard Paul Chek talking about clay and then I found you.

I started taking clay and in 2 to 3 months slowly the bleeding became normal, and the libido came back. My body felt a lot stronger, healthier and younger. I also had many healing crisis that lasted few weeks at the time, but I didn't stop taking clay although I reduced intake somewhat. — Maria T.

Highly Allergic and Sensitive

I wanted to say thank you very, very much for supplying this kind of product. I'm one of those people that is allergic to everything- including corn, and finding detoxifying and healing methods, or cleaning supplies that work as well as your products, is difficult! I drink liquid clay every day, and my severe reactions to perfumes seem to be highly diminished. I also drink a dose right after any exposure. My constantly toxic system feels really soothed. — Nikki F.

Lymph Gland Swollen and Painful

I have had extreme pain in my left arm and discovered a swollen lymph gland, a knot or swelling on the upper arm and another at the fold. The pain was in the shoulder and deep seemingly to the bone in the upper and lower arm extending to two middle fingers. One night it hurt me enough make a doctor's appointment but, in the meantime, I thought to cover my whole arm including the armpit in clay. The lymph node was extremely painful and upon touching it seemed much of the pain radiated from it. At first the clay seemed to intensify the pain, but it did ease the pain down to almost nothing. Upon removal of the wrap and clay, the lymph node swelling was diminished and pain down at least 75%. The doctor ordered a CT scan, and I've been waiting for them to call and schedule for almost 2 weeks. I am also drinking 1oz twice a day of liquid clay when I remember but most often once a day.

Right now, I'm seeing and feeling so much improvement, I may decline the CT scan. On the night of awesome pain, I wanted the scan to know what was going on in my body. With the healing I am experiencing using the clay, prayer and affirmations that I am perfectly healthy, I don't think I even want the CT. I have used clay minimally to this point all the while sharing the miracle of it with others. Now I can celebrate my personal experience that CLAY IS AWESOME! — Dena N.

Mammogram Report

I've been in the high-risk diagnostic mammography group for many years (due to family history. Two maternal aunts and my sister all had breast cancer at a young age. I've been getting mammograms since I was 30. Well, today when I showed up for my high-risk mammogram, they told me that I had "graduated" to the regular mammography screening group. I even had them double-check to be sure. That was good news - and bad news, because at the high-risk assessments you find out that day if you are clear or not. This regular group receives a letter in the mail in about a week to let you know if you need more studies or if you're okay. I kindly requested feedback sooner rather than later if possible. They told me they were all too busy --- but as I was leaving after the x-rays, they called me back (which give me a jolt) to let me know that they did find time and that I looked good! I went home and gave my little breasts a clay mask coat for an hour and now I'm sharing the good news with you. I really believe that drinking clay daily and using the mask is a healing aid like no other. And I don't have any bad reactions to it. How can I express my thanks any deeper? — Stephanie F.

Multiple Allergies

I am a consumer of this miraculous clay. I WAS literally allergic to almost all foods, scents, chemicals in products! Within DAYS of taking the clay I STOPPED reacting to most everything!! I thought I was dying, as I was losing so much weight due to not being able to eat much, nor truly gain absorption from the little I was eating. Thank you SO much for making this product! I have been telling everyone I know in my daily life, online and off and many are now gaining the same benefits from Leaky Gut, Multiple Chemical Sensitivity, Histamine Intolerance and more. — Michelle W.

Multiple Uses Working For Your Health

About ten years ago, I started using Calcium Bentonite Clay for a shoulder injury. A little skeptical, with a why not try it attitude, I started using it all over my shoulder, even in the arm pit, and then eventually up my neck and face and eventually all over my entire body. The first time I used it on the shoulder, I could tell a difference in my range of motion, and it made me excited as I could hopefully get out of pain and back to work soon.

But, it's so much more than that, I'm using it in my work as a massage therapist with a full body wrap, followed by a salt scrub in the steam room and let me tell you, your skin (largest organ in the body) is decadently silky and invigorating.

My dental cleanings are much easier using just a dab with your toothpaste. I have a sensitive tooth and occasionally it hurts so I pack clay around the tooth at night for one or two nights and it takes care of it.

I keep it in my beach bag and gave some to a woman who had a large spider bite on her thigh. She had tried Benadryl and a steroid creme; I had her glob it on and 30 minutes later she couldn't believe how much the swelling had gone down.

Even sipping the clay, it feels as though you are pouring ancient medicine into your body to do what it needs to do. Drinking the clay, curbs my sugar cravings which automatically boosts the immune system. Aside from cleaning your gut or as a result, it gives me clarity, more energy and better skin.

The pulling properties of this Calcium Bentonite Clay are simply amazing! - Kimberly M.

Multiple Benefits - Lower BP, Hypothyroid & Digestion

My husband and I have been drinking and using the clay topically for over 2 1/2 years. The health benefits have been subtle, consistent lower blood pressure, my hypothyroid medication has been cut in half, no chronic sinusitis, improvements in our digestion. We are in our mid 60's feeling well and strong. Thank you for such a great product. - Noreen T.

Multiple Chemical Sensitivities (MCS)

I have multiple chemical sensitivities (MCS) which includes sensitivities to many things including food, pollen, mold, etc. as well as chemicals. Has anyone mentioned to you that they are "allergic" or sensitive to and cannot tolerate clay taken internally? I know that clay can cause detox and it's sometimes difficult to determine if the symptoms are from detox or from sensitivity to the product. I'm currently taking only 0.25 tsp with each meal and not having any problems, but plan to increase to 0.5 tsp next week then 1.0 tsp the following week and may run into some problems with the higher amounts. Bill C.

Off Meds - Feeling Great

I have been using clay for almost 2 months and love the results. I use it for facials, hair mask, toothpaste and ingest it for general health. I am no longer on any meds, and I feel great. Believing and claying are the natural medications that I've needed all along. The clay is a natural healing source and natural is always better than the synthetics created by man. — Joanne P.

Post Cancer Recovery- More Energy, Hair Regrowth, Arthritis Better

We have only been using the clay for about 2 and 1/2 weeks. I had surgery in November 2019 for breast cancer which they got all the cancer with the surgery. I also had cancer on my left hand that was steadily getting larger and about the size of a dime. I was going to get it taken care of after the breast cancer but thought in the meantime I would put some bentonite clay on it hoping to take some of the soreness out of it. I did this faithfully for a couple of months and then noticed it was not nearly so red and sore. I continued putting the clay on it (I was not taking it internally at this time) and it continued improving until it is completely gone, just a slight scar.

My sister and I have noticed little improvements that are not really so little to us since we started drinking the bentonite clay. Since my surgery, I lost some of my hair and the hair around my temple has been extremely dry and brittle. It is getting soft now and starting to feel like normal hair. I have struggled with a lot of fatigue as well and I have been able to do more like I have a little more endurance. We both have painful arthritis and it has felt so far a little less painful. I have had a few skin rashes and acne coming out on my skin since starting the clay and know this is the toxins coming out. I put clay on them and they go away very quickly. We are excited about all that is happening since starting the clay and will continue to document our health successes. -Bonnie Å. from Norway

Pregnancy

I just gave birth to a baby boy two weeks ago. I took living clay all through my pregnancy and felt wonderful! Birth was the fastest and easiest out of all four kids, and he is wonderfully healthy and my most content baby. Also my recovery was the easiest yet. I highly recommend that pregnant women use this clay as part of their prenatal regimen! — Brieanne R.

Sickly No More

Growing up, every year I would get sick. The flu, a cold etc. I haven't been sickly it over 2 years now...not even a common cold!! I look back now at what I'm doing differently now and one major thing I have added is the clay! I have always been healthy...I eat a strict diet and exercise regularly but if I'm around anyone that is sick, I would almost always catch it. My skin looks better, and my bowels work great again too, and I have read that taking clay regularly actually helps soak up bacteria, fungi, and viruses! This might be a contributor as to why I haven't been sick?? The flu season here in Canada can be pretty nasty...especially this time of year. — Kevin A.

Suggestions for Toddlers

I just would like to say, I am not a doctor, but with much trial and error, in my opinion, I would not be too aggressive (regardless of age. Clay is extremely detoxing and can trigger herx (herxheimer) reaction that can be extremely unpleasant.

If I had a toddler, after considering the pediatrician's and/or Infectious Disease Specialist or whatever Healer (Naturopathic,etc.) plans of action, I would definitely include Calcium Bentonite (Living Clay) in the regimen.

I would give my toddler about a tsp of hydrated clay and observe. If all is well, I would give 2 tsps per day, again, observe . I would also paint the bottoms of her feet with a weak solution for a couple hrs during day in the beginning. Of course, I would discuss with doctors first. – Kevin M.

Unbelievable Energy

Just a quick note to let you know how totally IMPRESSED I am with the clay!! I have been feeling unbelievable energy (the Life Force kind!) since starting it AND no longer need any other supplements! It has cleared up a corner eye infection I've had chronically for over a year, AND a urinary tract infection I was coming down with - in only 2 days! -Laurie M.

Vertigo Relief

I am 56 years old, and usually am never sick, and have never had vertigo before. I was too sick to do a detox bath right away--though I knew that would help immensely. I just could not get it ready. So, I did drink a dose of clay in some juice. Then I put a clay mask on my face, neck and feet. I left this on for about an hour. This helped enough that I was then able to mix up the clay (2 cups of dry clay) and take a detox bath for 15-20 minutes. That evening, I did another clay mask on my face only.

I then did another clay bath a few days later. I think being more aggressive with the baths and masks (face and feet) would really see quicker results, possibly a bath a day or more a day. But I did get immediate relief from the vertigo, enough after the mask that I was able to ready the bath. And the bath was a big help. No more dizziness, just more feeling weak. We thank God for this clay every day! — Patty E.

MOUTH, TEETH AND GUMS

Abscessed Tooth

What a miracle! I had an abscessed tooth and was beginning to get the toxins spread into my throat and my ears. Within two hours after applying the powder clay to my abscess, it had drawn the infection out. I continued to apply it that night and the next day to fully heal the tooth, and I was infection free. Since the clay worked so well on my tooth, I decided to use it for a mask on my face, and wow, what a difference it made in my skin. — Laura G.

Brushing and Swishing With Clay

So, I brush with clay but my teeth have been getting sensitive, so I started swishing with liquid clay while I am in the shower. So far, I see whiter teeth and some of the sensitivity seems to be going away. While brushing with clay has helped my tarter and what tarter there is white, I am thinking that continuing swishing with clay for 15-20 minutes will do with the rest of the tarter and any other benefits. I am trying to keep my teeth from deteriorating. – Bev H.

Cold Sores

My husband has been plagued for many years with cold sores. He has found that putting clay on a threatening cold sore begins to dry it up overnight, becoming less active and diminishing irritation. Thanks! — Laura G.

Gum Infection

The other day my son had a big white ball of pus in the gum and a few hours before going to the dentist he put clay on. It burst and he was left with a tiny white dot. – Corrine M.

Pyorrhea

My pyorrhea finally got so bad my dentist told me all my teeth would need to be extracted. It seemed my teeth were fine but my gums would have to go. I began brushing my teeth and gums with hydrated Calcium Bentonite Clay and packing my gums in the evening at bedtime with dry powder. Today, one year later, my teeth are pearly white, and my gums are healthy pink and disease free. All thanks to Calcium Bentonite Clay. — Jan J.

TMJ Blocked Jaw-Worn Meniscus

I had a blocked jaw and a bit of pain, meaning that I could not open it totally, for 3 months, when I decided to consult. The dentist-surgeon said the meniscus was worn and he wanted me to have a mold in my jaw at night and if not efficient to operate, but close to the facial nerve and if he touched it I would have half of my face paralyzed.

I was scared, went home and put a little square poultice onto my meniscus every night. After 2 days, I had no pain anymore (never big pain) and after 5 days I could open my mouth normally.

Really, after that I should have gone to have an x-ray to see what happened to my meniscus????

Years later a physio told me could have been a muscle and the clay could have helped to relax it and I presume there is always this possibility that they could not see that with x-ray, but as my meniscus was worn, now 30 years later would be in pretty bad state, if the clay had not helped to reform it! –Corrine M.

Teeth Sensitivity & No Discoloration

I just received my clay order. I looked at your brochure, and it says nothing about brushing your teeth with it. That is my primary use of the product. I have had severe sensitivity to hot and cold on my teeth and gum problems as well as discoloration with age on my teeth and also small cavities. I have used this product for about 10 years. I now have no sensitivity to cold or hot, my gums and my teeth are healthy-no discoloration and at age 63 this is pretty good. – Cindy P.

Whiter Teeth

I find that clay shortens the duration of the pain of injuries. It has healed tooth pain for me very quickly. I brush my teeth with it and it gradually reduced the yellowness from antibiotics taken in childhood. — Sue A.

SKIN CONDITIONS

A Younger Looking and Feeling Me

The clay mask does wonders for my skin! Along with a vegan diet and daily green smoothies, the mask keeps my face looking youthful. Just recently my hairdresser complimented me saying, "You hardly have any wrinkles at all!" And yesterday a dental assistant complimented my facial skin as well. At almost 70 years of age, I especially value such compliments. The clay mask has also noticeably faded the age spots on my hands and shrunk the veins. Just wish I'd known about this simple but effective beauty treatment years ago. Many thanks, Perry A., for so freely sharing this wonderful "secret" with us! - Judy B.

Acne and Rosacea

I am so excited to have found something chemical-free that is helping my skin. I have been struggling with acne and rosacea for over 10 years and have tried so many prescriptions and over-the-counter products that were costly, chemical-laden and irritated my skin. In the past few months, I began making a clay mask, which definitely seemed to help, so I decided to try taking the clay internally. Once I started drinking clay, my skin showed even more noticeable improvement in under a week. I have my fiancé drinking it now as well, and his acne is clearing also! — Phoebe G.

Active Teen with Acne

My 14-year-old athletic son has been battling acne on his face and back for the past year. Five weeks ago, he started drinking 2 ounces of liquid clay in the morning and the evening. His acne now appears to be under control on his face, and his back has cleared up by about 70 percent. He has recently begun using the clay mask to augment the liquid regime, and we are seeing further results. He is now on a maintenance dose and plans to continue to make liquid clay part of his daily routine. — Donna H.

Bike Ride Chaffing

It all started with me participating in The Hottest Day in Austin Bike Ride. It was a 15-mile bicycle ride around Austin, in the middle of August, in the middle of the afternoon. I was wearing my swimming costume the whole day, and there was hardly a moment in the day when it wasn't at least damp. At the end of the day, my chode (or taint, if you will) was feeling the wear and tear I had placed upon it. The tops of my inner thighs were rubbing against my saddle during the ride, so they were singing the same song as my chode.

The next morning, I found myself wincing when I sat, and waddling around like a penguin. Taking off my underwear revealed a red, inflamed mess — and not the fun kind. I needed relief, as did my friends who went on the ride.

I looked for a Clay Detox Clay Powder for my swollen, throbbing taint. I figured if I used it for a few days, I would be in the clear. So, I made mud out of the powder, and gingerly applied it to myself, and I was soothed with IMMEDIATE RELIEF. I went from waddling around to walking/sitting normally. I was even back on my bicycle the next day! I've been raving about the stuff ever since. — Dan G.

Black Wart

Oh, I had a black wart appear on the side of my temple about a year ago ... darn thing was driving me crazy, as it made me look like I had a longer eyebrow on one side. The doctor couldn't get rid of it at all. I tried every OTC wart remedy available. Well,

I think you know where I'm going with this ... it's almost gone from applying the clay a few times a day. It's so faint now that I expect it will be invisible in the next few days. I will also show this to the doctor. — Georgene F.

Chicken Pox

My 22-year-old daughter came down with a serious case of chicken pox. She was very ill and covered from head to toe with pox, which nearly drove her crazy because of the itching and irritation. She mixed Calcium Bentonite Clay with water to a very thin film consistency and applied it to her entire body. In a matter of hours, the healing set in and she had complete rest and relief. Her recovery was fast and her skin remained lovely. The pox left no scars, which was a miracle. — Kit N.

Clay for Anxiety Relief

I have to tell you when I wake I have anxiety and I applied the clay mask to my vulva for my issue and in just a couple of minutes my anxiety subsided and I relaxed! It was/is wonderful. Bev H.

Cleansing Clay Mask Lessens Wrinkle

The mixture is thicker and easy to apply. My skin feels so soft and wrinkles are lessened. My niece uses the mask to help with her acne problem. She says it helps but does not totally clear the condition. - Patricia T.

Detoxing Dirty Cracked Fingers

It was suggested by a doctor friend of mine to ask you about this. I have been doing some detoxing with a couple ingredients alternating with use of the calcium bentonite clay. I was taking 2 or 3 times a day the 2 ounces of liquid clay. I now have fingers and nails that look like I've been digging in the dirt. I have not. And as much as I try to clean my nails and scrub with a brush this is the best I can get. Also, the cracks in my fingers are now dark as well as around each nail. I've soaked in soapy water, vinegar hydrogen peroxide and nothing changes it. (It is not painful or uncomfortable, just unsightly! If you have any thoughts on this I'd love to hear them. -Linda M,

Reply: Linda I would suggest you dip your fingers in the Clay Mask several times a day and let it dry and then wash it off and repeat. Perry

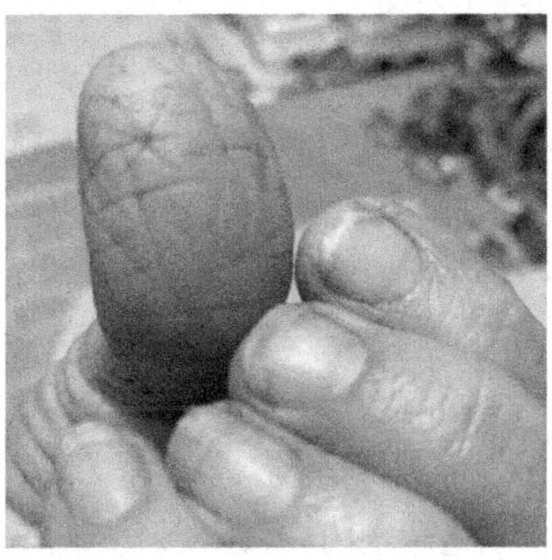

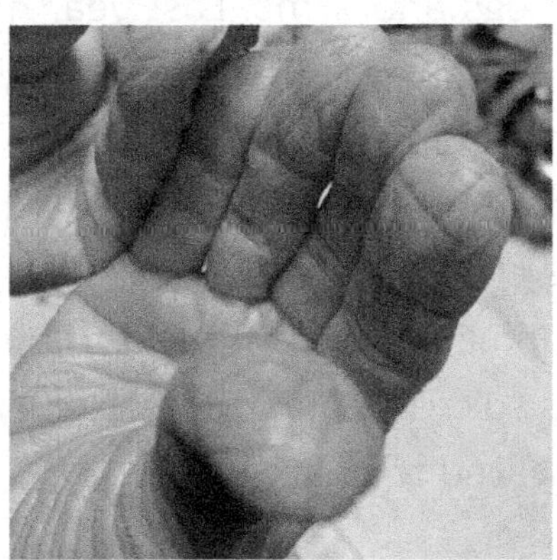

Linda: Yes it worked. Hands normal again thanks to your clay. - Linda M.

Grandson's Diaper Rash Gone in 1 Day

I just wanted to let you know that we used clay on our baby boy's diaper rash with quick success! He had a persistent diaper rash and our normal natural ointment did not solve the issue. We decided to try the clay on it after hearing about it on another on your zoom call. We applied it to the baby's bottom at bedtime and put on his diaper as usual. In the morning, when the clay was wiped away, his rash was completely gone We applied it to the baby's bottom at bedtime and put on his diaper as usual. In the morning, when the clay was wiped away, his rash was completely gone I'll put clay on just about any irritation. I keep a jar of clay mixed to the mask/poultice consistency for everyday use on bug bites, for facials, and whatever. As always, clay saves the day. I love this stuff! Best, Kim B.

Eczema – Severe Case

My mother is 83 years old. Mom would always talk about controlling her eczema. It was on the back of her neck and on the bend of her legs and arms. Last year my sisters started telling me that my mom, who generally walks about 1-2 miles every day, was not going out the door. This was because her skin was so messed up with eczema. What they described to me did not come close to what I saw when I got there to visit. She looked like an alligator from head to toe. Her skin, if you called it skin, was so crusty and brittle. Her eyes were red, and she was clearly scared to death.

Day 1: I made up a clay mask and covered her from head to toe. I allowed her to sit for 15 minutes or so. I put Mom in a 6-foot bathtub of water as hot as she could stand it. I put 3 full cups of clay in the tub and sat with her for 30 minutes, constantly pouring the water over her neck and chest. I had her drink cool water while sitting in the tub. When she got out, I patted her down and put Nutiva extra virgin organic coconut oil all over her, head to toe, wrapped her in a large towel and put her in the bed where she stayed for two hours.

Day 2: The next day we repeated the process. When I got there, she was looking better already. The bed had scales from eczema.

Day 3: She looked even better. She had another clay bath and was in there for about 15 to 20 minutes. Another coconut oiling down and back in bed.

Day 4: When I arrived, she quickly opened the door. What a smile! Here skin was smooth as a baby's butt. She is so happy. This was over a year ago and her skin is still smooth because she continues with her modified treatments. This summer my mother for the first time that I can remember attended the family reunion with a no-sleeve top! She strutted and danced all day. Oh, how happy all of us are! — Brenda J.

Hives and Headache

I must tell you how much clay has saved my bacon. The first night after taking this olive leaf extract that apparently is extremely potent. I broke out in hives all over my hips/thighs. They told me not to take any medications, let it all come out, so the only thing I had was the clay. I bathed in it twice a day with

1/2 cup and no hives after that. When I get a headache, I just take a bath and put some on my head and it's gone. Drinking it too. — Barbara H.

Plantar's Warts

I've been using clay on bandages on my feet and taking clay baths and foot baths, they are almost gone. I've got 3 of them that have been so severe that they were altering my gait and causing other foot problems — Linda W.

Poison Ivy

I was doing some yard work and noticed I had a little poison ivy. I put some clay mud on and went to bed. It looked much better the next morning, but I put some more hydrated clay on it. This morning the spots are almost gone. I had some poison ivy last year but didn't have clay and it got worse and spread and it took about a couple of weeks for it to disappear. Love the clay. — Chris S.

Poison Sumac – Quick Relief

I just had to tell you what happened to me this week. On Saturday, I got into some poison sumac. It was one of the worst cases my doctor had seen. It was all over my face, neck, arms and stomach. I was embarrassed to go out in public and of course, it was itching like crazy. After trying calamine lotion, witch hazel, oatmeal baths, etc. for 2 days, it only looked worse, not better! I thought, hey, I wonder if the clay will help. So, I decided to try it. I made it into a paste like I do for my facials and applied a very thin layer to the spots on my face, which I left overnight. In the morning, I was like a different person. All the redness and swelling was gone. The blisters were dried up! Some of the marks are still on my face, but they are faded, and you can hardly see them at all. WOW!! Just wanted to say thanks for an amazing product with so many awesome uses. — Morgan S.

Psoriasis No More

About a year ago I developed psoriasis localized to my underarms (literally in the armpits.) I spent months treating it with steroid ointment. It would relieve the sting and seemed to allow it to heal. However, as soon as I stopped using the ointment, within a week the burning, itchy scaling would return. The ointment did not cure anything, only lessened and masked the symptoms.

I discovered Bentonite clay while I was researching making my own tooth powder. I then found the Clay Information site, read about some of the amazing things clay could do and ordered some along with the Clay deodorant. I loved that they only sold food grade clay – I thought that it showed integrity in this company and didn't mess around with selling lesser clay for external use like some vendors – they only sell the best, period.

I started listening to Perry A's clay Q & A sessions and asked for her advice on using clay to treat my psoriasis. She recommended drinking clay, taking clay baths and using clay poultices. I followed a regimen of 2 to 3 clay baths per week and drank 4 oz of clay 3 to 4 times per day. This may be a bit of a high dose for some people to start with, but I approached this aggressively because I was so frustrated with the psoriasis and wanted it gone. I knew I could have a detox reaction, but I was okay with that.

I would get up in the morning, drink my clay and sip my coffee, then after about an hour or so I would drink plenty of water. I made sure to drink plenty of water throughout the day always leaving at least a 30-minute window before and after I drank my clay. I staggered my clay out for the remainder of the day with the last dose being right before bed. The only change to my diet that I made was to add green smoothies since I am on a program to lose weight this year. I drank at least one quart of green smoothie every day – sometimes two quarts. My thinking was that it would help with the detox and weight loss - plus, who couldn't eat more vegetables, right? I rarely did the clay poultices as I found the Clay deodorant worked great as a topical soother and since it has clay in it, I used that in place of the poultices most of the time.

Within a couple of days of following my regimen, I found that when I sweat, I would have a pretty strong odor. I also felt that I ran a little bit hot, not uncomfortably hot, but I would readily sweat lightly even if I wasn't doing strenuous activity. I believe this was my body detoxing. I think the green smoothies and a lot of water kept me from having any major detox symptoms.

Within one and a half months, my symptoms were completely gone and my skin was healed. That was over five months ago as of today 9/10/15. I have not had a single psoriasis break out since. I still take clay baths (because they are awesome!) and I do drink 3 to 4 oz of clay every morning. I still drink my green smoothies because between those and the clay, I feel great. Overall, I feel cleaner, my skin is brighter and softer. My hair also grows fast and is very healthy. Also, now that I am detoxed, when I do sweat it hardly has an odor. I attribute that to the clay.

I am a firm believer in calcium Bentonite clay - I love it and recommend it to everyone I know. Thank you, Perry A, for sharing all you know about this miracle from nature! — Kim E.

Shingles – No Pain

Last month I woke up one morning and thought I had a spider bite on my waist. It was bubbly like a new cold sore. I have been drinking clay (6oz) daily for 5 years now, and both my husband and I have not had the flu or a cold sore outbreak which we are both prone to.

I began applying wet clay to the area and in two days the rash spread so I went to the doctor, and he said it was shingles. He wanted to know how I was dealing with the pain. I said, "What pain?" He gave me a very expensive prescription (a seven-day course) and he told me he would call me in a prescription for when the pain started. I told him about clay, but he kind of just rolled his eyes, and said to expect the shingles to get worse, before better, and it would take 4 weeks or more for the shingles to run their course. I kept drinking the clay and I took the prescription, applying it topically at night before I went to bed and in the morning, and in the afternoon. I also used the clay mask. I put a lot on topically, morning, noon and night. I put plastic wrap on top and wore snug shorts to keep it in place. The pain never came. However it wasn't without discomfort as the clay did its job pulling and drawing the virus out. I could feel it. The shingles immediately stop spreading and were dried up and gone in two weeks to the day. All that was left of the shingles was a reddish tinge to the skin. They didn't even itch, which shingles painfully do.

The virus is aggressive, and I suspect if I hadn't been drinking clay, it would have been much worse. Long Live Clay. — Stacey B.

Shingles

A friend of mine put clay at an advanced stage of shingles, she was very skeptical. The shingles disappeared and the pain went away rapidly. — Corrine M.

Skin Lesion Removed

I want to share what I consider a clay miracle! I have a dry, raised age spot over my left breast that was the size of an oval dime. When I first introduced the clay and poultices, I began covering the spot and letting it dry and not really washing it off for 24 hours at a time. I did this a couple of times a week. Well, I want you to know that the spot is now one-half the size and where part of it has dried and scabbed off is new pink skin. I must say I am amazed and happy about this! — Susan S.

Red Rash & Severe Exhaustion & Fatigue

One of my important customers, Keisha, from Salts and Scents (Boston, MA) recommended your products to me and I recently made a purchase for the Detox Clay Powder. I just had to send an email to let you know what happened.

I had an unusual rash/red discoloring on various parts of my body, was suffering from severe exhaustion/fatigue. Keisha suggested that it was from a buildup of toxins in my system and suggested to try your product to "detox" my system and see what would happen.

It has been 1 week since using your products. I made a liquid version where I took 1 part to 4 parts water and blended it and drank it internally, took a bath with it, and used the clay mask. I started off drinking 1oz a day and worked up to 2/3 times per day. In the beginning I got a surge of energy, but then I took a turn for the worse - nauseous, lethargic - just felt horrific. *(Editor's notes notice she took a 1 to 4 ratio. Very concentrated. The correct blend is 1 to 8. This speeded the detoxing, and it was bringing up the toxins faster than they could be carried out of the body thus the Detox reactions. In a case like this slow down on the amount but do not stop. It is working.)

Today - one week later - I feel better than I ever have. The rash is GONE; I have energy and feel great. I was tempted a few days ago to call and yell at Keisha. I thought she poisoned me - but now that the worse has passed - I want to give her a big hug. It must have been my body detoxing and going through what it needed to do to get rid of the buildup. My skin looks so much better and people have noticed.

I hope I do not go through what I did again, it was awful. I am now a huge fan and plan on continuing to use your wonderful products. - Sherri W.

Skin Tumor on Arm

This thing had really grown a lot my family told me which I hadn't been aware of as I saw it every day. I used the clay almost 24 hours a day, changed it twice daily, for 2 weeks and the tumor shrunk down visibly every day. I stopped using the clay when the swelling was gone. Now I still have a scar or something similar, but it looks harmless, is flat and I don't cover it anymore. At night I used a bandage with lots of clay covering a big area.— Marion P.

This Clay is Awesome!

Nothing else has worked for over 2 years on the healing process of my skin infections until your clay withdrew toxins from the skin and the magic started happening. I used it externally and internally following the 21-day protocol. Currently, I am using it twice a day internally and I am using borax externally to finish off the infections. The two work really well together. Thanks for selling the clay!

- Jeffrey M.

Chapter Eleven

PETS, LIVESTOCK, WILDLIFE, FISH AND FOWL

Clay is beneficial to all of God's creations. If you are not sharing your clay with your pets, you are depriving them of good health. In Wild Health by Cindy Engle, we learn that most plant-eating animals eat clay to neutralize poisons in plants and seeds. Research has been done in feeding poultry, sheep, swine and cattle clay, all with amazing beneficial results. In addition, they have found clay in the feces of bears, tigers, wolves and raccoons and many rodents to suggest these animals also include clay in their diets. Gorillas, monkeys and chimpanzees, deer, tapirs as well as the macaws of Peru are clay eaters. What horse lovers haven't observed horses taking big bites of soil while grazing. Prize Koi fish are fed clay to enrich their color. Some animals also use clay topically. Elephants in Africa make a pilgrimage to clay deposits in shallow ponds and dig down to the clay and spray themselves to detox. Some goats and birds have been observed making casts of clay and grasses. It just makes sense to give your pets the wonderful healing powers of clay.

Clay has many benefits for pets. Bentonites in an animal's diet act as gut protectants (enterosorbents), which rapidly and preferentially bind aflatoxins from the digestive tract and thus reduce their absorption into the organism. (P. G. Grant and T. D. Phillips, 1998; Phillips et al., Characterization of clay-based enterosorbents for the prevention of aflatoxicosis, 2002) In that manner, adverse effect of aflatoxins on efficiency and liver function is minimized without marked defects in mineral metabolism of the animals (Schell, T. C. et al., 1993 a,b; Santurio, J. M. et al., 1999)

Clay can also help animals rid their bodies of poison in case of ingestion. Feed Calcium Bentonite Clay to pets that have eaten poisons, have diarrhea, are vomiting and have digestive issues, hot spots, skin irritations, mange, excessive scratching, puncture wounds, open sores, broken bones, parasites or signs of Candida. Give it to them to improve hair coat, weeping eyes, paw fungus, foot rot, warts, growths, joint problems and arthritis.

PROTOCOLS FOR PETS

Below are suggested daily maintenance protocols for pets but remember animals in the wild have free access to clay ponds, licks and wallows and instinctively monitor their own intake. They seem to know how much they need, so feel free to give them as much as they want. Do not, however, feed the clay in the dry form. Either give them the clay mask or the liquid clay.

Small pets under 10 pounds: 1 teaspoon of the clay mask mixed in their food twice a day.

Medium pets 10 to 50 pounds: 2 rounded teaspoons of the clay mask mixed in their food twice a day.

Large pets 50 pounds and over: 1 rounded tablespoon of clay mask in their food twice a day.

Horses and larger animals: 2 Tablespoons twice a day.

Pets that have ingested poison need doses 3 to 4 times a day until better.

Remember, clay is as good for your pets as it is for you and our environment. Now go give your pets some clay!

Chapter Twelve

PET TESTIMONIALS

CATS

18-year-old Constipated Cat Gets Relief

I have an eighteen-year-old cat that has had constipation much of her life. Believe me when I say I have tried every natural remedy I could find, and some not so natural. Being lactose intolerant, about a year ago I started using the Ayurvedic method of boiling milk to change it into a more digestible and nourishing substance. Just gave her a soup size spoonful morning and night. That gave some results for a while.

Recently I started using calcium Bentonite clay on myself and decided to put a very small bowl down for her. It looked like the water evaporated so I put a little more water in. A day or two later I found a bigger than tootsie roll stool in the litter box and was amazed. But this one incident was enough to impress me. — Elizabeth J.

Abscess on Cat's Spine

On a Thursday evening, I noticed a lump on my cat's spine and found a large area of pus. I cut the hair away and applied hydrated clay and Glad Press 'n Seal. The next morning, I re-dressed the wound with new clay. The pus was reduced greatly and even started to solidify. Took the cat to the vet that evening for an antibiotic shot, just to be on the safe side. I did not get all the clay off but good enough for the vet to look at the wound. Vet wanted to put in a stint. He did that before for drainage. It took a long time to drain and heal. I said no to the stint, too expensive for an unemployed person. The vet told me NOT to use the clay anymore. Of course I did not listen. I knew better. I placed new clay after vet visit. I replaced it Saturday morning. Wow, no pus, only an empty hole. Replaced it Saturday evening. I forgot Sunday morning. By evening, it hardened, so I had to add water and wait for it to re-hydrate. Monday morning, it was completely healed. — Sparky & Becky H.

Cat Eating Cat Litter Stopped when Offered Clay

We had a customer come in whose elderly cat was eating her clay cat litter. We recommended she start her on clay water as she was probably trying to detox from something. He bought the clay and added it to her water. She loved it and stopped eating her litter with all the other nasty stuff in it. — Diana D.

Cat Puncture Wounds

A friend's cat got into a fight with another cat. She used hydrated clay on the wounds and all healed without a trace of the fight. Cat wounds generally get very infected and require medical attention and treatment, not for this cat! — Katie M.

Cat Tumors Disappear with Clay

This summer I participated in a clay teleseminar and submitted a question about whether the clay could heal the large (cancerous looking) bleeding tumor on my cat's tail. When the vet shaved it, it looked like a rotten potato attached to his tail – much bigger than his actual tail, so it could not be removed – so the only thing they could offer was amputation. Well, I did not want to do that unless it meant life or death and there were no other options, so I started using the clay in the meantime just to stop the messy bleeding.

Well, long story short, my cat cooperated well with me applying the clay and it really helped stop the bleeding. However, in time an oozing hole developed where the bleeding used to be. I kept that hole packed with clay, and within an incredibly short time the entire huge tumor had just melted away. The hole is gone now. There is just a tiny bump left that I could feel at this point. I continue to apply the clay and will do so until there is no hint anything is left but his beautiful tail. Although my cat was never sick from this, he was acting rather old and depressed, but now he has the energy of a kitten again.

I gave a co-worker a small jar of clay for the same purpose as her cat also had a VERY large tumor on its neck. When I checked back last week, she said her cat's tumor had completely dissolved and was in fact also completely gone! — Brenda H.

Cat with Cysts

I have an elderly cat, Big Guy, who has been my companion for over 12 years. He's in good health except for a large cyst on top of his head near his ear. The vet won't remove it, as he doesn't want to do surgery on a cat his age if not necessary. Occasionally, I notice that Big Guy has been scratching the cyst, and it has bled a bit. This really worried me, so I started putting a dab of hydrated clay on it when he was quiet or asleep and didn't realize what I was doing! If he knew, he would promptly lick his paw and remove the stuff, but I figured that it wouldn't hurt his inside either! I notice that when I use this clay on the cyst, it gets smaller, the sore places dry up and he doesn't seem to be bothered by it. So, I'm going to keep using it on him as long as the cyst is there. — Jacq P.

Cat's Weepy Eyes Cleared Up

Just wanted to report that I've been giving my 3 oldest kitties hydrated clay mixed in with their food. One of them is a Persian, who has always had "weepy eyes." And I've just taken note of the fact that her weepy eye thing has cleared up and is gone!!! She had it all of her life. But the clay got it. — Jan

Rescue Cats Respond to Clay

I rescue Persian cats. They are now on clay water, and I add it to their food. They are very frisky and happy now, I can see a big difference in their eyes, they always have very runny eyes, but this is improving. Many cats that I get are severely ill, I will be bathing them in clay baths to detox them and will experiment with clay for ringworm. The protocol for treating cats with ringworm is very medicine intensive and extremely toxic. — Linda W.

DOGS

13-Year-Old Rescue Dog Chewing on Feet and Skin

I rescued an old dog who was probably about 13 yrs when I got her. Her skin stunk and was so black. She would chew herself until she bled. I had to stop her from doing that. So, she had to wear the cone for a year. But she would still manage to chew herself until she bled. Well. if I went to the vet for every time she broke the skin, I would be broke. What I decided to do was pat her wound down with clay. By the next morning, there was no swelling and by that night it was all healed up. It began to be a joke as I probably did this a hundred times over the last three years. She now doesn't wear a cone and still chews on herself but I just put a sweater on her. Her skin is not fully recovered but she is stronger and I know what to do if she starts chewing again. I put clay in her food also. I do a lot of other things but this is the clay story. -Rose B.

58 lb. German Shepherd Rescue Dog Rescued with Clay

I wanted to give you an update on my rescue dog, Kylie, since she has been using clay. As I mentioned before, she had been abused and feared everything when we first got her. She was a very tall German Shepherd who only weighed 58 lbs. I handled her trying to get weight on her but she had serious stomach issues. She was throwing up yellow bile in the mornings and would go into extreme dysentery. We got her up to about 69 pounds, which was not nearly enough for her size. We were at the Vet very often and she was on antibiotics for 3 months at a time, on several occasions. She got a yeast infection on the top of her paws a couple of times, and they were red and swollen and the hair was coming off. I had her on antifungal medication for the last time for over a month and it was not working. Our Vet bill has been over $2000 trying to remedy her problems

The man I buy the organic dog good from told his wife about it, as she is really into natural healing products and she was so kind to come with him to see what her problem was. She brought me a sample of the Calcium Bentonite Clay and I applied it to her feet and within a few days there was a great improvement and within 2 weeks it was completely healed. I started giving her the clay internally, I got a large size syringe from the drug store that would hold 15cc or 3 tablespoons at a time and started giving it to her morning and night. Within a few days the throwing up had stopped. Within the last 6 weeks she has had 2 more dysentery attacks but we were able to get it under control with clay and acidophilus. She is now digesting her food, and I took her over to the Vets office and weighed her yesterday and she was 77.2. I am going to wait a couple of weeks to make sure the dysentery problem is over and I am going to make an appointment to go in and talk to the Vet about the Clay. Juniece S.

Chloe's Enlarged Liver

My dog, Chloe, was developing an enlarged liver, and her liver enzymes were elevated. In the mornings, she would hunch over and move stiffly, and her belly was always hard. I researched and changed foods, but she received only minor relief from this.

I began giving her the hydrated clay through a syringe every night. After three days, her painful movements decreased, and she was more playful. Now her belly is soft and we can palpate without her crying out in pain. One of the most interesting things is that every night before I go to bed, I get my clay ready, and she comes and waits for me licking her lips. Now I just dip in and give her a spoonful, which she willingly licks off every bit ... I think she knows it makes her feel better, and she looks forward to having it. I'm so glad that the clay is helping her! — Justine F.

Clay Removed Plant Poison from Paralyzed Dog

My brother's dog was having this terrible problem with his back legs and could hardly get up, and when he did, his back legs were practically paralyzed. After going to the vet and taking antibiotics and then off to a special vet hospital, they did more blood tests, and he had gotten a condition which was from coming in contact with a certain plant which was paralyzing his hind legs. My husband told my brother about this clay he had and that we should try it in his dog food. Well, after a few days, he was starting to walk a little better and after a few weeks the dog was totally fine. What a miracle. The poison from the plant had left his body! — Carol N.

Doberman with Cancer Growth Between Eyes

Bodhi, my 1-year-old Doberman, had a cancerous growth between his eyes. We applied hydrated clay to the spot for a month, and the red scaly lump went away but was bald. Also, he fed him a tablespoon of hydrated clay in the morning and evening meals. The vet said that the hair would never grow back but the cancer would. We continued to put clay on the bald spot, and in a month the hair all grew back. Bodhi is now 2½ and cancer free and looking good! — Adrienne O.

Dog Bite - Puncture Wound

Gabbi was playing with another dog and the dog bit her foot and left a large canine tooth hole. After applying the hydrated clay, the wound healed in a few days and no infection. All the hair grew back, and you cannot tell that she was injured. — Katie M.

Dog with Cancer and Fatty Cysts

I have a 50-pound golden doodle 7 years old and Duncan had a cancerous tumor. We had taken him to the vet to have it remove and the vet told us they could not remove it all and it would possibly grow back. Duncan had a few lumps on his body in different areas, and this was of great concern to us. Our doggy daycare told us about calcium Bentonite clay and gave us the website to go read some of the testimonials. We fed Duncan a TBSP of hydrated clay in the morning and night in his food. After a month and a half all the tumors and lumps had disappeared. It has been more than a year now and nothing has returned, and our boy is happy and healthy. Now he won't eat his food without the clay mixed in it. Love the clay! — Kevin N.

Dog with Ear Infection

Callie was a one-year-old Shepherd at the time and had been to the vet several times for recurring ear infections. The infections were so bad she would not allow you to touch her head. Ear infections are less likely to happen in dogs when the ear stands up so this was very mysterious and was costing thousands of dollars at the vet. I started to feed Callie a tablespoon of hydrated clay in the morning and in the evening. After a month the ear infections disappeared, her coat filled in very nicely, she used to have an "old dog" smell that went away, and she did not seem to scratch as much. I can now touch her head without her shying away. I was so happy to see my dog pain free and calm. I love the clay! —Cheryl D.

Dog with Hot Spots and a Limp

I have a 6-year-old Shepherd/Husky cross named Yukia we adopted. He started to chew himself to the point he had removed a patch of hair and skin on in back over his hips. It was about 12 inches by 6 inches. We had no idea what was going on, and we spent thousands of dollars at the vet trying to help him. After many different types of medications and creams the vet told us it was auto immune and really nothing further, they could do for him. He had to wear a cone to keep him from doing further damage. Our dog daycare had told us about this calcium Bentonite clay and we thought we would give it a try. After 2 weeks feeding him 1 tablespoon of hydrated clay twice a day in his food and applying hydrated clay to the area it was healing amazingly well. After a month the skin had grown back in and there was hair starting to grow. Yukia no longer had to wear the cone of shame! He also had a limp in his back leg, the vet said would never go away and now it was gone as well. We notice that he no longer had a funny "old dog" smell to his coat. Overall a much happier attitude in general. The clay changed our dog's life and for that we are grateful! It is 6 months later and he is still very healthy and living life like someone left the gate open! — Lindsay B.

Dogs in Chemically Treated Yard

Last year after getting some work done in the yard I had to treat the lawn with a chemical pesticide which is something I usually never do. Having to go to an appointment I told my husband not to let the dogs out. Forgetting, he let them outside anyway. About four hours later I returned and saw them and learned they'd gone out almost immediately after I left and in a panic, I wrote the aboutclay forum for advice. Perry said to put them in clay water and leave it on them for 20 minutes before rinsing it off and to give them clay water by mouth. I put a cup of dry clay in the laundry tub of water and dipped each dog into it and left it on them for 20 minutes before rinsing it off and drying them. Each dog also got 6 ccs of liquid clay per 10 - 12 pounds of body weight. Not one of the 12 dogs got even slightly sick, and they not only walked, sat and laid on the newly treated grass but playing and wrestling they rolled in it. I'm so grateful I had the clay and the forum where I could get advice. — Mary Lee S.

Good Teeth Report on 13-Year-Old Pomeranian

I have a little 13-year-old Pomeranian. They have notoriously bad teeth. Last year my vet said that we may have to think about having her teeth scaled/scraped this year. But that is a surgical procedure, which would be hard on an elderly dog. So, I started giving her liquid clay with her dry food twice a day. I just pour some next to the food, same plate. She goes for the clay first, then the food! Anyway, we went back to vet this year and he was shocked to see how good her teeth looked! She acts like a puppy and is really healthy! — Marilyn A

Hair, Teeth, Breath, Kidney Stones and Energy Improvements for 8-Year-Old Dog

We have given Sassy clay daily (mix liquid in with her food) for almost 2 years now and her yearly checkups all ok. She is 8 now and is very healthy, active and since clay I have noticed an increased energy, no limp during cold weather and/or after lying around too long and no more urinary tract problems or kidney stones problems. She had surgery (pre-clay) and they said it could come back, it hasn't. Also noticed her teeth are cleaner, breath is better and hair is thicker. — Paul M.

Lab Recovers from Blood Parasite

My dog, Ryan (almost 11 yr old Lab) has been on clay (1 tablespoon per day mixed in his food.) for about 5 years and does remarkably well - never gets sick. For the last two years he has been slowing down, and I attributed it to getting old (he is my hearing assistance dog which, so he has a more active life than a pet). But in February all that changed. I had to take him to a vet - a first since moving to Lima, Peru over a year ago. He would not put any weight on one paw. Long story short - he had Erlichia which is a parasite that attaches to the red blood cells and causes severe anemia. His red cell blood count was down at 7 (normal is 12 - 17). After a session of acupuncture, a shot to the affected joint of an anti-inflammatory and a weekend of rest the vet couldn't believe how quickly he recovered. Erlichia causes joint problems and is very common in Peru. The vet was suspicious and asked to do blood work. Again, when the results came back, she was amazed that Ryan did as much as he did consider he was severely anemic. Now that the anemia is over, he is a different dog - it's as if he lost five years of his life, friends are amazed at the change in him. He also gets acupuncture treatments every two weeks. He is in his 9th year of working and shows no signs of slowing down. I know the clay plays a huge part in his general wellbeing and kept him going during his bout with Erlichia (which I think started about two years ago). My cat is also on clay and doing extremely well (he just turned 11). So now I understand how the clay helped Ryan while he had the Erlichic! — Hilary R.

Old Dog Can't Get Around Until Clay

My brother tries every home remedy and then sends me some. He was raving about this clay and taking it internally. I thought, "No way am I going to drink dirt!" So, I decided to try it on our

13-year-old dog, Max, who can no longer get up the stairs or jump on furniture. I mixed a teaspoon of hydrated clay in his food for 3 days. The third day I came downstairs and couldn't find him anywhere. I thought, OH MY Gosh, I have killed our dog with that stupid clay, and he has gone off somewhere to die. A short time later I was carrying the laundry upstairs and I heard this "thump, thump, thump" coming from my daughter's room. I opened the door and there was Max on the bed and thumping his tail in delight. I called my sister and told her to start taking the clay too, that this time Bob was right about his natural remedy. Now the whole family, critters and all, take clay. — Martha W.

Puppy with No Parasites Surprising the Vet

My puppy has only been de-wormed once, before I got her. I was supposed to de-worm her two more times, but I decided to give her clay instead. On our first visit to the vet, her stool was checked for parasites and guess what ... no parasites! The doctor couldn't believe that she was only de-wormed once. Hooray for the clay!!!! I continue to mix clay in her food every morning. Sometimes I give her a little extra when she sticks her nose in the duck poop! — Nancy F.

Parvo Rescue Pups Saved With Clay

I had taken in three rescue puppies from a littler of six. The other three went to another lady. All the puppies got Parvo. I treated mine with the recommended daily injection of Baytril from the veterinarian for five days, plus I gave my pups 1 tablespoon of the premixed liquid clay three times a day by mouth. My pups lived, and the rest of the litter that were only treated with Baytril died. The clay helped stop the diarrhea and the vomiting. — Cheryl P.

Tumor is gone!!!

It took 2 ½ months of applying the clay morning and evening (leaving it on until the next application). I have a sense it was more than just a non-malignant tumor having taken so long. I, as well as Zoe, am a very happy camper! Thanks for your help and support. The vet wrap used to keep it covered thinned hair and from her trying to scratch it, it is bald in a few places. I know it will just take time to grow back out. Feel free to share this with others, and I would be happy to answer any questions someone may have. - Janie D.

HORSES

Horse with Ostrich-Egg-Sized Bladder Stone

Luke had an egg-size stone in his bladder that was interfering with his ability to urinate. We started the horse on clay, and it seems to be working. Luke is no longer "leaking" constantly, seems to be more comfortable, is back working and tried to urinate on his own instead of letting urine just dribble out. This is extremely positive as it means there may be no bladder damages, and he still remembers what to do!!

We are excited. He will be going in for an ultrasound in a couple weeks to see how much the ostrich-egg-sized stone in his bladder has shrunk. If it has shrunk enough for ultrasound treatments to destroy it, that would be great, and if not, as long as there is a visible shrinkage, we know we are on the right track.

The horse now belongs in our school horse program. Have not

had a recent ultrasound of the lump in his bladder, but on the last one, it had decreased from 4 inches in diameter to 3 inches. I believe the lump to slowly be decreasing in size. The horse is much happier and can be used again as he is no longer in chronic pain. He's been saved from surgery so far and does not look like he will have to be put down.

Final report on Luke: With the latest ultrasound, the vet was unable to find any stone.

Here is the protocol:

I gave him a wet meal, like soaked beet pulp, added the dry powder to it and mixed it in. Started off with a cup a day and when we saw signs from the ultrasound that the stone was shrinking, dropped it to a 1/2 cup per day, and now that it is gone, down to a 1/4 cup as horses that get these stones are at danger of re-occurrence. Will likely, in about 6 months, drop him down to 1/4 cup every second day.

Took about 5 months before the stone shrunk from 4 inches to 3 inches and then another 5 months until it was gone. Granted, we were not doing an ultrasound every month, so it may have been sooner than 5 months once the stone started dissolving. Given the size of the stone, I was quite surprised that it was completely gone in just under a year. — Sharon H.

Lame Horse

After giving my horse clay for 3 days, his ankle is MUCH better. The swelling has gone down, and he no longer looks like he's suffering! He's holding his head up. He even ran a little bit this morning. All I can say is WOW! just WOW! Thank you for answering all my questions and soothing my nervousness about giving clay to my horse. I didn't know if the swelling was an infection or inflammation, but the clay solves both problems and worms him at the same time!!!! And it's non-invasive. Healing clay is amazing. Now my husband wants to try it since it worked so well for my beloved horse. — Areil M.

Sick Show Horse

My story starts in April with my daughter's show horse Dolly. She wasn't performing as she could. We had the vet check on her. He ran some tests and said she had a disease that would affect her for quite some time. We were very distressed, since my daughter had high hopes of going to the Palomino World Show in July to compete. She had been working hard nearly every day. We had to let Dolly rest for almost a month. In this time we prayed over her and gave her the clay in her feed every day. We had the vet check her in a month, and he said we had a sound horse, so Haley went back to riding Dolly and we went to the Palomino World Show, which Haley and Dolly won three World Championships and two Reserve World Championships. They also won the prestigious award of Golden Horse 13 and under. We still feed her the clay everyday i her feed. Thanks for telling us about this miracle clay" — Rebecca H.

OTHER ANIMALS

Holland Lop Elderbun With Abscess

I have a Holland Lop Elderbun named Jax. He will be on the 10th of February. In the last 1-1/2 years he has had three facial abscesses that I have had to treat with antibiotic injections for a 3-week period each time. I don't enjoy it and Jax certainly doesn't either. I was grooming him the other day and noticed that an abscess was forming just below his left eye. I put the clay on it for the last two days and it is resolving. — Melissa S.

Woodchuck with Broken Ankle – 5-Day Healing

While trying to rescue a baby woodchuck from being run over by a car, I inadvertently broke its ankle. It was squealing in pain, and the foot just hung and flopped around. It being Friday night, the vet was closed till Monday, so I made a soupy mixture of Calcium Bentonite Clay somewhere between liquid and hydrated so it would coat the leg thickly without me having to rub the clay on and maybe damage it more and then stuck the woodchuck's entire leg down into it. He stopped crying almost immediately so you could tell the clay eased the pain. Then I placed him in a small cage in a dim room so he could sleep. I noticed he licked some of the clay off his foot at that time, so he got some internally.

The next 3 days I dipped his leg and foot into the clay mixture once in the morning and again in the evening and kept him in the small cage with food near enough that he didn't have to walk to get it. I did not wrap the leg or set it in any way as I wasn't sure how to do it and didn't want to set it crookedly. Day 5 had him up and walking around and unhappy with his small quarters. The next day he was climbing in the cage. Both feet and legs are as good as new, and he's almost ready to be released back into the wild. Note: He likes the clay so much that I must put a small amount of hydrated on some of his food now or he tries eating dirt outside. — Mary Lee S.

Chapter Thirteen

RECIPES

Yes, you can cook with it, too!

Calcium Bentonite Clay can be added to just about any recipe. We encourage you to experiment and try adding clay to all your favorite smoothies and dishes. And when you create something great, please send us the recipe! We'll share it with all who are interested! You can email your recipes to Info@TheClayBook.com

Here are a few Calcium Bentonite Clay recipes to get you started. Bon Appétit!

Apple Clay Smoothie

I pulverize an apple in the blender with water and add about 4 ounces of liquid clay. I mix up the whole thing into a smoothie of about 8-10 ounces total and drink it in the evening. It has a calming and quieting effect and helps me go to sleep. It's a wonderful natural tranquilizer. I mix up a supply of about 8 cups of water to 1 cup of clay powder and keep it on hand for smoothies.

Banana Nut Muffins

Ingredients:

1¼ cup flour

1/4 cup Dry Powder Calcium Bentonite Clay

2 egg whites

1 cup mashed bananas

1½ tsp. baking powder

3/4 cup sugar

1/4 tsp. baking soda

1 Tbsp. vegetable oil

1/3 tsp. salt

1/4 cup chopped walnuts

1 tsp. lemon zest

Preheat oven to 350° F. Spray muffin tins with nonstick cooking spray. Stir together flour, Calcium Bentonite Clay, baking powder, baking soda and salt. In a medium bowl, beat egg whites slightly. Stir in bananas, sugar, oil and lemon peel. Add flour mixture and stir until just combined. Stir in walnuts. Fill muffin tins ¾ full. Bake for 20-25 minutes.

Banana Peanut Butter Chocolate Shake

1 frozen banana, peeled

1 cup milk

1 Tbsp. Dry Powder Calcium Bentonite Clay

1 Tbsp. peanut butter

3 Tbsp. chocolate syrup
(I use sugar-free)

2 ice cubes

Blend all ingredients until very smooth. Pour into a chilled glass and enjoy!

Berry Muffins

3/4 cup whole wheat flour

1 tsp. salt

1 cup all-purpose flour

1 tsp. cinnamon

1/4 cup Dry Powder Calcium Bentonite Clay

2 eggs, beaten

1/3 cup wheat germ

2 cups of half & half cream

2/3 cup white sugar

1 cup fresh blackberries

1 Tbsp. baking powder

1 cup fresh blueberries

Preheat oven to 400° F. Butter muffin pan. Whisk together flour, Calcium Bentonite Clay, wheat germ, sugar, baking powder, salt and cinnamon. In another bowl whisk together half &

half cream and eggs. Stir wet ingredients into dry ingredients, mixing until just combined. Fold in berries. Scoop batter into muffin pan cups 2/3 full. Bake in preheated oven for 20 minutes or until done.

Brownies

1½ cups unsalted butter

1/4 cup Dry Powder Calcium Bentonite Clay

1¼ cups unsweetened cocoa powder

2 tsp. vanilla

3 cups white sugar

1 cup chopped walnuts

1 cup flour

2 tsp. vanilla

1 tsp. salt

7 eggs

Preheat oven to 350° F. Line a 9x12 pan with foil and spray with cooking spray. In a saucepan over medium heat, melt butter. Stir in sugar until dissolved. Remove mixture from heat and beat in the eggs one at a time, mixing well after each addition. Stir in vanilla. Sift dry ingredients together. Add the flour mixture to the butter mixture and mix until combined. Stir in walnuts and spread batter into the pan. Bake at 350° F for 45-50 minutes. Do not over bake.

Chocolate Cake

3/4 cup flour

1/2 cup milk

1/4 cup Dry Powder Calcium Bentonite Clay

2 Tbsp. salad oil

2 Tbsp. cocoa

1 tsp. vanilla

2 tsp. baking powder

1/2 tsp. salt

3/4 cup chopped pecans

1/2 tsp. salt

Icing:

3/4 cup brown sugar

1¾ cup hot water

1/4 cup cocoa

Mix the first five ingredients. Add milk, oil and vanilla and stir and mix well. Mix in nuts. Pour into a greased 8-inch Pyrex pan. Mix icing and pour over the batter. Bake at 350° F for 35-40 minutes

Guacamole

2 ripe avocados

2 tomatoes, seeded and chopped

1 Tbsp. Hydrated Calcium Bentonite Clay

1/4 cup cilantro leaves, finely chopped

1 small red onion — chopped fine

1 jalapeño — seeded, diced

1 clove garlic — mashed

3 Tbsp. lime juice

Salt and freshly ground pepper

Halve and pit avocados and scoop flesh into a large bowl. Mash avocado with a fork and mix in the hydrated Calcium Bentonite Clay. Stir in remaining ingredients, combining well. Chill covered with plastic wrap for at least one hour and up to one day. Stir guacamole well and serve with tortilla chips.

Honey Water

2 cups of water

1 heaping Tbsp. of Dry Powder Calcium Bentonite Clay

4 tsp. raw honey

Put in a plastic or glass container with a plastic lid. Shake well and drink.

Oatmeal Cookies

1 cup shortening

1 tsp. vanilla

1 cup sugar

1 tsp. soda

1 cup brown sugar

1 cup flour

1/2 cup Dry Powder Calcium Bentonite Clay

3 cups

3-Minute Oatmeal

2 eggs, beaten

Cream shortening, eggs and vanilla; add sugar gradually, mix well. Mix soda, flour and Calcium Bentonite Clay and combine with the creamed mixture. Next, add oats. Form into small balls and bake at 375° F for 10-15 minutes. Makes 5 dozen.

Patty's Mexican Roll-Ups

2 – 8oz. cream cheese

1/2 cup chopped chives or green onions

3/4 cup sour cream

1 oz. liquid clay

1/2 tsp. garlic powder

Juice of one lime

1 – 4 oz. can chopped green chilies

1/4 to 1/2 cup Picante sauce

1 – 4 oz. can chopped black olives

Combine all of the above ingredients and spread on flour tortillas (10 in all). Roll each one separately into a log. Roll in plastic wrap. Put them in a plastic zip-lock bag and cool them in the refrigerator overnight or at least for a few hours. When ready to serve, slice each roll into about eight rounds and serve with Picante sauce.

Refried Bean Dip

Ingredients:

1 large can refried beans

Chopped red peppers

1 jar picante or taco sauce

Sliced olives (black)

1/4 cup Hydrated Calcium Bentonite Clay

Shredded cheese

Sour cream

Fritos or tortilla chips

Mix refried beans with picante sauce and Calcium Bentonite Clay. Spread on serving tray. Cover with sour cream and shredded cheese. Add chopped red peppers and sliced black olives. Serve with chips. Serves 8 to 12.

Sugar Cookies

1 cup sugar

1 cup shortening

1/2 cup Dry Powder Calcium Bentonite Clay

3 Tbsp. cream

2½ cups flour

1 tsp. vanilla

1½ tsp. baking powder

Blend dry ingredients together and add shortening. Mix cream and vanilla together and add to mixture. Chill the dough. Roll in a ball and mash with the bottom of a glass. Sprinkle lightly with sugar. Bake at 400° F for about 5-6 minutes.

Chapter Fourteen

THE FDA AND CALCIUM BENTONITE CLAY

At the time of its inception, the Food and Drug Administration (FDA) served the good of the people. However, the agency has come under the control of the companies that it is supposed to be monitoring. Long gone is the agency whose initial mission involved public health issues and the regulation of companies such as Bayer that want to sell aspirin in America.

Around the turn of the 20th century, all things "natural" in the health industry were a good thing. We felt it would serve the public good to monitor and do oversight on the new pharmaceutical companies, which were creating drugs that were synthesized and made from things known to be toxic to the human body. Simply put, it was the new "poison" pharmaceuticals being produced and the companies producing them that needed the oversight.

Today, loopholes in the original FDA plan have erupted like ripe boils. The pharmaceutical industry's influence gets exerted into the FDA oversight and the speed in which the agency works in a number of ways. In 1992 the Prescription Drug User

Fee act passed. The law allowed prescription companies to pay the FDA to speed up its review of a company's proposed drug. So in many ways, the FDA started looking upon the industry as its client, instead of the public and the public health, which should be the client. Another way in which the pharmaceutical companies intervene is by influencing the selection of leaders in its drug division who are spineless and gutless and who don't like controversy.

Additionally, the industry's influence has been allowed to grow considerably because of an absence of congressional oversight. In the past, when the FDA made a mistake, there would be a congressional hearing. What has happened to congressional oversight? Influence from big PHARMA interests' groups? There have been essentially one or two days of oversight hearings in 12 years, as opposed to maybe the previous 12 years with dozens and dozens of hearings. The FDA is getting away with no congressional oversight. Dr. Sidney Wolfe, director of Public Citizen's Health Research Group, describes today's FDA culture as "Please the industry.

Avoid conflict. Look upon our role as getting out as many drugs as possible." http://www.pbs.org/wgbh/pages/frontline/shows/prescription/hazard/independent.html

Bentonite Clays are, however, a horse of a different color. They are not a drug, and they are not a food. They are simply the Pathway to Healing by balancing, detoxing, stimulating, and alkalizing. They really don't fit the scope of the FDA guidelines. Until the FDA takes a serious look at how it works, it will never fit the perimeters of current FDA restrictions without going through some sort of cleansing process that would greatly reduce the functionality and efficacy of the product. The FDA guidelines are aimed toward poisonous medicines created in labs by pharmaceutical companies. These guidelines are not designed for natural clays made and designed by God. I have never heard of anyone dying from taking clay. I have never heard of clay destroying anyone's organs. A pure Calcium Bentonite Clay is not only safe but beneficial to the body.

According to the FDA, natural products must comply or be subject to fines or company closure. Before healing claims can be made by a company, the product must have scientific studies acceptable to the FDA. People in chat groups may share their experiences as long as they are not involved in marketing the product but may not give direct medical advice. The safe way to discuss natural Calcium Bentonite Clay is never to make any curative or medical claims but provide customers with outside resources that they can research themselves independently of any actual product marketing. Freedom of speech allows people to share their experiences without selling a product. "FDA Approved" means it has been tested and proved to make a specific claim as long as the public is informed of possible lethal and destructive side effects.

Personally, I think I'll go drink some clay.

Chapter Fifteen

CLAYTRONICS - THE FUTURE OF CLAY

CLAYTRONICS

Step into the future. What if there was a form of silica, readily available, that had even greater conductivity than the silicon used in the manufacturing of computers today? And what if that silica was self-cooling and could transfer data at more than 1,000 times the speed of today's norm? And what if that same silica had the inherent organic ability to act more like our biological brain than a binary piece of hardware, such as the brains of a computer today?

These questions are no longer simply questions. Today, these concepts are past the theoretical scientific model. They are proved and they are becoming tomorrow's reality. Calcium Bentonite Clay is all the buzz in the futurists' labs. The computer chip giants and the world's foremost robotics experts are moving toward creating a functional living cell "brain chip." Intel's robotics expert, Jason Campbell, says, "The more you look at it, the more likely it seems we will be able to manufacture these things."

Right now, researchers are investigating inventions that you and I cannot even imagine. Today, extensive research and experiments with Claytronics are being conducted at Carnegie Mellon University in Pittsburgh by a team of researchers that consists of Professors Todd C. Mowry and Seth Goldstein, as well as graduate and undergraduate students and researchers from Intel Labs Pittsburgh.

The science of smart matter is in its infancy, but early experiments have been encouraging. With the exploration of these new opportunities presented by chips and new materials, the future holds exciting potential. Some of these new materials are clay, wool, plant fibers and metals. One of the most interesting properties of new materials is their capacity to promote the dematerialization of products – that is, the use of less matter to accomplish a given task.

These living Smectite clays virtually replicate the body in its mineral composition. The most effective form of Calcium Bentonite Clays consists primarily of silica dioxide. When we look at the human brain, we find that it is silica that acts as the organic carrier of electrical impulses causing the brain to function, to compute, to cause action, thought, emotion, etc. Claytronic, using nanotechnology to create tiny robots called catoms, will enable three-dimensional copies of people to be emailed around the world for virtual meetings. When we look at a catom or Claytronic chip CPU, it is the silica that acts as the organic carrier of impulses, causing the computer processing unit to function, to compute, to cause action, thought, emotion, etc. This new science is the bridge between hardware and biology. Scientists are literally creating Living Chips! Imagine a virtual trip to the doctor's office via your phone where he could take your pulse and blood pressure while you relax at home. Beam me up, Scotty!

Could it be Calcium Bentonite Clay is the “magic stuff” of our collective futures? Could it be that Calcium Bentonite Clay is the body, mind and spirit of Claytronics? Could it be that Calcium Bentonite Clay is the ultimate curative for the human body? Could it be that Calcium Bentonite Clay holds the key to all of life itself? As the world reawakens to its seemingly curative abilities, science comes alive with discoveries that will propel our society from the Computer Age to the Claytronics Age.

Have you had your clay today?

Chapter Sixteen

HEALTH PRESERVATION AND LONGEVITY

How to look and feel younger for 100+ years!

Longevity, health and youthfulness – no three attributes are more greatly coveted than these in our society. More money is spent, more experts are consulted, and more energy is expended on this elusive quest than on any other.

I would contend that there is probably no one among those reading this book who is completely satisfied with both the way their body is aging (the speed, the look, the feel) and with their perceived appearance, their beauty. I want to suggest to you that you can reverse the aging process and change your appearance dramatically if you adopt the practices outlined in this chapter.

We will look at what makes our bodies age. We will discuss the difference between positive and negative ionic charged molecules and how they relate to the aging process. We will define the "dying process" and the "living process." And finally, we will outline the simple life plan that will add many, many years to your life – all the while remaining vibrant and alive.

Let's begin by taking a fun look at our beliefs about health. I can think of no better reflection of those beliefs than how we personally treat our own diseases and ailments. And what better evidence of that than to take A PEEK IN YOUR MEDICINE CABINET!

OK, be honest with me for a minute. If I were to slip into your bathroom unnoticed and peek in your medicine cabinet, what would it say about your state of health, and even more importantly, what would it say about your core beliefs about health itself?

Reach up to that mirror and swing it open! Let's start with the top shelf. There's Anacin, Excedrin, Excedrin P.M., Contac, Gelusil, Tylenol and a large old blue jar of Vicks. Then there's a bottle of Vivarin, a bottle of Serutan (that's Natures spelled backward) and two bottles of Milk of Magnesia – the regular that tastes like liquid chalk and the mint flavor that tastes like mint-flavored liquid chalk. And here's a large bottle of Rolaids standing close to its friend, a large bottle of Tums. And the Tums are standing next to a large bottle of orange-flavored Di-Gel tablets. What a trio of acid-indigestion piggy banks they make...

And oh my, look at that second shelf and all those vitamins. From A-Z and a few more in between. On the third shelf we find the utility infielders of the OTC medicine world. A variety of laxatives to keep the mail moving. Next we find Kaopectate, Pepto-Bismal and Preparation H, in case the mail moves too fast or painfully. Some Tucks to keep the mailroom tidy after delivery is made. Followed by a plethora of nasal drip inhibitors, Claritin, Zertec, and Dristan anchored by cough syrups, Nyqiul and Chloraseptic to make up the defensive line.

Then there is Oxy 5 for zits; Cortaid and Neosporin for skin care; and Visine and Murine for the eyes. That narrow shelf at the bottom known as the 'serious business' shelf. There is Valium, Percodan, Elavil and Daron Complex. Quite a picture of balanced health, aren't we?

Bentonite Clay? No, no, don't worry. I'm only joking of course. You couldn't really throw everything out in your medicine cabinet and replace it with Calcium Bentonite Clay, or could you?

As you ponder the remoteness of that even being a possibility, let's shift gears and look at our bodies on a cellular level. What is it that causes each cell to live or die at any given moment? Science has shown that the effects of detoxification on our body's cells are nothing short of miraculous. Time alone is not a disease or poison. It is the toxins that accumulate with time that the body cannot withstand and in turn causes deterioration. In other words, time alone is not the cause of death. Poisons are the cause of death of life forms.

So logically, by detoxifying your cells, a person can freshen up and grow healthier and younger than they once were by practicing this principle. Periodically detoxifying the body, drinking lots of fresh water and staying smart on nutrition can appear to work miracles. These amazing results are not miracles, just good science.

Amino Acids – Another Key to Agelessness

Amino acids are the building blocks of proteins, which are essential to life. They are a primary ingredient of most cell structures. Proteins are essential to all the chemical processes of the cells and thus are needed to rebuild the constant wear and tear on the human body. For instance, high-protein diets are especially vital during the growth years, during pregnancy and when tissues have been damaged by injury or disease.

Some research has shown that clays may have played an essential role in the formation of life. This hypothesis comes from experiments performed with clay to re-create the conditions under which amino acids may form proteins. The clay is thought to act as a catalyst for the formation of long peptide chains, or proteins. The summation is an easy one: these living clays capable of change are synonymous with life. These clays produce more peptides, and in turn, more protein amino acid links to life-forming peptide chains.

ARE WE FIGHTING THE WRONG WAR?

We view the problem of illness as something we should attack, something we should declare war on. The metaphor of declaring "War on____" is not limited to medicine. In recent years, we have declared a war on crime, a war on drugs, a war on AIDS, and so on. I do not believe that looking at disease from this perspective has been any more successful than any of the other "wars" we have declared. In fact, I believe a declaration of war ensures the problem will stay with us in perpetuity.

Our current health policy, dictated by the giant pharmaceutical companies, waits for a disease to occur and then attempts to kill and poison it out of our bodies in a full-frontal attack. Perhaps we are now realizing that after almost a 100-year failed experiments, this approach may not have proved itself to be in our best interest. Is it time today to resort to a more intelligent medical treatment system? Is it time to shift the emphasis to health preservation and longevity, rather than treatment of disease after the fact?

We have answered a few of the questions presented early on in this chapter regarding longevity. I now want to shift gears a bit and discuss the "ageless beauty" aspect of Calcium Bentonite Clay.

While beauty is only skin deep, the effects of Calcium Bentonite Clay touch your body on every level. As one young Calcium Bentonite Clay user told me, "It's helped me from head to toe, from stem to stern, and from all the way inside to all the way out." I don't think I could have said it better myself!

Today, spas and resorts around the world are touting Calcium Bentonite Clay as a true miracle. One Medi-Spa in California calls its Calcium Bentonite Clay facial treatments "Botox in a jar." The results are truly astounding. The good news is that you have a choice. You can choose to experience the age-reversing effects of Calcium Bentonite Clay at spas and resorts across the United States, or you can purchase Calcium Bentonite Clay online and enjoy all of its benefits for only pennies on the dollar in the privacy of your home. A complete line of Calcium Bentonite Clay-based beauty treatment products is now available to everyone.

Clinics and Medi-Spas are turning back time 10, 15, even 20 years for their clients in as few as three or four complete treatments. A comment from a client who had received four weekly Calcium Bentonite Clay treatments and who had also completed a 30-day full-body detox and internal cleanse said: "Look at me! In the past 30 days I have taken 20 years off the way I look and feel. My complexion is radiant – all of my wrinkles are gone! My body is firm and tighter, my energy level is up. I'm 52 years old and look and feel 29 again. Many of my friends aren't even recognizing me anymore. This is an absolute miracle in my life." You can even build your very own healthy "green" negative ionic charged house – or remodel the one you now own. The hottest new wall treatment on the market is a unique clay product that's all about adding a beautiful earth texture with a touch of color, while creating a healthier environment for you and your family. American Clay Earth Plaster provides the wonderful benefits of clay, which include longevity, mold-resistance without toxic fungicides, temperature moderation, dirt repellence, humidity control, sound attenuation and no volatile organic compounds. It's also backed by an eco-friendly philosophy. People are drawn to this clay plaster because it is "green," and there has been a huge response for this new product. Homeowners are hungry for something like this clay plaster – it is easy to use, environmentally friendly, gives warmth and offers even more versatility than plaster.

This book is jam-packed full of scientific evidence and real-life testimonies attesting to the miracle of Calcium Bentonite Clay. I could go on and on for pages playing the "Is it only a coincidence?" game. But all evidence clearly points to one thing – that ageless beauty and longevity are no coincidence when Calcium Bentonite Clay is used as a life practice – it is a truth!

So, if time alone does not cause the death of us at a cellular level, and assuming that poisons, toxins and the like do – what if we could consistently and completely rid our bodies of all poisons, toxins and any other environmental maladies of our own creation?

Remember a belief is just a thought we keep thinking. Choose another thought. Choose to live to be 100 + years old! Choose to feel young while doing so! Choose to take responsibility for your health and lifestyle choices! Choose Calcium Bentonite Clay! The only remaining question should be.....

Will you choose to have clay today?

RESOURCE LISTING

This book is intended as a resource to inform the reader of many of the various uses for Calcium Bentonite Clay. It is not intended as a sales or marketing tool, or for product endorsement. FDA and FTC regulations prohibit this type of endorsement when discussing curative or treatment methods.

The reference listing below is intended to refer to you sources of information that may assist you in your search for the best Calcium Bentonite Clay available today.

Our first suggestion is to do an online search for "Calcium Bentonite Clay." The results of this search should give you several sources, which I would recommend either email or phone with any questions you may have. And remember to ask the questions outlined in the book to ensure that you are getting the best available product. In a recent search for "Calcium Bentonite Clay," I learned there were more than 401,000 hits for those search parameters. A search for "Living Clay" turned up 11,880,000 hits. I also learned that the top companies, in my opinion, came up in the top five or six listings in this search as well.

In addition to online search, we also want to refer you to some excellent independent resources for further information on Calcium Bentonite Clay. These sites and listings offer a wealth of information and possibly offer further suggestions as to what and where to buy the best available Calcium Bentonite Clay. They are as follows:

www.BentoniteClayInfo.com
www.AsYouLikeIt.com
Benefits of Calcium Bentonite Clay - YouTube, Karen J. Adkins
Earth Cures, Raymond Dextreit, Translation by Michel Abehsera, Carol Publishing Company, 1977, 1997
The Clay Cure, Ran Knishinsky, Healing Arts Press, 1998
Heal Yourself Naturally, Nancy Stine, 2012 e-book
Handbook of Clay Science, 2nd Edition,Volumes 1 & 2, edited by F. Bergaya and G. Lagaly, 2013.
The Healing Clay, Michel Abehsara
The Clay Disciple, Cano Graham

Above all else, I encourage you to take responsibility for your own health. Don't allow another day to pass without Calcium Bentonite Clay in it. I promise you will experience a better quality of life as soon as you make the choice to use clay on a daily basis, and you just may live to be 100+ and still look and feel young.

Now, go eat some clay!

BIBLIOGRAPHY

[1] Abehsara, Michel. The Healing Clay, 1979

[2] Alexander, Kathryn. Dietary Healing, The Complete Detox Program, 2013

[3] American Diabetes Association http://www.diabetes.org/diabetes-statistics/complications.jsp

[4] Annals of the N.Y. Academy of Science*, Vol. 57, page 678*

[5] Aylward and Findlay. SI Chemical Data [Unknown Binding], 1987

[6] Benedict, Ruth. Patterns of Culture. Native American proverb, 1934

[7] Bergaya, F. and Lagaly, G. Handbook of Clay Science, 2nd Edition, Volumes 1 & 2, 2013

[8] Butenandt, Adolf. Nobel Prize winner 1939 for Chemistry. Proved that life cannot exist without silica. Research conducted at Columbia University, 1972

[9] Carrel, Alexis, M.D. The Rockefeller Institute for Medical Research. Sustained the life of cells from a chicken embryo. 1912

[10] Clark, Linda A. Know Your Nutrition, Keats Publishing (No-

vember 1984), http://treeoflifecenterus.com)

[11] Cousens, Gabriel, M.D. Remedies for Radiation, 2013

[12] Damrau, Frederic, M.D. Medical Annals of the District of Columbia, 1961

[13] Dextreit, Raymond, Earth Cures, Translation by Michel Abehsera, Carol Publishing Company, 1977, 1997

[14] Dioscorides, Pedanius, De Materia Medica (Regarding Medical Materials, a five-volume book), 70 A.D.

[15] Duncan, Lindsey, ND, CN, Nutritionist

[16] Earnest, C.N. Thermal Analysis of selected Illites and Smectite Clay Minerals Part 1, Lecture notes in Earth Sciences. Berlin: Springer-Verlag, 1991

[17] Emerson, Ralph Waldo, Selected Essays, Lectures and Poems, a Bantam Book, 1990

[18] Gibson, Sheila and Gibson, Robin. Homeopathy for Everyone, Harmondsworth, England: Arkana, 1987

[19] Goldstein, Seth of Carnegie Mellon University and Mowery, Todd of the Intel Research Lab – Pittsburgh. Claytronics: A Scalable Basis for Future Robots, 2004

[20] Cano Graham, The Clay Disciple

[21] Grant, P.G. and Phillips, T. D., 1998; Phillips et al., Characterization of clay-based enterosorbents for the prevention of aflatoxicosis, 2002

[22] Harney, Corbin. The Way It is, Blue Dolphin Publishing,

1995

[23] Hoffman, Wendell H. Energy to Heal, 1992

[24] Hogan, Paul, et al, "Economic Costs of Diabetes in the U.S. in 2002," *Diabetes Care* 26 (2003): 917-32.

[26] Hunter, John M. and Horst, Oscar H. "Religious Geophagy as a Cottage Industry: The Holy Clay Tablets of Esquipulas, Guatemala," National Geographic Research 5 No.3 page 26. 1989

[27] Jang, Miriam. Article, Breakthroughs in the Evaluation and Treatment of Autism, 2009

[28] Jensen, Bernard. Guide to Diet and Detoxification, 2000

[29] Katz, Dr. David L., director of the Prevention Research Center at Yale University, *Huffington Post* Article,

[30] Kervan, C. Louis. Biological Transmutation (from the French 1966 edition). Translation by Michel Abehsera, 1979

[31] Kennedy, B. A., Surface Mining, 2nd Edition, 1990

[32] Knishinsky, Ran. The Clay Cure, Healing Arts Press, 1998

[33] Lee, Natasha. "Could Detoxification Be the Fountain of Youth?" Nutritional Research for Peter Gillham's Nutritional Center

[34] Lipson, Steven M. and G. Stolzky. "Specificity of Virus to Adsorption to Clay Minerals." Canadian Journal of Microbiology 31, 1985

[35] Luo, Dan. Cornell University study, "Was Clay

the Birthplace of Life?" November 2013 http://www.science20.com/news_articles/was_clay_birthplace_life-123856

[36] Marshall, Barry James, professor of Clinical Microbiology at the University of Western Australia, and Warren, Robin. Study on Helicobacter pylori (H. pylori), The Medical Journal of Australia, 1985

[37] Martin, Paul R. "True Carpal Tunnel Syndrome," Neuro Diagnostics, McHenry, Illinois, 1996

[38] Martin, Robert T. Cornell University, Physico·Chemical Properties of Soils, American Society of Agronomy Inc., publisher. Madison, Wisconsin, 1965

[39] Meschino, James, a doctor of chiropractic, is a fellow of the Academy of Anti-Aging Research and an associate professor at the Canadian Memorial Chiropractic College.

[40] Millot, Georges. "Clay," Scientific American, April 1979

[41] Mineral Co., Bentonite Properties, http://www.mineralco.net/index/product/productdetail/9

[42] Monash University, Groundwater and Environmental Engineering, The Characteristics of Clay, September 17, 2003 http://misclab.umeoce.maine.edu/boss/classes/SMS_618_2003/Characteristics_of_Clay.pdf

[43] Musafira, Anjou and Chazot, Pascal. Clay Cures, 2006

[44] National Geographic documentary: http://www.natgeoeducation video.com/film/247/the-body-snatchers January 2000

[45] Paraquat Health and Safety Guide, World Health Organization, Geneva 1991

[46] Price, Weston D.D.S., Nutrition and Physical Degeneration, 1938

[47] Schell, T. C. et al., 1993 a,b; Santurio, J. M. et al., 1999

[48] Random House College Dictionary/Bentonite Rock

Revised Standard Version of the Bible, Genesis 2:7, Job 33:4, John 9:6 through John 9:15

[49] Shearer, Arran; et al, "Predicted Costs and Outcomes from Reduced Vibration Detection in People with Diabetes in the U.S.," *Diabetes Care* 26 (2003): 2305-10; and Adam Gordois, et al, "The Health Care Costs of Diabetic Peripheral Neuropathy in the U.S.," *Diabetes Care* 26 (2003): 1790-95 www.geoengineer.org/files/ClayMineralogy-Sivakugan.ppt

[50] Siegfried, Tom, The replicator: create your own body double, New Scientist http://www.isi.edu/robots/press/claytronics_new_scientist_11_june_2005.pdf

[51] Sivakugan, N., Clay Mineralogy N. [58] Smith, Alexander Graham Cairns, H. Hartman -Biotransmutaions.

[52] smith,Alexander Graham Cairns, H. Hartman- Biotransmutation.

[53] Stump, Jullus a renowned German physician

[54] Szostak, Jack W. Howard Hughes Medical Institute (HHMI), "Clays as Catalysts," Science. Vol. 302, Oct. 24, 2003

[55] Thackara, John, Smart matters, Doors of Perception, htt

p://www.doorsofperception.com/notopic/smart-matters/

[56] Ubick, Suzanne, Mud, Mud, Glorious Mud http://research archive.calacademy.org/calwild/2005winter/stories/mud.html

[57] U.S. Food and Drug Administration http://www.cfsan.fda .gov/~dms/grasguid.html#Q1

[58] U.S. Government Bureau of Mines Booklet #609

[59] Wikipedia, https://en.wikipedia.org/wiki/Enzyme

[60] Wolf, Sydney, M.D. Director of Citizen's Health Research Group, How Independent is the FDA?, http://www.pbs.org/wgbh/pages/frontline/shows/pres cription/hazard/independent.html

[61] Wikipedia, https://en.wikipedia.org/wiki/Enzyme

[62] Xerox Palo Alto Research Center, Digital Clay Modules, http://www.sciencephoto.com/media/344445/view

http://honors.byu.edu/content/activated-sodium-bentonite-h igh-affinity-sorbent-aflatoxin-b1-and-cholera-toxin

ABOUT THE AUTHOR

Perry A~

Perry A's background is as diverse as the clay she loves talking about. From city girl to country girl and points in between, the lifelong Texan earned a Bachelor of Science degree in Animal Science from Texas Tech University. Her background in chemistry, biology and veterinary science contributes to her knowledge base for understanding the intricate workings of clays. At Texas Tech she was a member of the Zeta Tau Alpha social sorority and was on the university's rodeo team. She was selected by her peers as the first woman to win Texas Tech's prestigious "Aggie of the Year Award" and was the 1958 Texas

Tech Rodeo Queen.

After graduating, she married her college sweetheart, had two daughters and lived in the small farming community of Seymour, Texas. The marriage ended after 27 years, and her first job as a probation officer opened her eyes to the fact that she could motivate people. She went on to become a successful motivational keynote speaker and has written several books under her speaker name, Perry A~.

She became a student of clays in the early 1990s after being introduced to a green Calcium Bentonite Clay. Her passion and curiosity led her away from her speaking career and on a new journey of research and discovery into the amazing healing potential of Calcium Bentonite Clays. She has been an advocate for this clay ever since.

In her second clay book, Calcium Bentonite Clay: Nature's Pathway to Healing, she simplifies complex chemistry and research data while introducing readers to the intriguing properties of Calcium Bentonite Clay. She has an extensive library of science journals and reference books and is a member of the Clay Mineral Society. Today, she gives interviews and lectures about using and mixing clays, as well as writing articles, blogs and books on the subject. To say that she is passionate about educating people to this age-old curative is an understatement.

In addition, Perry A~ encourages readers to challenge their long-held limiting beliefs about their bodies' ability to heal. "After all," she says, "a belief is just a thought you keep thinking, and body ALWAYS follows mind. Choose to believe that every day in every way, you are getting better and better and better."

Being a people person, she loves the opportunities that being the "Clay Lady" has given her to connect with people. "Making new friends from all over the world is the most exciting and rewarding part for me," she says. "A good clay will win friends and influence people. All I do is get it in or on people, and the clay does the rest. It is all about the results! The rest is history, and they become clay lovers for life."

To contact Perry A~ email perrya@perrya.com or call 512-773-0335. To sign up for Perry A~'s Tips and Testimonials and Perry's Weekly Power Thoughts, send your full name and email to perrya@perrya.com. To learn more about Calcium Bentonite Clay, go to www.BentoniteClayInfo.com for articles, testimonials and interviews.

Made in the USA
Coppell, TX
04 February 2026